P9-BYE-268

JEWISH PHILOSOPHY IN A SECULAR AGE

Jewish Philosophy
in a
Secular Age

Kenneth Seeskin

STATE UNIVERSITY OF NEW YORK PRESS

Published by
State University of New York Press, Albany

© 1990 State University of New York

All rights reserved

For information, address State University of New York
Press, State University Plaza, Albany, NY 12246

Library of Congress Cataloging-in-Publication Data

Seeskin, Kenneth, 1947–
Jewish philosophy in a secular age / Kenneth Seeskin.
  p.   cm.
Bibliography: p.
Includes index.
ISBN 0-7914-0104-9.—ISBN 0-7914-0105-7
    1. Philosophy, Jewish. 2. Judaism—20th century.   I. Title.
B154.S39   1990
181'.06—dc19   88-37125
                                                        CIP

10 9 8 7 6 5 4 3 2 1

To my parents,
Ethel and Philip Seeskin

Contents

Preface

This book has two objectives: to get secular philosophers to pay more attention to Jewish philosophy and to get Jewish philosophers to pay more attention to secular philosophy. One can think of the book as a kind of dialogue: an ongoing discussion among Plato, Aristotle, Maimonides, Judah Halevi, Descartes, Spinoza, Kant, Kierkegaard, Cohen, Buber, and Rosenzweig. Although not philosophers in the technical sense of the word, the prophets have also contributed to this dialogue, as have contemporary thinkers like Rawls, Rorty, Fackenheim, and Schwarzschild. From a historical perspective, such a dialogue is an impossibility, but from a philosophic one, it is not. Religion bids us to turn away from the transitory and focus on the eternal. It is hardly surprising, then, that the status of eternal truth is an eternal question.

To sustain the dialogue motif, and to reach two separate audiences, I had to make a number of editorial decisions. It was impossible to present an overview of the thought of each thinker I discuss. Since it was not my purpose to write a compendium of the history of Western philosophy, I have concentrated on selected texts and themes. In each case, there was material I had to leave out. A reader who wants a fuller treatment of Maimonides, Spinoza, Kant, Cohen, or Buber should consult secondary sources devoted to the thought of these figures. In the same way, I have tried to avoid esoteric questions and to refer to sources which are readily available. As in all of my philosophic writing, I have tried to present ideas in a readable fashion and to keep the use of technical terms and foreign words to a minimum. Citations from Maimonides' *Guide of The Perplexed* are from the Pines translation.

There are a number of people and institutions I would like to thank. Material from chapters 2, 3, and 6 was presented to the Academy for Jewish Philosophy and can be found in the publications of its proceedings. I wish to thank its members and especially its talented Director, Norbert Samuelson, for providing a stimulating environment in which to test new ideas. Portions of chapter 7 were published in *Philosophy and Literature* in 1987. I wish to thank its editors, Denis Dutton and Patrick Henry, as well as its publisher, Johns Hopkins University Press, for allowing me to use that material here. A number of individuals read portions of the manuscript or contributed to my understanding of the issues discussed within it. In alphabetical order, they include: James Edie, Seymour Feldman, Steven Katz, Menachem Kellner, Barry Kogan, David Levin, Shlomo Levine, Thomas McCarthy, John McCumber, Michael Morgan, David Novak, Norbert Samuelson, Samuel Todes, Meredith Williams, and Michael Williams.

There are three people I can thank but cannot possibly repay. Under the circumstances, I have no choice but to live with a lifelong debt of gratitude. They are: Manfred Vogel, friend, colleague, and my first teacher of Jewish philosophy; Steven S. Schwarzschild, friend, philosophic ally, and the person who enabled me to see the great affinity between Judaism and Platonism; finally Joseph Edelheit, friend, teacher, critic, and, in many ways, the person who encouraged me to write this book.

Chapter One

Introduction

1. The Problem of "Jewish" Philosophy

The notion of an inquiry that is both Jewish and philosophical has long been problematic. Philosophy is not indigenous to Judaism. With the exception of Philo, whose direct influence lay mainly with Christianity, Judaism did not produce a genuine work of philosophy until the tenth century. Even then, Jewish philosophy was largely a response to an external source: Islamic influence. Many regarded this response as suspect. By the thirteenth century, a controversy arose on whether Maimonides' rationalistic version of Judaism was heretical. The controversy is still with us. For some, Judaism demands surrender to the will of God, so that any attempt to devise a philosophic justification is misguided. For others, Judaism is a culture and does not need philosophic argument to claim legitimacy. Not surprisingly, one can still pick up a book on Jewish philosophy and find the author replying to the charge that the investigation is somehow *un*-Jewish.[1]

The reason this charge still has force is that philosophy is by nature a secular enterprise. It seeks a truth that is universal and eschews claims of ethnic or religious particularity. To many people, however, Judaism is not a universal phenomenon. As committed a student of Jewish philosophy as Isaac Husik questioned whether a religiously oriented philosophy is possible in the modern age. According to Husik philosophy is neutral with respect to Judaism or any other religious tradition: "There are Jews now and there are philosophers, but there are no Jewish philosophers and there is no Jewish philosophy."[2] Husik is hardly alone in thinking this. Many American universities have no program or department identified with Judaism. Those that do often have trouble demarcating a subject that is Jewish and philosophical in a clear way. There is either secular philosophy, which takes no official notice of Judaism, or something called "Jewish thought," which takes no official notice of Descartes, Mill, Nietzsche, Wittgenstein, or Heidegger. In cases where the

1

term "Jewish philosophy" is used, it often refers to contributions made in the Middle Ages, thereby confirming Husik's point.

Part of the problem concerns definition. Is Jewish philosophy supposed to be philosophy written by, to, or about Jews? Is it a philosophy *of* Judaism or a Jewish reflection *on* philosophical subjects? In a recent study, Jürgen Habermas tried to locate a distinctively Jewish strain in people like Husserl and Wittgenstein.[3] He assumed, innocently enough, that if they were Jews who wrote philosophy, their philosophy was Jewish. To find that strain, however, he had to resort to a high level of generality and make use of sources which his "Jewish" thinkers may never have seen. But for the circumstances of his birth, Husserl would not be associated with anything Jewish—at least not on the basis of his written work. As for Wittgenstein, he was not born a Jew, was not raised as a Jew, and has had very little impact on Jewish thought. In fact, Wittgenstein's impact is substantially less than that of Kant, even though Kant had no Jewish ancestry and some pretty unflattering things to say about Judaism as a religion.[4] So not every philosopher of Jewish ancestry has made a contribution to Jewish philosophy, and not every person who has influenced Jewish philosophy has Jewish ancestry. Put otherwise, a Jewish author may not write as Jew; a gentile author may formulate ideas which Jews find appealing. There is, then, a great danger in defining Jewish philosophy in ethnic terms.

A second suggestion is that if Jewish philosophy is not simply philosophy written by Jews, it is philosophy written *to* them—philosophy which presupposes Jewish training or is directed to readers who are self-consciously Jewish in their outlook. But here, too, there is a problem with universality. There is no such thing as a philosophical truth accessible to a single religious community. This was as true in the Middle Ages as it is now. Maimonides insists, for example, that the canons of rationality used to interpret Scripture be acceptable to the people of every nation.[5] Rationality is the common possession of the human race because the entire human race is created in the image of God (*Guide* 1.1). It follows that if love of God culminates in an intellectual apprehension of divine perfection, in principle there is no reason such apprehension should be limited to Jews or any other community. If the arguments of the *Guide* are valid, they are valid for everyone. It is hardly surprising, then, that many of the classics of Jewish philosophy—the *Guide* included— have been appropriated by general audiences. The works of Philo, Spinoza, and Buber, for example, have found greater acceptance outside the Jewish community than inside. This is as it should be. If

Jewish philosophy has uncovered important truths about God, the human condition, or created existence, these truths should be of interest to everyone. A person may follow Hermann Cohen in using Jewish sources, but this does not mean, nor did Cohen intend it to mean, that the conclusions are parochial in nature. In Cohen's words: ". . . it would have been an irreparable mistake in our arrangement if we were to limit and confine the religion of reason to the Jewish religion because of its literary sources. This limitation would be an insoluble contradiction to the signpost of reason."[6] What Cohen is saying is that Jewish philosophy must first succeed as philosophy if it is to be legitimate—otherwise, it is nothing but a form of preaching to the converted.

Unlike Husik, Julius Guttmann stresses the continuity between modern Jewish philosophy and that of the Middle Ages:

> Philosophy maintains, through crises and polemics, a unique type of continuity. A striking testimony to this is the development of Jewish philosophy, which maintains its linkage with the past despite the abyss which divides the Middle Ages from modern times. The selfsame problems are reformulated in the thought of modernity; and the new Jewish philosophy has, in all its trends, learned from the solutions offered to these problems by the great philosophers of our past, from Maimonides on the one hand, to Judah Halevi on the other. This connection is felt no less in the development of modern Jewish philosophy itself, despite the differences and oppositions among the various schools and trends.[7]

The problem with Guttmann's account—a problem suggested by the title of his book, *Die Philosophie des Judentums*—is the idea that Jewish philosophy is a philosophy *of* Judaism. A philosophical masterpiece like the *Guide* is more than a series of claims about a particular religion. For example, its discussion of the limits of human knowledge goes far beyond anything to which Judaism is committed, even if we grant that Maimonides is not writing for the common people. Like Cohen, Maimonides makes ample use of Jewish sources. But Maimonides admits that his interpretation of these sources is determined in large part by the direction of a philosophic argument.[8] Prove to him that the world is eternal and he would propose a reading of Genesis which denies a literal theory of creation. Such a proof, if it could be found, would have no more claim to being Jewish than the writings of a contemporary astrophysicist arguing for the same thing. It is therefore misleading to say that the *Guide* is a philosophy *of* Judaism. It is at least that, but it is also a philosophy of the human attempt to comprehend the divine.

I conclude that we cannot define Jewish philosophy simply in terms of ancestry, audience, or religious content. The reason is that all of these are irrelevant to its status *as* philosophy. A more promising suggestion is to follow Steven S. Schwarzschild and define it in terms of its orientation.[9] The price we pay for making this move is that we will no longer have anything appropriately labeled "Jewish" philosophy. Instead we will have philosophy done in a Jewish way or philosophy that contains, to quote Schwarzschild, a characteristic "Jewish twist." Schwarzschild bids us to emphasize the philosophy being espoused rather than the ethnic background of the person espousing it. On this view, philosophy is "Jewish" by virtue of transhistorical ideas that secular thought will sometimes arrive at on its own. For simplicity's sake, I will treat "Jewish philosophy" and Schwarzschild's "philosophy done in a Jewish way" as synonymous.[10]

To pursue Schwarzschild's suggestion, philosophy done in a Jewish way is characterized by two theses which a gentile can assert as easily as a Jew. In general terms, they are (1) the Primacy of Practical Reason, and (2) the Transcendence of the Rational.

The Primacy of Practical Reason asserts that the central philosophic category is that of conduct, what ought to be done. Logic, metaphysics, and epistemology are legitimate to the degree that they help us clarify the duties and aspirations we face as moral agents. It is a well-known fact that the sacred literature of Judaism contains little in the way of metaphysical speculation. This is true not only for the Bible but for later commentaries as well. The reason there is not much *meta*physics is that there is not much physics either.[11] The prophets took notice of the heavenly bodies and of events like floods and earthquakes. But there is no serious effort to explain these phenomena in terms of universal laws. Everything in nature is a consequence or effect of God's will. It follows that the real drama is not between humanity and the environment but between humanity and the Creator. This is another way of saying that the real drama is moral. The Creator is first and foremost a God of righteousness who demands righteous behavior from His people. When Moses asks God to show him His glory (Exodus 33.18), God responds by making His *goodness* pass before Moses. Repeatedly God identifies Himself with morality. Thus the words of Deuteronomy 16.20: "Justice, justice shall you pursue!" Even when Jewish philosophers appropriated metaphysical arguments from others, their work retained a strong ethical bias.

The Transcendence of the Rational, which might also be called "anti-incarnationism," asserts that it is impossible for the ideal to be realized in a sensuous medium. This principle is the philosophic equivalent of the basic Jewish conviction that God is separate from the world and cannot be depicted with images of things found in the world. According to Deuteronomy 5.8: "You shall not make for yourself a sculptured image, any likeness of what is in the heavens above, or on the earth below, or in the waters below the earth." In this respect, the second thesis is similar to the first: God is never *in* heavenly bodies or earthly phenomena but is a moral will who stands *above* them. In philosophic terms, this means that everything in the world is fallible and subject to critique. The most that can be claimed on behalf of anything in the world is that it strives for the ideal; but to strive for something is to admit that one does not have it. In this way, Jewish thought is appropriately described as messianic. Instead of defending the world as it is at present, it puts forward a standard which has not been achieved and may never be achieved until the end of time.

To the degree that these principles are characteristic of Jewish thought, a certain number of revisions are in order. Husserl did not accept the primacy of practical reason. According to some interpretations, Spinoza identified God with nature and therefore denied transcendence. On the other hand, Socrates; on many interpretations, Plato; and—on virtually every interpretation—Kant accepted both. Ironically, Habermas is much closer to accepting them than many of the people he classifies as "Jewish." No doubt, there is something paradoxical in saying that Plato, Kant, and Habermas were doing philosophy in a Jewish way. But the paradox is no greater than that which arises when someone says that it is impossible to study contemporary French philosophy without reading Marx, Nietzsche, or Heidegger; impossible to study Nietzsche and Heidegger without reading the Greeks; impossible to study contemporary American philosophy without reading Frege, Russell, and Wittgenstein. Technically Marx does not qualify as a French philosopher, but to anyone familiar with the development of French thought in this century, there is no intellectual mileage to be made by insisting on a technical definition. If French thinkers appropriated Marx, if they found his work well suited to their purposes, if they produced significant commentaries on it, then from the standpoint of the intellectual historian, Marx is a central figure for French philosophy, no matter where he was born or in what language he wrote.

The reason such "paradoxes" arise is that philosophic argument does not always respect ethnic, national, or religious boundaries. That is why we should be wary of sticking to these boundaries too closely. We can see this by considering the outlines of the medieval "synthesis" of faith and reason. Faced with the charge that philosophy is un-Jewish, Saadia replies that since the God who laid down the commandments is the same as the God who endowed us with the ability to reason, there is no ground for supposing that the two are in conflict.[12] Pursued to its final stage, reason will confirm what the prophets disclose in the sacred books. If we add that reason is a universal faculty, it follows that the people of any nation can confirm the teachings of Judaism. If, for example, Judaism teaches that God created the world *ex nihilo*, why should other people not be able to discover this for themselves? And if they do discover it, why should their arguments not be part of the study of Jewish philosophy?

In this day and age, we are not likely to hear many philosophers talking about reason in so abstract a fashion or claiming that reason "confirms" a religious doctrine. Still, the fact of independent discovery has to be taken seriously. If some gentile thinkers stand to Jewish philosophy as Marx stands to French, there is no basis for insisting on a tight, ethnic characterization of the former. Whether one argues that such thinkers are "Jewish" in their outlook or that Jewish philosophy is part of a wider tradition of intellectual development is immaterial. The fact is that there is a natural progression from Plato to Maimonides, from Maimonides to Kant, and from Kant to Cohen. There are, of course, other thinkers of note in the gaps that separate these figures: Plotinus, Saadia and the Kalam school, ibn Gabirol, ibn Daud, Gersonides, and Leibniz, just to name a few. But if Schwarzschild is right, any philosophy done in a self-consciously Jewish way will be a running dialogue with these four primary people. We should keep in mind, however, that no philosophic tradition can claim to be the custodian of what every Jew believes. To say that Jewish thinkers typically accept certain views is not to say that they always do, or that there is something unholy about those who do not. Alternative readings of Jewish philosophy are available. Husik and Guttmann have already been mentioned. Other people would claim that the rationalistic tradition exemplified by Maimonides and Cohen has been replaced by the existentialism of Buber and Rosenzweig, the neo-orthodoxy of Soloveitchik, or the Holocaust theology of Fackenheim. According to Michael Wyschogrod, it is not transcendence but immanence which is the core of Judaism, and not just immanence but embodiment.[13] In what follows, I will express broad sympathies with Schwarzschild. My major reason for doing so is that his characterization affords the best hope for making Jewish philosophy of interest to more than Jews. I believe strongly that Jewish philosophy must not become an inward-looking subject tied to a specific culture. At best, it not only borrows from thinkers outside the Jewish community but influences and reinterprets them as well.

My quarrel with Schwarzschild has less to do with Judaism than it does with philosophy. Assume Schwarzschild has correctly identified the "Jewish twist." Most discussions of Jewish philosophy proceed on the assumption that at least one term is clear: philosophy. The problem is to say how philosophy can take on a Jewish character. What if it should happen that things are reversed—that we have a pretty good idea of what makes something Jewish but a rather vague one of what makes it philosophical? In this case, the tail might well be wagging the dog. It is to this possibility that I now turn.

2. The Problem of Philosophy Simpliciter

To an outside observer, the current state of philosophic inquiry must seem puzzling in the extreme. The current debates have less to do with God, sense data, or the prospects for happiness than they do with the legitimacy of the philosophical enterprise itself. According to Richard Rorty, traditional philosophy was undermined by three thinkers who called into question the standard notions of rationality: Dewey, Wittgenstein, and Heidegger.[14] Each of them offered a way of disengaging from the old metaphysical tradition of which they were once a part: Dewey from Hegel, Wittgenstein from Russell, Heidegger from Husserl. The result, according to Rorty, is that we live in a post-philosophic culture in which old paradigms like pure reason, the external world, the disembodied or self-transparent subject, and the "given" element of human experience have collapsed. It is now impossible to talk about concepts without talking about their historical development; to talk about obligations without talking about the specific interests they serve; to talk about sense impressions without talking about the mind's way of interpreting them; to talk about the conscious without talking about the preconscious or unconscious. These additions are more than courteous bows to modernity, for they deprive philosophy of what has long been its primary justification: the ability to confront an unconceptualized reality face to face.

For Rorty, the seeds of philosophy's destruction were planted by one who was himself a philosopher: Kant.[15] Once we recognize, as Kant wanted us to, how much the mind contributes to experience for experience to be intelligible, we put ourselves in the position of seeing that (1) it is impossible to identify that aspect of human experience which is somehow given, that is, which has no taint of "interpretation"; and (2) it becomes very possible to imagine that if certain conditions had obtained, the world would look a lot different than it now does. In short, by drawing attention to the conceptual scheme by which we interpret experience, Kant raised the question of alternative conceptual schemes. Not that Kant himself took such alternatives seriously; he thought he was setting forth the necessary conditions for any ordering of experience. If, however, we follow Hegel in thinking that our conceptual scheme has a history, then, according to Rorty, we are left with the conclusion that our way of ordering experience is only one of many. What is more, we may find ourselves with no all-inclusive set of concepts by which to translate from one conceptual scheme to another. In this situation, there is no Archimedean point on which to secure a certain or presuppositionless beginning. Philosophy can explicate the concepts we use, but it cannot make the traditional claim of confronting reality face to face. As Rosenzweig said a generation before Rorty, the person who strives for presuppositionless knowledge only shows how many presuppositions he or she has.[16]

In defense of Rorty, it is worth noting how much philosophy has been a series of retreats from claims of indubitability. If the sixteenth and seventeenth centuries put an end to certainty about God, the eighteenth century put an end to certainty about the immediate content of experience, the nineteenth century to certainty about the laws of thought, the twentieth century to certainty about the distinction between language and the world. In fact, the history of philosophy is the best evidence available for denying that an Archimedean point can be found. The problem is that unlike mathematicians, philosophers have always allowed themselves the freedom of starting over. Instead of building on their predecessors, philosophers have often returned to the foundations in an effort to construct the edifice of human knowledge anew. In the case of Russell, Moore, and Husserl, they returned to the foundations several times in the space of a single career. Each of these efforts was accompanied by a promise that presuppositions had been abandoned and reality confronted face to face.

But here Rosenzweig's criticism has real force. Why have so many philosophers felt the need to start over? Why is the history of philosophy not cumulative? To put this in a different way, if the foundations of human knowledge are clear in and of themselves, why have so many people experienced difficulty in identifying them? If, on the other hand, they are not clear and generate considerable controversy, in what sense are they foundational? Each time someone takes us back to the foundations, we are led to believe that previous thinkers were looking at the world with a jaundiced eye. But after repeated attempts to start over, it is difficult not to come to the conclusion that all efforts to identify foundations are "jaundiced" in the sense that they involve a large measure of interpretation. It is not that Descartes, Locke, Hume, Russell, or Husserl were blind to facts which an unbiased inquiry would reveal. It is that no one can identify the place at which acquaintance with reality stops and interpretation begins.

What, then, becomes of the discipline which promised an unbiased account of the world? In the early pages of *The Star of Redemption*, Rosenzweig argues that philosophy has broken with its past: hence the reference to "new thinking." We may question how radical the break was in light of the Hegelianism that pervades the rest of his book. In any case, this much is clear: Rosenzweig helped to usher in an age in which the future direction of philosophy is very much in doubt. For Rorty and Derrida, philosophy based on the traditional dualisms of subject/object, analytic/synthetic, empirical/a priori, language/world is simply over. There is no discipline that determines the bounds of rationality for all human knowledge, no discipline that has any claim to being in possession of "first truths." Here is Rorty's description of what a post-philosophical culture would be like:

> *A fortiori*, such a culture would contain nobody called "the philosopher" who could explain why and how certain areas of culture enjoyed a special relation to reality. Such a culture would, doubtless, contain specialists in seeing how things hung together. But these would be people who had no special "problems" to solve, nor any special "method" to apply,

abided by no particular disciplinary standards, had no collective self-image as a "profession." They might resemble contemporary philosophy professors in being more interested in moral responsibility than in prosody, or more interested in the articulation of sentences than in that of the human body, but they might not. They would be all-purpose intellectuals who were ready to offer a view on pretty much anything, in the hope of making it hang together with everything else.[17]

In this way, the all-purpose intellectual will replace the secular philosopher just as, in Rorty's opinion, the secular philosopher once replaced the theologian.

Not everyone has taken such a radical view. For people like Gadamer and Habermas, philosophy is not dead but in need of transformation.[18] For Gadamer, this transformation would lead to a historically based hermeneutics; for Habermas, a broad-based social commentary. In both cases, philosophy could retain its status as a discipline with identifiable standards and some sense of being a profession. But it would not be a discipline patterned on Cartesian notions of rationality. It would be "practical" in the sense that ideas like meaning and truth would be connected with human interest, desire, or activity. Such a practical turn is evident in Gadamer's appropriation of the Aristotelian concept of *phronesis*, a type of rationality distinct from demonstrative science (*episteme*) on the one hand and production (*techne*) on the other. In Habermas, it is evident in the universal pragmatics that looks at communication from the standpoint of the agent involved in it. In both cases, there is constant recognition of the fallibility of the philosophic enterprise: an attempt to have rationality without indubitability. For Stephen Toulmin, philosophy would become "practical" in an obvious way: it would forsake theory construction and return to the case-book method of teaching ethics. It would rediscover what is usually known as casuistry and emphasize the rhetorical dimension of ethical arguments. Instead of striving for necessity and universality, it would direct its attention to the timely and the appropriate.

I do not wish to take sides in the end-of-philosophy debate or predict where philosophy will be in fifty years. My reason for bringing in Rorty, Derrida, Habermas, et al. is to point out that however we define what it means to do philosophy *in a Jewish way*, there is first the problem of what it is to do philosophy at all. In fact, if we look at Jewish philosophy since Rosenzweig, we will find that Rorty's description of the all-purpose intellectual is not far from the truth. Is there a single method or set of problems common to Buber, Kaplan, Heschel, Soloveitchik, Levinas, Schwarzschild, Fackenheim, Borowitz, or Hartman? I suggest not. Their interests range from biblical studies to legal matters, from theological inquiry to the discussion of concrete decisions, from the autonomous subject to the horrors of Auschwitz. Some of their work reads like poetry, some like social commentary, some like traditional philosophy. It is hardly surprising, then, that people do not know whether to call it Jewish philosophy, Jewish theology, Jewish thought, or philosophy done in a Jewish way.

To return to Schwarzschild, if there is disagreement on what counts as philosophy, there will be disagreement on what counts as philosophy done in a Jewish way. On the other hand, it is noteworthy that Jewish thinkers did not have to wait for the latter part of the twentieth century to take seriously the goals of interpretation and critique. Insofar as anyone writes as a knowledgeable Jew, there is no possibility of beginning philosophy *de novo*. Centuries of text and commentary have to be consulted. Continuity with previous thinkers, though not the only consideration, is certainly an important one. No knowledgeable Jew has to be told what Alasdair MacIntyre told the philosophic community in *After Virtue*: that we are born with a past.[19]

In one respect, taxonomy is unimportant. It matters little whether a work is classified as philosophy, theology, or something else. The issue is whether it is illuminating. In another respect, the difficulties we have encountered in saying what Jewish philosophy is should make us cautious in setting its goals. There is no longer any question of effecting a synthesis between Judaism and an established body of knowledge called philosophy—unless one means the results of a particular philosophic school. Nor is there any question of using philosophy to demonstrate the superiority of Judaism to other religions. The goals of philosophy have become more interpretive than demonstrative. According to David Lewis, it is rare that philosophical theories are ever refuted conclusively: "Once the menu of well-worked-out theories is before us, philosophy is a matter of opinion. . . ."[20] Lewis cites the results of Gödel and Gettier as counterexamples. It is significant, however, that he does not cite the "results" of Aristotle, Anselm, Descartes, Locke, or Kant. The truth is that Aristotle did not destroy Platonism once and for all, nor did Anselm destroy atheism, Descartes destroy skepticism, Locke destroy innate ideas, or Kant put an end to the scandal that philosophy has no proof for the external world. So while Lewis may have overstated his case by proclaiming it a matter of opinion which of the well-worked-out theories to adopt, he is right in suggesting it cannot be decided by demonstration. To some philosophers, this conclusion will seem profoundly unsettling. Take away demonstration and you take away the heart and soul of philosophy. To those like Gadamer, Habermas, and Toulmin, however, the move from demonstration to interpretation and critique is all for the good.

To see this, we need turn no further than Maimonides. Contrary to what some people expect to find when they open the *Guide*, Maimonides does not offer a systematic treatise in metaphysics. There is no formal discussion of axioms and postulates, no mention of being *qua* being, no attempt to reconstruct human knowledge from the ground up. The main questions raised by the book are hermeneutical: how to get beyond the literal meaning of biblical terms and parables to the truths they contain. At *Guide* 2.2, he tells us:

> Know that my purpose in this Treatise of mine was not to compose something on natural science, or to make an epitome of notions pertaining to the divine science according to some doctrines, or to demonstrate what has been demonstrated in them. Nor was my purpose in this Treatise to give a summary and epitomized description of the disposition of the spheres, or to make known their number. For the books composed concerning these matters are adequate. If, however, they should turn out not to be adequate with regard to some subject, that which I shall say concerning that subject will not be superior to everything else that has been said about it. My purpose in this Treatise, as I have informed you in its introduction, is only to elucidate the difficult points of the Law and to make manifest the true realities of its hidden meanings, which the multitude cannot be made to understand because of these matters being too high for it.

Maimonides' sources are Scripture and rabbinic commentaries on the one hand, the philosophic tradition on the other. But it would be wrong to think that the *Guide* is a "synthesis" in a simpleminded way. Scripture cannot be read in a literal fashion and requires considerable effort on the part of the interpreter before its hidden meanings can be made clear. The proofs advanced by philosophers are not always convincing. Since, according to Maimonides, words like *existence, unity,* or *incorporeality* have totally different meanings when applied to us and to God, the interpretation of these proofs may be as difficult as the interpretation of Scripture. All this is a way of saying the *Guide* is not an axiomatic treatise à la Euclid but an extended exercise in interpretation and critique. Certainly this is true in regard to creation and providence—two areas where Maimonides thinks demonstration is impossible. Instead of culminating in a body of demonstrably certain results, the *Guide* forces us to solve hermeneutical questions of our own.

As for Cohen, his religion of reason is a philosophical construction derived *out of the sources of Judaism.* In this respect, it too is a hermeneutical exercise. Biblical religion, rabbinic literature, the prayer book, even the historical experience of the Jewish people are the material on which Cohen reflects. By calling the final product a religion of reason, all he means is that he has produced a refinement or crystallization of what these sources contain or imply. Because it is an idealized version of Judaism, it is not a description of the day-to-day activities of practicing Jews. It stands to those activities as an ideal democracy stands to the give and take of a working parliament. It is a version of Judaism which does not ignore the original sources but attempts to strip away elements of myth, superstition, or historical particularity. So while the task of the book is theory construction, the goals of interpretation and critique are never far from view. It is an interpretation because it reformulates material in a philosophically perspicuous way, a critique because it leaves out what reason finds impossible to accept.

It must be emphasized again that Maimonides and Cohen are the major figures in Jewish philosophy according to the view here adopted, and that view is selective. There is as much disagreement in the Jewish world as there is in the world at large—a fact which should surprise no one. I am prepared to admit, with Rorty, that there is at present no single method or subject matter over which the philosopher can claim mastery. *A fortiori,* there is no single method or subject matter over which the Jewish philosopher can claim mastery. I make no claim to exclusivity. On the contrary, my claim is one of continuity with a tradition. It is the tradition that affirms the two principles set forth in the previous section. I submit that despite the definitional problems encountered thus far, such continuity is enough to make the inquiry both Jewish and philosophical.

3. Judaism and the Elimination of Metaphysics

According to Rorty, the most significant event of the twentieth century is the destruction of the metaphysical tradition which began with Parmenides. From a Jewish perspective, however, there is a respect in which this development is beside the point. To the degree that practical reason holds sway over Jewish thought, metaphysics is at best a marginal enterprise. The explanations for this difference are various and range from the nature of biblical religion to the grammatical structure of Semitic languages to the rabbinic understanding of textuality.[21] These explanations have led some people to conclude that there is a radical split between Jewish thought and Greek: that despite the attempts at synthesis, the two are discontinuous. I am unsympathetic with these claims for a variety of reasons. Platonism has, and continues to have, a strong appeal for Jewish thinkers. Let us recall that Plato assigned Goodness a unique status in the world of forms—superior to Being in power and dignity (*Republic* 509B). Let us also recall that Plato does not allow the philosopher who has escaped from the cave to contemplate the eternal truths in private. The philosopher must return to the cave and assist the other prisoners—much as the prophets were instructed to return to the city, however sinful it might be. Finally let us recall that more than any other thinker in the western tradition, Plato warned about the seductive nature of representational art. But even if we move beyond Plato, the idea of a radical split between Athens and Jerusalem is questionable. Notice, for example, that one of the features which distinguishes ancient Greek skepticism from that which flourished in the sixteenth and seventeenth centuries is that the former has a strong practical dimension. Where the distinction between Athens and Jerusalem is legitimate is on the whole question of metaphysics. Even when Greek philosophy was introduced to Jewish intellectuals in the tenth century, it is hard to find Jewish thinkers preoccupied with Parmenides' question or the question which defines Aristotelian first philosophy: What is being *in itself?*

The typical Jewish response is to proclaim the question invalid. Maimonides asks us to think of God not as a being with an essence but as an agent who acts for a purpose (*Guide* 1.54–58). In keeping with this view, Buber contends that God's disclosure of Himself at Exodus 3.14 must be understood in a way which does not commit the Bible to a statist ontology:

As reply to his question about the name, Moses is told: *Ehyeh asher ehyeh*. This is usually understood to mean "I am that I am," in the sense that YHVH describes himself as the Being One or even the Everlasting One, the one unalterably persisting in his being. But that would be abstraction of a kind which does not usually come about in periods of increasing religious vitality; while in addition the verb in the Biblical language does not carry this particular shade of meaning of pure existence. It means: happening, coming into being, being there, being present, being thus and thus; but not being in the abstract sense.[22]

Buber's suggested translation of *Ehyeh asher ehyeh* is "I am and remain present." The significance of this rendering is that the link with Eleatic metaphysics is broken. God is not the one who *is* but the one who *does*. As Cohen argues, the place of being is taken over by action.[23]

The shift from being to action is not just a neo-Kantian legacy. It is evident in as committed a phenomenologist as Emmanuel Levinas. Levinas agrees with Heidegger, Rorty, and the other antimetaphysicians that the essential feature of Greek philosophy is its preoccupation with the intelligibility of presence. Being is what can be exposed or revealed to the mind in perfect clarity. Levinas maintains that while Heidegger struggled with this model, he never really escaped from the conviction that presence is the ultimate philosophic category. Put otherwise, there is no practical turn in Heidegger. For Levinas, on the other hand, a person's ethical relation to another person is prior to his ontological relation to himself or even to the rest of the world. In regard to God, he claims:

> The God of the Bible cannot be defined or proved by means of logical predications and attributions. Even the superlatives of wisdom, power, and causality advanced by medieval ontology are inadequate to the absolute otherness of God. It is not by superlatives that we can think of God, but by trying to identify the particular interhuman events that open towards transcendence and reveal traces where God has passed. The God of ethical philosophy is not God the almighty being of creation, but the persecuted God of the prophets who is always in relation with man and whose difference from man is never indifference. This is why I have tried to think of God in terms of a desire, a desire that cannot be fulfilled or satisfied—in the etymological sense of *satis*, measure.[24]

The concern with the practical dimension of divine perfection, coupled with the insistence on a transcendent God, makes Levinas thoroughly Jewish in his outlook. Though Husserl, too, was born a Jew, it is Levinas who has earned a position in Jewish philosophy.

It will be objected that all this talk about the antimetaphysical tendencies of Jewish thought or the difference between Hebrew and Greek plays into Rorty's hands. The fact that a culture could produce art, literature, social institutions, even philosophy, without Eleatic assumptions shows that those assumptions are not as clear and distinct as some have claimed. If they are not, Rorty is in a stronger position to argue that Western metaphysics is bankrupt.

If Rorty maintained that Western metaphysics is bankrupt and *therefore* we must concentrate on the ethical dimension of human existence, there would be no argument. The truth is, however, that despite his railing against Plato, Descartes, and Kant, or his willingness to adopt the label "pragmatist," Rorty is a product of the very thing he seeks to undermine. The issues which concern him are the standard philosophic fare: meaning, truth, disembodied subjects, the status of scientific knowledge, representation. Granted he is not trading one theory for another but calling into question the need to theorize about such things in the first place; still, he speaks as if traditional philosophy and metaphysics are the same thing. In reading him, one gets the impression that the Enlightenment thinkers had a lot to say about meaning and truth, but only a few scattered remarks about values and institutions. He gives lip service to the fact that their theories changed the face of European society but seems comparatively uninterested in how or why this happened. His view is typical of Anglo-American philosophers in this century. Since meaning and truth are the central issues in philosophy, they are the main reason for studying the history of philosophy. What Locke says about primary and secondary qualities is more important than what he says about toleration; what Hume says about causality is more important than what he says about the passions; what Kant says about the analytic/synthetic distinction is more important than what he says about the regulative employment of the ideas of reason.

This approach prevents us from seeing that for many of the Enlightenment thinkers, theories of meaning and truth were not put forward as ends in themselves: they were weapons in the war against unlimited monarchy and dogmatic orthodoxy. It is therefore misleading to suggest that Spinoza, Locke, Hume, and Kant were engaged in the same philosophic enterprise as Frege, Russell, or Quine. Ironically, Rorty is the last person who should succumb to the idea that all great philosophers were involved in the same project. No one has done more to attack the idea that philosophy is a single discipline characterized by unbroken lines of development. For many of the Enlightenment thinkers, revised opinions about meaning and truth were integral parts of a social program stressing liberal values like individual rights, religious toleration, and the ideal of universal humanity. Unfortunately, Rorty has little to say about the social dimension of their thought. And unlike Dewey, he has no radical social program of his own. His eye has been trained to look beyond such programs to the metaphysical planks which support them—the purpose being to argue that the planks are rotten.

There is an attempt to alleviate this problem in Rorty's latest book, *Contingency, Iron, And Solidarity.* Unlike his earlier writings, the essays in this volume deal with political themes like community, utopia, cruelty, and personal freedom. But here, too, meaning and truth are never far from view. Rorty's image of utopia is that of a place where people recognize how contingent their linguistic categories are. They abandon notions like truth, rationality, or moral obligation for ones like metaphor or aesthetic preference. The result is a "poeticized" society in which people do not appeal to deep level truths to support their rejection of Nazism, Stalinism, or other forms of political brutality. They see that their revulsion to brutality is really a cultural artifact and thus a contingent matter. Traditionally, utopias are places where the poor are fed, the abused protected, the captive freed, the young educated, and the injustices that plague modern societies eliminated. But in Rorty's utopia, these ideals are pushed to the back of the stage. A person who looks through Rorty's book hoping to find moral indignation at society's injustices will be disappointed. He is not trying to correct society's ills as much as he is trying to alter our discourse *about* them. If he is a reformer, his efforts are directed mainly to the meta level.

To be sure, Rorty is against cruelty. But despite two essays on the depiction of cruelty in novels, he does not have much to say about the political institutions needed to eliminate it. The reason is clear: his objection to cruelty must stay clear of ideas like human dignity, human rights, and universal humanity. The theories that support liberal social institutions are texts and thus contingent associations of words. Worse, they are associations that take us back to metaphysics. Having given up any attempt to improve or enlarge on these texts, the philosopher in Rorty's utopia will move out of the public sphere and concentrate on private matters like self-fulfilment and self-creation. The possibility that a poetically inspired philosopher like Heidegger could promote brutality is not really an issue for Rorty. It could be said, therefore, that Rorty has no radical social program because he does not think philosophers should be in the business of devising them. What business should they be in? Once again we come back to the same theme. Philosophers should be in the business of helping us get the metaphysical monkey off our backs. This is the ill *par excellence*, the primary condition Rorty's utopia is designed to correct.

On the elimination of metaphysics, Rorty credits Kant with the realization that there are no descriptive truths behind natural science: no domain over which metaphysics holds sway.[25] But unlike Kant, Rorty does not attack knowledge to make room for faith. He does not want to transform philosophy from a speculative to a practical discipline, at least not if practical philosophy is in the business of grounding the value judgments or social practices we live by. There are for Rorty no moral facts or deep-level truths on which these judgments or practices are based. When it comes to behavior, he is content to recommend what he calls "the Socratic virtues—willingness to talk, to listen to other people, to weigh the consequences of our actions upon other people."[26] In short, he admires the virtues of conversation but resists the need to ask what must be true for successful conversation to be possible. An answer to the latter would take us back to traditional philosophy, and the need to show that the European form of life is "more than European." His primary examples of people who fed this need are Plato and Kant, the two primary examples of gentile thinkers doing philosophy in a Jewish way. According to Rorty, Plato and Kant are responsible for the myth that philosophical method can take the place of deliberation—that morality involves consulting one's memory of the Good or having one's behavior subsumed under a rule.[27] The source of the myth is the belief that moral judgments or social practices need a philosophic explanation to be legitimate, that they must take account of a unique set of truths about human agents. But this notion of legitimation is an illusion: "All the Platonic or Kantian philosopher does is to take the finished first-level product, jack it up a few levels of abstraction, invent a metaphysical or epistemological or semantical vocabulary into which to translate it, and announce that he has *grounded* it."[28]

Notice the reference to metaphysics, epistemology, and semantics. It is as if Rorty has identified a trio of old friends and can now
sing the familiar songs. There is no domain for metaphysics to
study, truth is not the sort of thing which can have an essence,
meaning does not require a theory. A person who never read Plato
or Kant would come away with the impression that they were apol-
ogists for their own cultures, that they sought to legitimate the
Athenian or Prussian understanding of morality by showing that it
has its roots in "pure reason." This is part and parcel of the traditional philosopher's urge to show that the European form of life is
more than European. The fact is, however, that neither Plato nor
Kant did any such thing. Far from being a legitimation of Athenian
society, the *Republic* is a stinging rejection. Its purpose is to show
the reader how *few* judgments and practices in Athenian society can
stand rational scrutiny. It was, after all, Athenian society which
convicted Socrates. To suggest that Plato was satisfied with something called "the European form of life" is to overlook the extent to
which his ideal society, too, is a program for reform, a paradigm
rather than an abstraction. Plato thinks the classes in the ideal state
will be analogous to the divisions in the soul, but the analogy is
rough and hardly constitutes "correspondence with reality" as later
epistemologists used the term. Its relation to any existing society is
a complicated question, which two millennia of scholarship have
still not resolved.

Part of Rorty's problem is his use of structural metaphors:
foundations, grounds, jacks, and the like. This terminology suggests
that all traditional philosophy can be understood along Cartesian
lines. Put otherwise, philosophy is simply science carried on at a
more abstract level: it accepts the world as it is but seeks a more perspicuous explanation for why it is so. It is clear from Rorty's writings
that he regards the differences between Plato, Kant, and Descartes
as unimportant. Sometimes he talks about the "Platonic-Kantian
notion of grounding," sometimes about the "Cartesian-Kantian
pattern," sometimes about "traditional, Platonic, epistemologically-
centered philosophy," and sometimes about "systematic philosophy," by which he means the tradition which includes Plato, Kant,
and Descartes. What is missing from Rorty's understanding of traditional philosophy is the extent to which the Platonic and Kantian
portions of it are revisionary, that is, the extent to which they seek a
target rather than a ground. Hilary Putnam makes this point in *The
Many Faces of Realism*.[29] Kant is not simply providing arguments for

the proper ordering of the formal and material principles of morality; he is providing an image of the world which inspires them and without which they would not make sense. To use a religiously charged but nonetheless appropriate term, Rorty has ignored the extent to which the thought of Plato and Kant is messianic.

According to Kant, Plato was right in thinking that reason has a natural tendency to transcend experience by finding ideas to which no empirical object can coincide.[30] Although the perfect state may never come into being, this fact has no tendency to show that the idea of the perfect state fails as an archetype. The mistake is to ontologize the archetypes by conceiving of them as objects in a supersensible domain. Provided we make the move from theoretical to practical, from entities to ends, Kant thinks we can accommodate Platonic philosophy, and transcendental ideas, without lapsing into metaphysics. The transcendental ideas have no constitutive employment and therefore cannot support claims of knowledge. They refer to a perfect rather than an actual ordering of experience and in that sense are aspirations. The fact that they are useful aspirations does not justify any claim of "correspondence with reality," a term which neither Plato nor Kant employs. Kant, then, is a primary case of someone who has made the "practical turn." From Rorty's point of view, however, Kant's turn is still objectionable. Although Kant has eliminated some of the trappings of classical metaphysics, he retains the elements of necessity and universality. The aspirations Kant is talking about arise from the nature of reason itself. He therefore thinks of philosophy as more than contingent. Rorty suggests Kant has undermined one species of dogmatism only to fall prey to another. The *First Critique* disposes of natural theology. But by claiming necessity and universality for his ethics, Kant, on Rorty's interpretation, makes the same mistake as the theologians: he attempts to reduce rationality to a rule, to argue that there is a fixed procedure for determining moral choices.[31] For Rorty, this is wishful thinking. The life of reason is nothing but the life of deliberation, which is to say Socratic conversation. There is no possibility of replacing deliberation with "method."

The differences between Plato and Kant, on the one hand, and Rorty, on the other, have less to do with metaphysics, epistemology, and semantics than they do with a fundamental conviction that the world is in need of repair. Plato and Kant are suspicious of any morality derived from sense experience. At best, the senses can tell us what the world is, not what it could be or ought to be. For the person with a vision of a different world, there must be a way of giving content to ethical judgments without relying on descriptive claims. Thus Callicles tells Socrates in the *Gorgias* (481b): "Are you serious or just having fun? For if you are serious and what you say is true, our lives would have to be turned upside down and everything we are doing is the opposite of what we should be doing." How could Socrates convince people that the world *is* upside down and the overwhelming majority of Athenians wrong about what they believe? He needed a method which would allow his respondents to consider new and unimagined possibilities without the burden of satisfying popular opinion.[32] That need led him to postulate the theory of recollection, a theory which maintains that our idea of Goodness is not derived from sense experience but brought to conscious awareness through questioning. In Kant, the need to find a nondescriptive basis for ethical judgments led to the discovery of transcendental philosophy. In both cases, the move to the a priori was undertaken not to stifle moral choice but the opposite: to liberate it from reliance on the status quo. Therein lies the point: Rorty is much happier with the status quo than the people he criticizes. He may not wish to defend every inch, but he never suggests that the world is upside down. His writing is critical, not messianic.

From a Jewish perspective, this debate is significant because it leads directly to a discussion of Hermann Cohen. Rorty's criticisms of Plato and Kant are essentially the ones modern Jewish philosophers have made against Cohen's notion of a religion of reason. It is too abstract. It is too optimistic. It tries to show that a particular form of life is more than just a form of life, that it has its roots in pure reason. It is, in effect, nothing but a version of Judaism "jacked up" by a philosophic vocabulary. As a form of culture, Judaism does not need a philosophic defense. The reply is, once again, that Cohen's religion of reason is neither a description of Judaism nor a glorification. In some cases, for example, claims of ethnicity, it is as sharp a criticism of Jewish attitudes as Plato's *Republic* was of Athenian. In fact, Cohen's writing is unabashedly messianic. It is in the concept of messianism that Cohen thinks idealistic philosophy and biblical religion come together. Note, for example, that Callicles' remarks to Socrates could just as easily have been directed to Amos or Jeremiah.

As Cohen sees it, Plato's great achievement was to create the space in which ethics could flourish: the intelligible world. Plato's intelligible world is beyond the sensible but not as a limit that the sensible world approaches. According to Cohen, Plato's thought is not future-directed:

Plato's political idealism, therefore, does not recognize a future proper, insofar as it would be a new peculiar creation and development. The beyond which he grants to the good means only that the good is beyond the being of the world of the mathematical and physical sciences. It does not mean, however, a beyond with regard to the past and present of the historical experience in the development of the peoples. The latter beyond, however, in distinction from the eschatological one, is the clear meaning of the messianic future.[33]

From Plato's ethics of transcendence, "passing over millennia, a straight road leads to Kant." Here Cohen suggests that the purpose of transcendental philosophy is not to make final pronouncements about experience but to set before us the infinite task of clarifying it. To the degree that experience falls short of the ideas reason constructs, philosophy is future-directed: it puts before us a reality we can conceive but do not yet have. For Cohen, then, the Hegelian dictum is wrong: the real is not the rational—it approaches the rational as a function approaches its limit.

We are back to the two principles which characterize Jewish philosophy: the primacy of ethics and the transcendence of the rational. Because the world is imperfect, the task of human beings is to bring it into closer conformity with the ideal. Deny transcendence and, in Cohen's opinion, you are forced to accept the world as it is. Deny the priority of ethics and you get a throwback to Greek ontologism. Put them together and you get what Cohen calls "religious reason" or more accurately, the religion of reason. If Cohen is right, the impetus behind Plato and Kant is religious. What motivated them is what Kant refers to as the "spiritual flight" from the physical world. This insight, which seemed obvious to Cohen, would strike many contemporary philosophers as outrageous. For much of this century, philosophers have tried to perpetuate the image that their discipline is an extension of science, not theology. Like Descartes, they are involved in "underwriting" the results of the physicist or mathematician. It is hardly surprising, then, that Plato and Kant are taught in modern universities as people who contributed to the Cartesian project, a project which insists on its secular prerogatives.

But Kant knew very well what he was talking about. The theme of spiritual flight as well as the principle of *imitatio Dei* are clearly articulated in the following passage from the *Theaetetus* (176a–c):

We should attempt to flee from this world to the next as fast as possible. That means becoming like God as much as possible, which means becoming righteous and holy with the help of wisdom. But it is no easy matter to persuade people that the reasons for fleeing wickedness and pursuing virtue are not what the majority of people say. It is not that one should avoid the *appearance* of being bad and attain that of being good. . . . God has no taint of evil whatever, only perfect righteousness; and nothing is more like God than one of us who becomes as righteous as possible.

This passage will become critical when I discuss Maimonides. For the present, notice the emphasis on behavior and the commitment to transcendence.

To his credit, Rorty sees that his quarrel with Plato and Kant cannot be resolved in a way which avoids circularity. But he leaves little doubt that history is on his side. He believes that by the twentieth century, attempts to ground this or criticize that were "shrugged off" by those whose activities were being grounded or criticized.[34] This may have been true for Russell, Husserl, and other people wedded to the Cartesian view of philosophy, but it is not true for Cohen. Rather than an underwriting of the existing order, Cohen's religion of reason became exactly what he intended: a model for a new one. Today it would be hard to characterize emancipated Judaism, with its emphasis on social responsibility and Jewish identity in a mass culture, without going back to him. For better or worse, his writing had enormous social consequences. On the other hand, the fact that his religious works have not had the wide acceptance of Buber's casts doubt on their claim of universality. So history crossed up both the pragmatist and the rationalist: the pragmatist for thinking that transcendental ideals do not change people's lives, the rationalist for thinking that once understood, they have the power to change everyone's.

4. Plan of the Present Work

I have described the present work as a running dialogue with a particular tradition, and in that respect have borrowed Rorty's notion of conversation. I do not intend this work as a historical study. Good secondary literature on the figures that make up this tradition already exists. Nor do I intend it as a systematic treatise. It is rather a discussion of selected issues in the philosophy of religion whose purpose is to carry this tradition forward. It needs to be said that one can defend the rationalist tradition without claiming one has established the parameters for all future discourse on the subject. One can have rationality without indubitability; one can reject demonstration in favor of interpretation and critique. If I am right, interpretation and critique have always been the Jewish philosopher's metier. What makes this book possible is that increasing numbers of secular philosophers are claiming to do the same thing.

Interpretation and critique cannot be done in an intellectual vacuum. So I am not going to defend the tradition which runs from Plato to Cohen by starting with the axioms of Platonic philosophy and trying to arrive at their counterparts in *Religion of Reason*. My approach will be the opposite: to understand this tradition by seeing how people have tried to overthrow it. To continue with the notion of dialogue, I will try to show how this tradition has responded to a long line of critics. From a philosophical standpoint, the critics come in a variety of shapes and sizes: Aristotle, Descartes, Spinoza, Hume, Kierkegaard, Buber, the ethical intuitionists, and Fackenheim. Some argue that this tradition is too enamored of rationality, others that it is not enamored enough. In one way or another, all are opposed to the idea of a free and rational agent whose will can be understood according to ethical principles.

The discussion will begin in what might be considered the enemy's camp: Aristotle and the doctrine of analogy. I do this to show why the Aristotelian view of God is problematic and why our only hope of understanding God is to replace metaphysics with ethics. But to make this argument, it will be necessary to wade through a fair amount of metaphysical argument. The central claim will be that this argument turns on itself. All one gets from an attempt to understand God as a being in Himself is a confession of ignorance. The remaining topics in the book are chosen to allow the critics to have their say. Thus the objections of Descartes and Spinoza can best be understood by looking at the issue of divine causation; those of Kierkegaard and Buber by looking at revelation; those of the intuitionists by considering the nature of ethical reasoning; that of Fackenheim by discussing the problem of evil. For the most part, the critics are presented in chronological order. The critical portion of the book begins with Aristotle and ends with Fackenheim. On the other hand, the book will attempt to show that there are philosophic themes that reappear in different epochs. To the degree that it succeeds, we will be able to say, with Cohen, that religious reason has a share in the eternal.

Notes

1. See, for example, Louis Jacobs, *A Jewish Theology* (New York: Behrman House, 1973), 10–1. This is not a criticism of Jacobs's work. The fact that so gifted an author finds it necessary to answer the charge that philosophy is un-Jewish only shows that the charge is still being made. For further discussion of this problem, see Erich Unger, "Modern Judaism's Need for Philosophy," in Arthur A. Cohen (ed.) *Arguments and Doctrines* (New York: Harper & Row, 1970), 146–58.

2. Isaac Husik, *A History of Medieval Jewish Philosophy* (1916; rpt. New York: Harper & Row, 1966), 432. The obvious reply to Husik is that the problem has nothing to do with modernity: philosophy was *always* neutral in this sense. Cf. Husik's remark (300) on Maimonides' attempt to reconcile philosophy and biblical religion. For a position similar to Husik's, see Menachem Kellner, "Is Contemporary Jewish Philosophy Possible?—No," in N. Samuelson (ed.), *Studies in Jewish Philosophy* (Lanham, Md.: University Press of America, 1987), 17–28. Notice that Kellner makes a distinction between Jewish philosophy and modern Jewish thought. For criticism of Kellner, see Barry Kogan, "Jewish Philosophy in the 1980s: A Response to Kellner," in Samuelson, 29–41. Finally, see Michael Wyschogrod, *The Body of Faith* (New York: Seabury Press, 1983), 52–53.

3. Jürgen Habermas, *Philosophical-Political Profiles*, trans. Frederick G. Lawrence (Cambridge: MIT Press, 1983), 21–43.

4. See *Religion Within the Limits of Reason Alone*, trans. T. M. Green and H. H. Hudson (1943; rpt. New York: Harper & Row, 1960), 116–17.

5. See *Guide* 3.31 as well as "Helek: Sanhedrin, Chapter Ten," English translation, in Isadore Twersky (ed.), *A Maimonides Reader* (New York: Behrman House, 1972), 407. For further study, see the excellent discussion of Maimonides' view of philosophy in David Hartman, *Maimonides: Torah and Philosophic Quest* (Philadelphia: Jewish Publication Society, 1986): 32–33: "Against this approach [one which separates thought from action or dismisses the unity of *halachah* and *aggadah*] Maimonides appeals to the Torah, arguing that the Torah itself indicates the existence and legitimacy of universal criteria of truth:

> For this is your wisdom and your understanding in the sight of the nations which shall hear all these statutes and say, "Surely, that great nation is a wise and discerning people" (Deut. 4.6).

If there are specific Jewish criteria of truth, how could this promise be realized? If what counts for truth in this community is to be based exclusively upon rabbinic authority, how can the Torah expect those who are not bound by that authority to marvel at and appreciate the wisdom of the commu-

nity? There must exist, then, independent criteria of truth which neither
Jew nor non-Jew can ignore." Deuteronomy 4.6 is also a significant text for
Cohen and will be discussed in greater detail below.

6. Hermann Cohen, *Religion of Reason Out of the Sources of Judaism*,
trans. Simon Kaplan (New York: Frederick Ungar, 1972), 8. For further discussion of Cohen's method, see Wendell S. Dietrich, *Cohen and Troeltsch:
Ethical Monotheistic Religion and Theory of Culture* (Atlanta: Scholars Press,
1986), 5–18.

7. Julius Guttmann, *Philosophies of Judaism*, trans. David W. Silverman
(New York: Schocken Books, 1973), 451.

8. *Guide* 2.25. That is why it is wrong to say, as Leo Strauss does, that
"one begins to understand the *Guide* once one sees that it is not a philosophical book—a book written by a philosopher for philosophers—but a
Jewish book: a book written by a Jew for Jews. Its first premise is the old
Jewish premise that being a Jew and being a philosopher are two incompatible things. Philosophers are men who try to give an account of the whole
by starting from what is always accessible to man as man; Maimonides
starts from the acceptance of the Torah. A Jew may make use of philosophy
and Maimonides makes the most ample use of it; but as a Jew he gives his
assent where as a philosopher he would suspend his assent (cf. II,16)."
Maimonides does give his assent to things on which, *qua* philosopher, he
would suspend judgment. But that is only because philosophy does not
have, or does not *yet* have, an acceptable demonstration. In areas where a
demonstration exists, Maimonides' Judaism is transformed to satisfy the
needs of his philosophy. Put otherwise, philosophy is needed if we are to
know when to interpret the Torah literally and when not to do so (see, for
example, *Guide* 2.25 on the issue of corporeality). And if it is decided that a
literal interpretation is impossible, philosophy is needed to decide the direction in which a proper interpretation should move. The price one pays
for interpreting the *Guide* as a Jewish book rather than a philosophic one is
esotericism. For Strauss's position, see *Persecution and the Art of Writing*
(Glencoe, Ill.: The Free Press, 1952), 38–94 as well as "How to Begin the
Study of *The Guide of the Perplexed*," in *The Guide of the Perplexed*, trans.
Shlomo Pines (Chicago: University of Chicago Press, 1963), xiv. For criticism
of Strauss, see Marvin Fox's review in *Journal of the History of Philosophy* 3
(1965), 265–74 as well as the longer study by David Hartman in *Maimonides*,
3–138. If all esotericism is committed to is that (1) most people are incapable of understanding philosophic argument, and (2) philosophic argument
cannot be limited to simple demonstration, then it is unobjectionable. Any
number of philosophers have used dialectical arguments to advance their
position and have warned that they are not writing for a popular audience.
But it does not follow that they are trying to withhold important information or that one has to make use of secret devices to get at it.

9. Steven S. Schwarzschild, "An Agenda for Jewish Philosophy in the 1980s," in Samuelson, *Studies*, 101–25.

10. Schwarzschild, "Modern Jewish Philosophy," address read at Valparaiso University, April, 1986.

11. For a good discussion of this point, see Manfred Vogel, *A Quest For A Theology of Judaism* (Lanham, Md.: University Press of America, 1987), 11.

12. For an English translation of this passage, see *The Book of Beliefs and Opinions*, Introduction, trans. S. Rosenblatt (New Haven: Yale University Press, 1948), 28: "Our Master, blessed and exalted be He, has namely given us complete instructions in regard to our religious requirements through the medium of His prophets. [He did this] after [first] confirming for us their possession of the gifts of prophecy by means of [sundry] miracles and marvels. Thus He has enjoined us to accept these matters as binding and observe them. He has furthermore informed us, however, that, if we would engage in speculation and diligent research, inquiry would produce for us in each instance the complete truth, tallying with His announcement to us by the speech of His prophets. Besides that He has given us the assurance that the godless will never be in a position to offer a proof against our religion, nor skeptics [to produce] an argument against our creed."

13. Wyschogrod, *Body of Faith*, xv, 11–14, 100–104, 212–13. Wyschogrod goes to some length to distinguish the incarnation of God in Israel from the Christian view of incarnation in Christ. But the thrust of the book makes it a rival to the present study. One point of similarity is the problem of defining "Jewish philosophy" (40–43).

14. Richard Rorty, *Philosophy and the Mirror of Nature* (Princeton: Princeton University Press, 1979), 5ff.

15. Rorty, *Consequences of Pragmatism* (Minneapolis: University of Minnesota Press, 1982), 3ff.

16. Franz Rosenzweig, *The Star of Redemption*, trans. W. W. Hallo (New York: Holt, Rinehart, & Winston, 1970), 3. On the issue of confronting reality face to face, see Rosenzweig's comment on the identity of thought and being, 17: "Philosophy fed theology on the identity of reasoning and being as a nurse might drop a pacifier into the mouth of a babe to keep him from crying."

17. Rorty, *Consequences*, xxxix.

18. For further discussion of how Gadamer and Habermas fit into the end of philosophy debate, see the introduction and relevant chapters of K.

Baynes, J. Bohman, and T. M. McCarthy (eds.), *After Philosophy: End or Transformation?* (Cambridge: MIT Press, 1986).

19. MacIntyre, A., *After Virtue* (Notre Dame: University of Notre Dame Press, 2d ed., 1984), 266–67.

20. David Lewis, *Philosophical Papers,* vol. 1 (Oxford: Clarendon Press, 1983), x–xi. For further discussion, see Alasdair MacIntyre, *After Virtue,* 266–67.

21. For the connection with biblical religion, see Guttmann, *Philosophies,* 17. For the connection with language, see Thorleif Boman, *Hebrew Thought Compared to Greek,* trans. J. L. Moreau (London: SCM Press, 1960), 27–73 and Steven S. Schwarzschild, "On Jewish Language," unpublished manuscript. Boman's central thesis is that the Hebrew world is dynamic and the Greek world static. One represents things from the point of view of the agent, the other from the point of view of the observer. The problem is that Boman paints in broad strokes and often succumbs to linguistic determinism. The grammar of a language may help us to understand the structure of a person's thought, but grammar alone cannot be decisive. Despite the Parmenidean resistance to dynamism, and its effect on Plato and Aristotle, there are indications that for the Greeks, too, being implies activity. See *Sophist* 247d–e, where power (*dynamis*) is offered as the mark of the real, and *Metaphysics* Theta, 1–9, where being is understood in terms of act. For the connection with the rabbinic understanding of textuality, see Susan Handelman, *The Slayers of Moses: The Emergence of Rabbinic Interpretation in Modern Literary Theory* (Albany: SUNY Press, 1982), and Jose Faur, *Golden Doves with Silver Dots: Semiotics and Textuality in Rabbinic Tradition* (Bloomington: Indiana University Press, 1986).

22. Buber, *Moses: The Revelation and the Covenant* (New York: Harper & Row, 1958), 51—52. Cf. Cohen, *Religion of Reason,* 42–43, 94. Note the Septuagint's rendering of this passage: *ego eimi ho on.*

23. Cohen, *Religion of Reason,* 94. For a more detailed discussion of this point, see "Charakteristik der Ethik Maimonis," in the reprint of *Jüdische Schriften* vol. 3 (New York: Arno Press, 1980), 238–48.

24. See "Dialogue with Emmanuel Levinas," in Richard A. Cohen (ed.), *Face to Face with Levinas* (Albany: SUNY Press, 1986), 31–32.

25. Rorty, *Consequences,* 383–84.

26. Rorty, *Consequences,* 172. Notice that throughout this essay Rorty assumes there is a wide gulf between Socrates and Plato. Socrates is a humanist committed to the values of conversation; Plato is a rationalist who thinks all moral questions can be answered by applying mechanical procedures. It is doubtful, I think, that the dialogues would support so sharp a contrast.

27. Rorty, *Consequences*, 163–64.

28. Rorty, *Consequences*, 168.

29. Putnam, *The Many Faces of Realism* (LaSalle, Ill.: Open Court Press, 1987), 51.

30. *Critique of Pure Reason*, A313/B370-A319/B375.

31. Rorty, *Consequences*, 164. cf. MacIntyre, *After Virtue*, 221: "The notion of escaping . . . into a realm of entirely universal maxims which belong to man as such, whether in its eighteenth-century Kantian form or in the presentation of some modern analytical moral philosophies, is an illusion and an illusion with painful consequences. When men and women identify what are in fact their partial and particular causes too easily and too completely with the cause of some universal principle, they usually behave worse than they would otherwise do."

32. See, for example, *Crito* 49d–e and *Gorgias* 472b–c.

33. Cohen, *Religion of Reason*, 292.

34. Rorty, *Consequences*, 174.

Chapter Two

The Positive Contribution
of
Negative Theology

1. The Attraction of Negative Theology

This chapter does not purport to be a complete survey of negative theology in Judaism. Anyone who desires to read such a study is invited to consult the classic article by Alexander Altmann on the divine attributes.[1] What I propose is a treatment of certain themes in negative theology as developed by three thinkers: Maimonides, Descartes, and Kant. In this way, I shall treat one thinker central to Jewish philosophy, one thinker clearly outside it, and one thinker who, though not Jewish by birth, had a decisive impact on it. All three claim there are important respects in which God is unknowable.

The central claim of negative theology is that God is unlike anything in the world, that He is radically unique. According to Hermann Cohen, it is God's uniqueness more than His oneness that is at the root of monotheism.[2] A worldview which replaced the pantheon of Mt. Olympus with a single god of limited power or knowledge, say Zeus or Poseidon, would not be monotheistic as Judaism understands the term. Monotheism properly so called requires not only a single deity but a deity who stands apart from everything else, thus the words of Isaiah 40.25: "To whom then will you liken Me, that I should be equal?"

But to say that God cannot be compared to anything in the world is to raise a philosophic problem: how to characterize something that stands apart? Can the logical and metaphysical assumptions that pertain to created existence also pertain to the Creator? Aristotle maintains that words predicated of things in different categories cannot be predicated in the same sense (*Topics* 107a3–17).[3] Thus *clear* means something different when predicated of a color and a musical note, *sharp* something different when predicated of a

31

musical note and a knife. If we apply this claim to God, we arrive at the conclusion that words like *wise, powerful,* and *living* are not used univocally of God and His creatures. If they were, God would be in the same category as His creatures, which would destroy His uniqueness. Yet all Aristotle says is that these words cannot have the *same* meaning; he leaves open the possibility that there is some sort of analogy. In other words, Aristotle is not committed to the view that *knowledge* is applied to humans and God homonymously, having nothing in common except the name. For if there is nothing in common except the name, God would be beyond human comprehension and there would be no science that investigates Him.

It is not surprising, then, that in the *Metaphysics,* Aristotle stresses divine perfection but not inscrutability. On the contrary, God is not only an existent thing but a cause or principle for the explanation of everything else. At *Metaphysics* 1026a23–32 (cf. 1064a28 ff.), Aristotle distinguishes first philosophy, or theology, from both physics and mathematics. Mathematics investigates things that are immovable but that do not exist separately. Physics investigates things that exist separately but are not immovable. If there were not an immovable substance, physics would be first philosophy. If there is an immovable substance, the science that investigates it will be prior to all others. This science investigates one being, but owing to the unique character of this being as primary and as first principle (1064a35–7), it falls to this science to investigate being universally, that is, being *qua* being. Since Aristotle thinks he can demonstrate the existence of an immovable substance, the science which investigates this substance is the most universal science of all; in short, theology is first philosophy. Clearly the identification of theology with first philosophy assumes that the subject matter of theology is knowable. As Wolfson points out, Aristotle ascribes multiple predicates to God—thinking, living, being pleased, causing motion, lasting eternally—without ever suggesting that these predicates compromise the simplicity of the divine substance.[4]

On the other hand, Aristotle is aware that God does not live or think the way we do. So terms like *lives* or *thinks* cannot be synonyms. But if God is to be investigated scientifically, neither can they be homonyms. Aristotle needs something between the two extremes. The standard solution is to invoke "predication by reference" or what Aristotle calls predication *pros hen.*[5] According to this doctrine, words like *substance, unity,* or *thought* have different meanings when applied to different things; but all of these meanings refer to a primary meaning or form (*Metaphysics* 1003b14–15). Aristotle's example of predication by reference is health. Although health is not formally present in a diet or a complexion, we may describe them as "healthy" since one is productive of health, the other a sign of it. Both meanings are intelligible by reference to the primary meaning, which is the health of a body. It follows that *healthy* has neither the same meaning in all three cases nor a completely different one. There is ambiguity but not so much that the things described as healthy cannot be investigated by a single science. We can also have predication by reference when something *is* formally present in two things but in different degrees. Consider thought. This activity is formally present in humans; but to understand it, we must refer to the primary instance of it in God, who is always thinking. Again, *thought* is neither a synonym nor a homonym. The ambiguity in question is systematic and falls within the province of a single science. Although the scholastic philosophers referred to predication by reference as *analogy*, Joseph Owens is right in saying that Aristotle distinguished them.[6] Properly speaking, analogy involves four terms: A is to B as C is to D.[7] In the interest of simplicity, I will follow scholastic usage. The classic expression of predication by analogy in Jewish philosophy is found in Gersonides' *Wars of the Lord* (132–33).[8] At the end of this chapter, I shall argue that there is one group of terms for which Gersonides' argument is unavoidable. But we must first understand why the doctrine of analogy cannot be true for all terms.

There are two problems in holding that there is an analogy between God and His creation. First, analogy implies similarity. If terms are predicated of God and humans by analogy, God cannot be radically unique. Second, we can assert an analogy between a map and the territory it depicts, an individual and the state, or a machine and a large institution because we have independent experience of each. But since we do not have independent experience of God, we have no grounds for claiming that His knowledge bears any resemblance to ours. This argument is reminiscent of one that Berkeley uses in the *Three Dialogues*. Hylas supposes there is a resemblance between our ideas and the material objects that cause them. But Philonous gets him to see that if we have no contact with those objects, we have no grounds for asserting the resemblance. Even if such objects existed, they could not have the properties we normally ascribe to them because those properties are descriptive of ideas. The culmination of this argument is the famous Berkeleyan dictum that only an idea can resemble another idea.

I take the central thesis of negative theology to be that only a conditioned object can resemble another conditioned object; no conditioned object can resemble God. Thus God cannot have any of the properties we attribute to things in the world. He is *sui generis*, beyond the grasp of a finite intelligence. It may be the case, therefore, that Scripture applies multiple attributes to God: life, thought, power, and so on. As we understand these things, they are all different. But since God cannot admit plurality in any respect, these properties cannot inhere in God the way they inhere in other things. According to Maimonides (*Guide* 1.57), "He exists, but not through an existence other than His essence: and similarly He lives, but not through life; He is powerful, but not through power; He knows, but not through knowledge." When it comes to God's existence, life, or power, all we can truly say is what He is *not*: He is not existent in the way that His creatures are; not living, powerful, or wise, in the way they are. By turning positive predications into denials, all we do is stress God's uniqueness, a uniqueness so radical that nothing else in the universe offers a basis on which to infer knowledge of His essential nature.

We can agree with Isaac Franck that the unknowability of God does not necessarily lead to mysticism.[9] To say that God cannot be grasped by a finite mind is not to say that finite minds have special, extrarational modes of access to Him. This sort of mysticism is compatible with the unknowability of God, but not one of the thinkers I wish to consider adopts it. In fact, all three are commonly described as rationalists in one way or another. But their rationalism prevents them from saying that God's essential nature is amenable to scientific demonstration. Although there are no clear anticipations of negative theology in Plato, it is not surprising that this theory has found support among philosophers in the Platonic tradition. If God is unlike anything in the world, we cannot construct a theology on principles derived from experience. Put otherwise, there is no inference which leads from natural phenomena to God. Substantial portions of the *Guide of the Perplexed* attempt to show that accepted theories of God and creation are wrong for just this reason. If there is no analogy between God and His creation, neither is there an analogy between the world as it is at present and the world at its inception. To the degree that negative theology rejects arguments from analogy, it opens itself to the charge that it amounts to skepticism: the principle which underlies all existence is beyond human comprehension.[10] On the other hand, one cannot be a total skeptic and participate in a religious tradition. This chapter attempts to show how the charge can be answered.

2. Maimonides Contra Aristotle

Maimonides' negative theology is perhaps the most interesting aspect of his thought because it allows us to see the extent to which he parted company with Aristotle. If God were knowable, He would be subject to definition. But any definition compromises divine simplicity. If the definition asserts that God embodies an essence, it implies there is a cause anterior to Him, as rational is anterior to man. If it identifies God by genus and specific difference, it introduces multiplicity. If it asserts that God is a substratum to which accidents are attached, it introduces multiplicity once again. With respect to relation, Maimonides adopts a view of equivocation much stronger than that taken by Aristotle. If it is true, as Aristotle indicates in the *Categories* (6b37 ff.), that relations imply reciprocity, then to say that God has a relation to any of His creatures is to say that He is like them (*Guide* 1.52):

> The subject of investigation and speculation is therefore the question whether there is between Him, may He be exalted, and any of the substances created by Him a true relation of some kind so that this relation might be predicated of Him. It is clear at the first glance that there is no correlation between Him and the things created by Him. For one of the properties of two correlated things is the possibility of inverting the statement concerning them while preserving their respective relations. Now He, may He be exalted, has a necessary existence while that which is other than He has a possible existence, as we shall make clear. There accordingly can be no correlation between them. As for the view that there is some relation between them, it is deemed correct, but this is not correct. For it is impossible to represent oneself that a relation subsists between the intellect and color although, according to our school, both of them are comprised by the same "existence." How then can a relation be represented between Him and what is other than He when there is no notion comprising in any respect both of the two, inasmuch as existence is, in our opinion, affirmed of Him, may He be exalted, and of what is other than He merely by way of absolute equivocation. There

is, in truth, no relation in any respect between Him and any of
His creatures. For relation is always found between two things
falling under the same—necessarily proximate—species,
whereas there is no relation between the two things if they
merely fall under the same genus. On this account one does
not say that this red is more intense than this green or less or
equally so, though both fall under the same genus, namely
color. If, however, two things fall under two different genera,
there is no relation between them in any respect whatever, not
even according to the inchoate notions of common opinion;
this holds even for cases in which the two things fall in the
last resort under one higher genus. For instance, there is no
relation between a hundred cubits and the heat that is in pep-
per inasmuch as the latter belongs to the genus quality and the
former to the genus quantity. There is no relation either between knowledge and sweetness or between clemency and bit-
terness, though all of them fall under the supreme genus
quality. How then could there subsist a relation between Him,
may He be exalted, and any of the things created by Him,
given the immense difference between them with regard to the
true reality of their existence, than which there is no greater
difference?

Aristotle argued that univocity is not preserved across categorical
lines; Maimonides' position is that it is not even preserved across
generic lines in the same category. If so, the entire scheme of the
Categories is inapplicable to God.

    If there is no relation between God, whose existence is neces-
sary, and His creatures, whose existence is contingent, there is no
possibility of asserting an analogy. It is *not* true, therefore, that
God's existence is more stable than ours, His life more permanent,
His power and wisdom more perfect (*Guide* 1.56). These claims imply that there is a basis for comparison—something Maimonides is
at pains to deny. What, then, do we say about statements like "God
exists" or "God is powerful"? They seem to be meaningful and to
convey more information than a tautology like "A is A." According
to Maimonides, the only sense we can attach to them is the corresponding negations: "God is not absent," "God is not weak."

    Here it is necessary to say a few words about negation. In the
first place, ordinary language is not an infallible guide to what is
a negative and what is a positive quality. We can see this by considering the following pairs of terms: infinite/perfect, undying/eter-

nal, spiritual/incorporeal. Although one appears to be positive and the other negative, in normal parlance they are synonymous. Thus a word like *one* may *look* positive but be used of God in a negative way.[11] If Maimonides is right, the same is true of *wise, good, living,* and the other divine attributes. As applied to us, they designate a positive quality; but just the opposite is true as applied to God. Hence the logic of discourse about God is different from that about humans.

In the second place, the negation Maimonides is talking about is exclusionary.[12] If I say, "This book is not blue," I am talking about an attribute which, though it does not belong to the book, could. From a logical standpoint, there is no difference between the negative judgment, "This book is not blue," and the positive one, "This book has a color somewhere else on the spectrum." There is nothing to be gained in using the negative formulation, and if this were the sort of negation Maimonides had in mind when he claimed that God has no positive attributes, his position would be trivial. Since every book has a color, when we say this book is not blue, we imply that it is something else. But "God is not weak" cannot mean that God has a place on the scale of which weakness and normal strength are the termini—even the highest point. Rather, it must mean that God is not on the scale at all; His power is utterly unlike ours. Maimonides makes this point with the example, "This wall does not see"(*Guide* 1.58). Seeing is inapplicable to walls. While the surface grammar of "This wall does not see" resembles that of "This wall does not keep out trespassers," the negations involved are quite different. All we can infer from "This wall does not see" is that seeing and blindness belong to things in a different category. Similarly, "God is not weak" implies not only that God does not admit of a privation, but that *He does not admit of a normal perfection either.* That is why Maimonides claims it is *not* true that God is more powerful than we are.

It follows that turning positive statements like "God is powerful" into negative ones like "God is not weak" is more than a stylistic exercise. The latter is a perspicuous way of representing what the former conceals: that our ground for holding this claim is not a clear understanding of omnipotence but the recognition that however *we* conceive of weakness or strength, God's power is different. We distinguish knowledge from power, and power from life. But our ability to distinguish them has no tendency to show that they are distinct in God. The true nature of our understanding is thus better expressed as a negation. In this respect, the proper analysis of "God is powerful" would be "God is not weak and we have no comprehension of what His power is like." The latter part of the conjunct indicates that "God is powerful" cannot be an axiom in a divine science. For even if we regard it as true, it does not meet the conditions Aristotle sets forth for the premises of a scientific demonstration, one of which is that it provides knowledge of the essential nature of the subject (*Posterior Analytics* 1.6).

What is true of God is also true of the heavenly bodies or intellects: the supposed analogy between the human knower and the divine object known is faulty.[13] In particular, Maimonides pursues two lines of attack against the classical Aristotelian position: (1) we cannot assume that what is true of the sublunary world is also true of the heavens, and (2) we cannot assume that the principles needed to explain the world as it is at present afford any understanding of its origin. It may be said, therefore, that Maimonides' strategy is not to replace the Aristotelian science of the heavens with one of his own but to deny that we have positive knowledge of the heavens at all.[14] We can take measurements of the heavenly bodies and say that they are composed of matter and form; but since the matter is not the sort we are familiar with on earth, we cannot conclude that the heavenly bodies have properties similar to terrestrial objects (*Guide* 1.58). In Book Two of the *Guide* (19 & 24), he argues that there is no known principle under which the motion of the heavenly bodies can be subsumed: some rotate from east to west, some from west to east; some rotate at one speed, some at another. According to the conclusion of 2.24, "regarding all that is in the heavens, man grasps nothing but a small measure of what is mathematical. . . ." In the case of God, we have a being who is not composed of matter at all. So anything we infer about the relation between potency and act in humans would have no application to God.

Consider an example. The Aristotelian philosophers assume that if God created the world in time, He would have to move from potency to act, and this would imply that He had undergone a change. Maimonides replies (*Guide* 2.18) that this argument works only for corporeal objects that have active and passive components. The Aristotelians themselves admit that it is possible for a purely active being to have intermittent effects depending on the disposition of the material that receives its action.[15] A fire that bleaches something at one moment may blacken something else at another. In short, there is no reason to suppose that all change is brought about by an agent moving from potency to act. If so, the Aristotelian argument that God would have to move from potency to act is invalid. Thus the word *action* is used homonymously in relation to God and to forces residing in material bodies. If there were an analogy between them, Aristotle's argument against creation would be persuasive. Maimonides' point is that the circumstances surrounding divine action and material action are so different that no analogy is possible.

We reach the same conclusion if we try to infer something about the origin of the world from knowledge of its current state. Here Maimonides asks us to imagine that a man is taken away from his mother at an early age and raised by his father on a deserted island. From a knowledge of his own anatomy, he would not be able to deduce anything about the science of reproduction or gestation. His present condition would provide little help in determining how he came to be (*Guide* 2.17). But difficult as this inference might be with respect to a human fetus, it is nothing compared to the inference we would have to make with respect to the origin of the world. Creation, after all, is not the same as change. In change, a substratum loses one accident and takes on another. But the substratum itself persists through the entire process. In creation, there is nothing, or nothing definite, which remains the same: we go from nonexistence to existence. There is no reason to think that creation and change can be explained by a common set of principles. It follows that the arguments of the Aristotelian philosophers are an attempt to extend metaphysical ideas like act, potency, and change beyond the limits of human understanding. That these principles are applicable to earthly phenomena, Maimonides has no doubt (*Guide* 2.22). But when applied to things beyond the earth, they amount to speculation. Worse, they amount to speculation dressed up as knowledge. To save the reputation of Aristotle, Maimonides claims that not even Aristotle believed he had a demonstration of eternity (*Guide* 2.15). From the standpoint of historical accuracy, Maimonides is almost certainly wrong. But he is not wrong in pointing out that the origin of the world cannot be understood by examining the changes of individual things within it. At the very least, the Aristotelians have given no reason to think it can.

Looking ahead to Kant, we can say that Maimonides set strict limits to what we can know scientifically.[16] In the First Antinomy, Kant shows that when it comes to the creation of the world, *either* of two contradictory theses can be proved. In effect, Maimonides argues for the converse: that *neither* of two contradictory theses can be proved. But there is clearly a point of agreement: human reason cannot know that the world was created or that it was not. There are reasons for preferring creation that will be discussed in the next chapter. But intellectual honesty requires us to admit we do not have anything approaching a demonstration; creation is a subject on which human reason must pause (*Guide* 1.71). This is a drastic conclusion, because if we cannot prove that the world was created, theology has no definitive answer to the single most important question it is supposed to address. To see why, we must keep in mind that there is more to the creation issue than a theory about the origin of the world. As Maimonides presents the debate, creation provides the theoretical foundation for miracles, revelation, providence, and the rest of the biblical worldview (*Guide* 2.25). By contrast, eternity provides the foundation for cosmic determinism, a view that Maimonides thinks renders the Torah void. The debate over creation is therefore a debate over radically different conceptions of God. If the debate cannot be settled by demonstration, no one can know for certain which conception of God is true.

The unsettling nature of this result has troubled people for centuries. In Book Six of *Wars of the Lord*, Gersonides tries to show that the arguments for creation *are* conclusive—though it should be understood that the creation he is talking about is not *ex nihilo*. On the other hand, there is a persistent school of thought that maintains that Maimonides was secretly committed to a doctrine of eternity.[17] The chief reasons for reading him as a precursor to Kant are philosophic: (1) he did in fact expose weaknesses in the Aristotelian position, and (2) his own arguments on behalf of creation are not decisive.[18] I see no reason, therefore, why we should not take him at his word. The central question posed by theology is beyond the limits of human reason to resolve conclusively.

3. Maimonides and the Status of Religious Truth

How, then, does Maimonides avoid skepticism? If there is no analogy between God and His creatures, between the creation of the universe and changes of things within it, how can one talk about religion without falling into a pit of nonsense? On the issue of creation, Maimonides proposes a change in modality: from what we can know to what it is rational to believe. By his own admission, Maimonides' arguments in favor of creation do no more than tip the scales. If someone were to insist on rigorous standards of proof, Maimonides would have little choice but to embrace skepticism.

One of the main contributions of the *Guide* is to show that we can work with less stringent standards provided we are self-conscious about what we are doing. In this context, "self-conscious" means that we do not claim greater rigor for our arguments that what they deserve, that we recognize when human reason has reached its limits, and that we do not aspire to go beyond them. Such is the lesson Maimonides draws from the Talmudic passage (*Hagigah* 14b) where four rabbis enter the garden of paradise (*pardes*) but experience very different results (*Guide* 1.32). One died, one went insane, one became an apostate, one emerged unscathed. Maimonides interprets the parable as saying that the four were exposed to divine or esoteric matters. What enabled one rabbi, Akiba, to enter and return in peace is that he did not attempt to overreach himself in the study of these things. Maimonides concludes that "human intellects have a limit at which they stop." With respect to creation, Maimonides does not show that the beginning of the world is an established fact; all he shows is that it is a possibility (*Guide* 2.18). As long as this is true, miracles, revelation, and providence are possibilities as well. In a word, the biblical worldview is possible. One can believe it without sinning against reason. More to the point, one can believe it without misrepresenting one's epistemological position. Although some will regard these conclusions as too weak, they are all that Maimonides set out to establish—that philosophy and Judaism are compatible.

On the issue of God, he proposes a shift from essence to action. If we cannot talk about what God *is*, we can talk about what He *does*. The difference is that the latter does not concern God as He is in Himself but His consequences or effects—the things which flow from or emanate from God.[19] Since God does not admit plurality, He cannot be the subject of a normal proposition. But we encounter no such problem if we move from God Himself to His effects on the world. We have seen that it is possible for one thing to have multiple effects, for example, the fire that bleaches and blackens. Provided we keep the thing and its effects separate, we can attribute multiplicity to the latter without compromising the simplicity of the former.

The reason this point requires a move from the metaphysical to the practical is that the things that flow from God, the things that we have some hope of comprehending, are the thirteen moral attributes or *middot* (literally: measures). To put this in a different way, the only sense we can make of God is that He is the one whose actions have beneficial consequences for human beings and the rest

of created existence. In this respect, the moral attributes are not aspects of God's nature as much as they are norms for humans to live
by.[20] There is no possibility of going from the effects of God's activity in the world to knowledge of the essential nature which produces them. As Maimonides is fond of pointing out, not even
Moses could see God's face but had to settle for intermediaries, that
is, God's goodness (Exodus 33.23; cf. *Guide* 1.37, 38, 54). As far as
human beings are concerned, the moral attributes are all we have.
We cannot infer from "God *does* good" to "God *is* good."

This result seems paradoxical because for human agents, the
inference from "X does good" to "X is good" is straightforward.
Again we face the problem of God's uniqueness. Once we say that
God is good, we introduce the multiplicity of subject and predicate.
The advantage of action oriented vocabulary is that we avoid the
problem of talking about God as He is in Himself. We can admit
skepticism on God Himself and drop to the level of effects one or
more steps removed from God. Arthur Hyman writes:

> Suppose it is the case that (1) there exists an empty room in
> which there is found some being "X," (2) the parts of a watch
> are introduced into the room, (3) nothing miraculously hap-
> pens in the room, and (4) after some time a finished watch is
> handed out of the room. From these conditions we can infer
> that the being "X" has the ability to produce a watch, though
> we do not know the essential nature of "X" nor any property
> of "X" which enables it to construct a watch.[21]

In one respect, Maimonides has made a concession to the doctrine
of analogy. Actions flow from God that resemble just and merciful
actions performed by human agents. The point is, however, that the
analogy is not between us and God but between the consequences
of His actions and the consequences of ours (*Guide* 1.54). And even
here, we cannot press the analogy very far. Moral action in humans
come from dispositions in the soul. Since we have no grounds for
asserting such dispositions in God, the nature of the "X" that produces the actions remains a mystery.

We can see how Maimonides would answer an objection raised
by Gersonides and Aquinas.[22] Why are some names applicable to
God and others not? Why, for example, can we not say that God is
corporeal? He cannot be corporeal in the way we are; but if *corporeal*
is a homonym, the fact that corporeality implies imperfection in us
would have no tendency to show that it implies imperfection in

Him. For all we know, divine corporeality might be a perfection. By the same token, why can we not say that God is cowardly, or arrogant, or anything else? As long as we qualify these claims by saying that the terms in question are homonyms, we avoid the charge of blasphemy. If corporeality presents a problem, vices like cowardliness or arrogance present a worse one. Why not attribute moral imperfections to God since, once again, a quality that represents an imperfection in us might not do so in Him?

In regard to corporeality, Maimonides would point out that the prophets do not ascribe to God anything that the multitude regard as a deficiency (*Guide* 1.47). The reason is simple: religious language has many functions. Not only must it state the truth, it must evoke proper emotions and convey an attitude of reverence. Even if a word like *corporeal* is predicated homonymously, to say that God is corporeal would invite confusion.[23] We do not have to adopt an esoteric doctrine to see that the connotations of certain words are such that no sacred literature can apply them to God without misleading the average worshipper.

In regard to words like *cowardly* or *arrogant*, Maimonides would invoke the principle of *imitatio Dei*.[24] We have seen that this principle is articulated by Plato in the *Theaetetus*. More important, for Maimonides' purposes, it is also found in Leviticus 19.2: "Ye shall be holy; for I the Lord your God am holy." Maimonides interprets the passage as follows (*Guide* 1.54):

> For the Utmost virtue of man is to become like unto Him . . . as far as he is able; which means that we should make our actions like unto His, as the Sages made clear when interpreting the verse, *Ye shall be holy*.

What is significant about this interpretation is that Maimonides takes the principle in a behavioral rather than an ontological way. It is not that we become like God in the sense that our nature comes to resemble His. That is impossible. Rather, it is that our actions bring about results similar to the ones brought about by His. If the consequences of divine activity are such that unborn embryos are protected against harm from external forces, God is called merciful. It follows, according to the principle of *imitatio Dei*, that we are obliged to protect our children from harm. In this way, God serves as a moral exemplar. But it does not follow that by protecting our children, we come to resemble God. Like Moses, we cannot get beyond intermediaries.

If Maimonides is right, the intermediaries are enough to up-hold a standard of behavior and therefore the body of Jewish law. We do not need metaphysical speculation to make sense of the religion. Once it is shown that the biblical worldview is possible, all we need is the moral attributes of God. The crux of Maimonides' interpretation is that we can retain the principle of *imitatio Dei* and still admit to ignorance about God as He is in Himself. It follows that everything we say about God is either (1) a statement about His actions, or (2) an exclusion negation. Classical metaphysical propositions like "God exists" or "God is one" would have to be interpreted according to (2). We could regard them as true and im-portant; but since *unity* and *existence* are homonymous terms, these propositions cannot provide the foundation for a divine science in Aristotle's sense.[25] There is no science of homonymy. In the last analysis, such propositions are meaningful because they assert the uniqueness of God and our inability to know Him.

4. Maimonides' Intellectualism

According to the interpretation proposed above, the only pos-itive knowledge we can have of God is ethical in nature. It pertains to His actions rather than His essence and is needed to uphold the principle of *imitatio Dei*. It will be objected that any suggestion of a practical turn in Maimonides is inconsistent with his account of hu-man perfection and the intellectual love of God. The issue is whether human perfection culminates in ethical action or theoretical reflection. If, as I have argued, Maimonides undermined the possi-bility of a divine science, there is a strong reason for preferring ac-tion over reflection: there is nothing of a positive nature for the theologian to reflect on. In his introduction to the *Guide*, Shlomo Pines attacked the idea of a practical turn:

> As Maimonides points out in the last chapter of the *Guide* (III 54), man should endeavor to imitate Him in this respect (i.e., by performing acts of justice, mercy, and good judgment). This statement has sometimes been interpreted as meaning that— in contradiction to the whole trend of his thought and to many definite assertions occurring in the *Guide* and even in the chapter in question—Maimonides at the end adopted the quasi-Kantian idea that the ordinary moral virtues and moral actions are of greater importance and value than the intellec-tual virtues and the theoretical way of life. It seems to me that

a study of this last chapter and of the chapter preceding it (III 53 as well as of I 52) cannot but show that this explanation is completely false.[26]

Maimonides does maintain that the moral virtues are a preparation for the intellectual (1.54). The chief intellectual virtue is the love of God which, in Maimonides' opinion, is proportional to the knowledge of Him. Pines's original view was that this intellectualism undercuts negative theology. If intellectual virtue is the primary human perfection, it cannot be true that the only positive knowledge we have of God is ethical. There must be some sort of knowledge of God's essence.

But to sustain his objection, Pines had to follow Strauss into the misty realm of esoteric interpretation. After emphasizing the importance of metaphysics, Pines admitted the *Guide* does not look anything like a systematic treatise; a reader possessing all the qualities Maimonides requires could obtain from the text no more than what Pines termed "an inkling" of physical or metaphysical knowledge.[27] Worse, Pines attributed to Maimonides a secret doctrine of analogy to get metaphysical knowledge into the picture. The negative theology so prominent in Book One becomes a "smokescreen" which, in Pines's original view "may not hold up to close scrutiny."[28] Unfortunately we were not told *why* it will not hold up or what we are likely to find when we look behind the smokescreen. One can only guess that it would have been the standard medieval view of God as found in the Arabic philosophers and Gersonides. When Maimonides departs from the prevailing opinions of his day, people fond of esoteric interpretation typically assume he is being disingenuous. The problem is that without negative theology, Maimonides loses much of his originality as a thinker. He was not the first person to follow the *via negativa;* it can be traced back to Dionysius, and before him, to Clement and Plotinus. Maimonides' contribution consists in the rigor with which he applied it, in particular the view that the Divine attributes are homonyms. Take away negative theology and the *Guide* is not just an esoteric book but one whose philosophic significance is greatly in doubt.

The main argument Pines gave for regarding Maimonides' negative theology as a smokescreen is the theory of intellection presented at *Guide* 1.68. There Maimonides accepts the Aristotelian theory according to which the intellect in action, the idea in the intellect, and the act of forming that idea are one and the same.[29] Put otherwise, when the intellect forms an idea of an object, the intellect, the act of forming the idea, and the idea formed are one. Therefore it is true to say that the intellect is what it apprehends. According to Maimonides, this analysis applies to God, whose intellect is always in action, and to humans when the intellect moves from potency to act. But if this is so, two consequences seem to follow: (1) we have some positive knowledge of God, and (2) the structure of divine apprehension is the same as the structure of human. Both consequences are suggestive of a doctrine of analogy.

It is significant, however, that in a more recent publication, Pines has changed his mind.[30] According to the later view, there are two very distinct levels of human comprehension in Maimonides' epistemology: that of the natural world and that of the heavens. In the first case, the mind is presented with a composite of matter and form in sense or imagination. The faculty of insight abstracts the form and actualizes it in the mind of the knower. It is in this sense that the mind becomes identical with what it apprehends. In the second case, that of separate forms or intelligences, the mind can apprehend nothing. For if a human mind were to apprehend the form of a heavenly body, it would, in the act of apprehension, become identical with that form. In short, there would be no difference between the human mind and the intelligence (celestial body) it comes to know: the limitations imposed by the human condition would vanish. But this conclusion, as Pines himself notes, is at odds with the view Maimonides espouses at *Guide* 3.9: "Matter is a strong veil preventing the apprehension of that which is separate from matter as it truly is. . . . [W]henever our intellect aspires to apprehend the deity or one of the intellects, there subsists this great veil interposed between the two." Pines concludes that Maimonides' comments on divine intellection are probable at best and therefore "the analogy that is drawn in the chapter [1.68] between God's and man's intellection does not and probably is not intended to prove anything."

Still, Pines's original position raises an interesting question. Suppose there is a single theory of intellection which includes our knowledge and God's. Suppose, in addition, that there are significant features of dissimilarity such as those spelled out at *Guide* 3.20: (1) God's knowledge remains one even though it embraces different kinds of objects, (2) God's knowledge extends to things not yet in existence, (3) God's knowledge includes the infinite, (4) God's knowledge remains unchanged even though it comprises the knowledge of changeable things, (5) God's knowledge of future contingents does not determine their outcome. At what point do we emphasize the differences and at what point the similarity? Maimonides insists that similarity does not extend across generic lines. The proponents of analogy insist that if a single theory of intellection covers both, we have a case where God represents the primary instance of the thing in question while we represent a derivative one. Insofar as contemporary philosophers have abandoned the notion of categories and category mistakes, the question is unanswerable. Rather than accuse Maimonides of putting forward a secret doctrine, it would be better to conclude that the concept of similarity is not sufficiently precise to say whether *knowledge* is used analogously or homonymously. Gersonides tries to resolve the issue in favor of analogy. But the fact that later thinkers took this option is no reason to accuse Maimonides of hiding the truth. His account of negative theology may be imprecise, but it is not insincere. The point Maimonides wants to drive home is that we have no idea how God contemplates the universe or how knowledge, will, and power are one in God. Again, if relation implies reciprocity, there is no relation between God's knowledge and ours—even if we assume that God is one with the object of His thought.

What, then, becomes of contemplation and the dozens of places where Maimonides claims the purpose of the Torah is to instill true opinions in the mind of the worshiper? For example, consider this passage from *Guide* 3.27:

> His [human] ultimate perfection is to become rational in actu, I mean to have an intellect in actu; this would consist in knowing everything concerning all the things that it is within the capacity of man to know in accordance with his ultimate perfection. It is clear that to this ultimate perfection there do not belong either actions or moral qualities and that it consists only of opinions toward which speculation has led and that investigation has rendered compulsory.

The passage would constitute strong evidence for the intellectual interpretation were it not for the phrase "that it is within the capacity of man to know." Such qualifications are frequent in the *Guide* and suggest that when Maimonides talks about intellectual perfection, he is not speaking loosely.[31] Intellectual perfection is the highest human virtue, but any reasonable interpretation of it must take into account what Maimonides says about the *limits* of human knowledge elsewhere in the *Guide*.

Recall Maimonides' discussion of the four rabbis who entered paradise. Akiba entered and returned in peace because he did not aspire to things which lie beyond the reach of the human intellect. So while he achieved perfection, in *our* terms his achievement is more critical than speculative: he recognized exactly how far his arguments carried him. In a word, his knowledge is negative: it imposes limits. The key to understanding this view of human perfection is to see that negative knowledge is still knowledge. Here Maimonides follows a long line of thinkers who stress the value of knowing that one does not know. In the *Apology* (23a–b), Socrates sums up a lifetime of philosophic inquiry by admitting he has not found the answers to his questions and that when it comes to the knowledge a god possesses, human knowledge is of little or no value. This conclusion is consistent with the history of his life, for while he professed an abiding trust in god, he never claimed to have knowledge of "higher matters."[32] The closest he comes to defining piety in the *Euthyphro* is to say that it is a species of justice.

We would be misinterpreting Socrates if we did not see that the recognition of one's limits is for him a significant achievement—perhaps the most significant a person can have. According to Maimonides (*Guide* 1.59), it may take a lifetime of study to see why the attributes investigated by an earthly science cannot be applied to God. Yet such study would bring us *closer* to Him and to the perfection we seek:

> You come nearer to the apprehension of Him, may He be exalted, with every increase in the negations regarding Him. . . . For this reason a man sometimes labors for many years in order to understand some science and to gain true knowledge of its premises so that he should have certainty with regard to this science, whereas the only conclusion from this science in its entirety consists in our negating with reference to God some notion of which it has been learnt by means of a demonstration that it cannot possibly be ascribed to God.

In sum: we understand God when we realize that nothing in the world can be compared to Him. Human perfection consists not in piercing the veil but accepting it.

It follows that the knowledge Maimonides is talking about is critical or second-order knowledge: a form of learned ignorance. According to Maimonides, critical knowledge is the epistemological counterpart of admitting God's uniqueness. Again from *Guide* 1.59:

"The knowledge of Him consists in the inability to attain the ultimate term in apprehending Him." But where does learned ignorance lead? Not to quietude. The *Guide* would make no sense unless contemplation of one's limits led to contemplation of God's moral attributes and thus to the 613 commandments. Again, the reasoning is Socratic. If knowledge of things above and below the earth is not accessible to us, we must set our sights on something else: the knowledge necessary to live a virtuous life. In this way, the pursuit of knowledge and the pursuit of virtue are identical. So it is no accident that at *Guide* 3.11, Maimonides accepts the classic formulation of the Socratic paradox. Nor is it an accident that God's moral attributes are brought back to center stage at the end of the book (*Guide* 3.54):

> It is clear that the perfection of man that may truly be gloried in is the one acquired by him who has achieved, in a measure corresponding to his capacity, apprehension of Him, may He be exalted, and who knows His providence extending over His creatures as manifested in the act of bringing them into being and in their governance as it is. The way of life of such an individual, after he has achieved this apprehension, will always have in view *loving-kindness*, *righteousness*, and *judgment*, through assimilation to His action, may He be exalted, just as we have explained several times in this Treatise.

Although very few people may be able to reach this state, *in principle* it is open to everyone. As Isadore Twersky wrote, "this minority is not a closed caste, the goal remains open and universal and this special kind of *imitatio Dei* is a true mirror of Maimonideanism."[33]

We may conclude that intellectual perfection is both critical and practical in nature. Looking backward from the twelfth century, we can draw parallels between Maimonides and Plato; but it should also be clear why, looking in the opposite direction, we can draw parallels between Maimonides and Kant. There are dangers in reading one philosopher through the eyes of another—particularly when they are separated by more than five hundred years. We can respect the differences between them and still admit that they had similar intuitions about the limits of human reason. The chief advantage of this reading is that it avoids esoteric interpretation. Maimonides' contribution can be stated in terms which leave no doubt about its significance. While it is true that Maimonides speaks cryptically and employs dialectical arguments, so have any number of great thinkers. He takes it upon himself to reveal doctrines that the untrained eye would never find in Scripture, but what is surprising in that? Of course, Maimonides is not as rigorous as Kant. He relies on the Aristotelian notion of categories. He agrees with Aristotle's view of the sublunary realm. His quarrel with Aristotelian metaphysics is based on dissatisfaction with existing arguments rather than an attempt to set forth the preconditions of all future knowledge. Still, Maimonides offered a critique of what passed for knowledge in his day. To this extent, he showed the world that it is possible to disengage from the doctrine of analogy and still put forward a credible form of religion. The next step in this account is to consider someone whose critique went beyond anything Maimonides could foresee.

5. Descartes and Voluntarism

Descartes' place in this discussion is based on a letter to Mersenne written in 1630:

> The mathematical truths which you call eternal have been laid down by God and depend on Him entirely no less than the rest of His creatures. Indeed to say that these truths are independent of God is to talk of Him as if He were Jupiter or Saturn and to subject Him to the Styx and the Fates. Please do not hesitate to assert and proclaim everywhere that it is God who has laid down these laws in nature just as a king lays down laws in his kingdom. There is no single one that we cannot understand if our mind turns to consider it. They are all inborn in our minds, just as a king would imprint his laws on the hearts of all his subjects if he had enough power to do so. The greatness of God, on the other hand, is something which we cannot comprehend even though we know it. But the very fact that we judge it incomprehensible makes us esteem it the more greatly; just as a king has more majesty when he is less familiarly known by his subjects, provided of course that they do not get the idea that they have no king—they must know him enough to be in no doubt about that.[34]

This doctrine amounts to the claim that God's will is absolutely free. The propositions we regard as necessary depend on that will as much as finite creatures do. So just as God was free to create or not to create the world, He was free to create a world in which the

Pythagorean Theorem is true or one in which it is false.[35] Although *we* cannot understand how the Pythagorean Theorem could be false, this is only a fact about us. As Harry Frankfurt put it: "That our minds cannot conceive such things signifies nothing beyond itself, however, except that God has freely chosen to create us like that."[36] What looks like a necessary truth about the world is actually a truth about human psychology. God is not limited by what our minds are capable of understanding.

The crux of Descartes' view is, once again, the uniqueness of God in a monotheistic universe. To limit God's will, in particular, to limit it to what human beings are able to understand, is to break the boundary that separates God from His creatures, to treat Him like the Greek gods, who were limited by the Styx and the Fates. This does not mean that the Pythagorean Theorem is false, only that God *could have made it so*. The power of God is infinite and incomprehensible. As Descartes tells Arnauld, we can never say that something cannot be brought about by God.[37] I cannot imagine a mountain without a valley, but I should not presume that God cannot make one. All I can say is that He has given me a mind which cannot conceive of such a possibility. It follows that there is nothing in the Pythagorean Theorem or any other necessary truth which makes it inherently necessary or its opposite inherently impossible. God might have given me a mind which finds the denial of the Pythagorean Theorem as compelling as I now find its assertion. And He might have created a world in which its denial is not just compelling but true. The limits of human reason are just that: limits of *human* reason. They present no obstacle to an omnipotent God.

To the suggestion that his view is incoherent—that we cannot understand what it means to suppose that the *im*possible is possible—Descartes has a ready reply. There is no point in asking *how* God could have made the Pythagorean Theorem false or two times four not equal to eight; Descartes freely admits that we cannot understand it. Here his position is a variant on a scholastic principle: we can know *that* God's power is limitless without being able to understand what limitless power implies. In a letter to Mesland, he writes:

As for the difficulty of conceiving how it was a matter of freedom and indifference for God to make it not be true that the three angles of a triangle were equal to two right angles, or generally, that contradictions cannot exist together, one can easily remove it by considering that the power of God cannot have any limits. . . .[38]

According to Frankfurt, it is a mistake to think we can offer a logically coherent account of what God can do. God exists, but the nature of His existence or His power is beyond comprehension. In fact, it is dangerous to suppose that the truths we consider necessary afford some sort of purchase on God. As human beings possessing finite minds, all we can do is stay within the bounds of rationality. But we should not be so bold as to think that these limits also apply to God.

Descartes' view has had few, if any, proponents in Jewish philosophy. The standard Jewish position is the one adopted by Maimonides in the *Guide* (3.15).[39] That which is logically impossible is so necessarily and for all time. It does not limit God's power to say that He can create only what is logically possible. To insist that His power must extend to the logically *im*possible is to fall victim to incoherence. This does not mean that in individual cases it is always an easy matter to decide whether something is impossible. It may be that we consider some things impossible owing to a lack of imagination. The boundaries of human imagination do not restrict God's power. But if it could be shown that something actually is impossible, that its incomprehensibility has nothing to do with the weakness of our imagination but applies to the nature of the thing under discussion, then it is not within God's power to create it.

Why the reluctance to extend God's power beyond the limits of human reason? That God's knowledge and power are beyond comprehension Maimonides would be the first to admit. But his position is that it does not limit God's power to say that He can do only what is logically possible. Maimonides would be right if there were reason to suppose that God's apprehension of necessary truths is fundamentally like our own. If, when God thinks the Pythagorean Theorem, He apprehends something that cannot be otherwise, then there is a reason for saying He *wills* it as something that cannot be otherwise. On this account, God's knowledge is more vast than ours, but He shares something very important with us: the same principles of rationality.[40] We can then be sure that if something is incoherent to us, it will be incoherent to God. No limit is implied if God cannot create what He Himself cannot conceive.

Notice, however, that the position just described assumes a basic similarity between our knowledge and God's. If both operate according to the same principles, then while the extent of God's knowledge is beyond our comprehension, its basic structure is not. There is, as it were, an isomorphism between our knowledge and His: the necessary propositions we know are a subset of those known by God. There is little question that Maimonides would want to affirm such isomorphism. The question is, once again, whether the similarity is enough to overturn his insistence that *knowledge* is a homonym. Remember that for Maimonides, it is *not* true that God's knowledge and power are greater than ours. As late as *Guide* 3.20, he still insists there is no relation between them, no doctrine of analogy that would enable us to identify a common core of meaning in *wise* as applied to us and as applied to God. If so, how can we use our knowledge to infer something about God's? How can we say that because we regard something as necessary, God must regard it that way too? From the fact that something is an essential part of human wisdom, I submit that there is no conclusion we can draw about its status for God. All we can do is follow Descartes in saying that God has endowed us with a mind that cannot conceive its denial.[41]

To make this clearer, let me sketch three possible positions:

1. *Analogy.* The propositions we regard as necessary are also necessary for God. Although He knows much more than we do, there is some overlap between His knowledge and ours.

2. *Agnosticism.* The propositions we regard as necessary may or may not be necessary for God. He may regard them as necessary, possible, or false. We simply cannot know.

3. *Cartesianism.* Both the propositions we regard as necessary and their denials are possible for God. Since God is omnipotent and can do anything, necessity does not apply to Him. He could make the Pythagorean Theorem false just as easily as make it true.

If there is no relation between our knowledge and God's, then the only alternatives open to us are (2) and (3).

In the above-mentioned passage in the *Guide*, Maimonides claims that only someone ignorant of mathematics would believe that God could make a square with a diagonal equal to the side. But it is noteworthy that between Maimonides and Descartes, there are no mathematical propositions in dispute. Descartes' question concerns the applicability of mathematical propositions to God. On what grounds, then, can Maimonides say that God cannot make a square with a diagonal equal to a side? By his own admission, Maimonides has no positive knowledge of God's nature. It would seem, therefore, that the only basis for his claim is the fact that such a possibility is incomprehensible *to us*. But this point is not in dispute either. No one is arguing that we can understand how God might do this. The issue is whether we can offer *our* inability to understand something as a reason for saying that God cannot do it. The distinction between reason and imagination will not help. For even if someone could show that there are purely rational grounds for regarding something as impossible, we must establish an isomorphism between human reason and divine before we can say what Maimonides wants.

Lacking any positive knowledge of God, we cannot even begin to establish this isomorphism. We can, of course, *believe* what we want about God's apprehension of necessary truths. But appealing to the same intellectual honesty which Maimonides cites in his discussion of creation, we have nothing approaching a demonstration that God apprehends these truths as we do. Nor will we ever have one, because to know how God apprehends necessary truths, we would have to have a mind like God's. As Maimonides himself claims at *Guide* 1.59, God is not an object of human comprehension: none but God can comprehend God. So the inertia of Maimonides' negative theology points directly to the agnostic alternative. The fact that he regarded the truths of mathematics as certain is not evidence of esotericism or inconsistency. All it shows is that he did not carry his critical arguments to their extreme. That required another philosopher of genius.

According to Frankfurt, there are reasons for moving beyond agnosticism to full-strength Cartesianism.[42] Whatever status the necessary truths might have in God's mind, Descartes considers it a mistake to think that His mind has any causal effect on His will. Since willing and knowing are the same in God, there is no act of thought or reflection prior to the first exercise of His will. There is, then, nothing external to His will that can exert any influence over it. But here, again, the inertia of Maimonides' position points in the direction of agnosticism. Although knowing and willing are the same in God, we have no positive knowledge of either one or of the precise way in which they are connected, a point we will examine further in the next chapter. For the present, we are forced to admit that when it comes to what God can or cannot do, human reason must again pause.

Part of what people find unappealing about Descartes' position is the suggestion that God might have created the world in an arbitrary fashion, so that behind the truths we regard as necessary there lurks absurdity. In the case of Jewish philosophy, the problem with Cartesianism is its practical consequences. It is but a small step from the voluntaristic God of Descartes to the ethically indifferent God of *Fear and Trembling*. A position that stresses the primacy of ethical reason cannot admit ethical indifference. To put this in a different way, Maimonides could admit agnosticism in regard to mathematical and metaphysical truths, but he could not permit such agnosticism to spill over into ethics. God's moral status must be preserved or the whole concept of *imitatio Dei* will be lost.

Still, there is an aspect of Descartes' position which can be seen as carrying on the work of Maimonides and the negative theologians. Since there is a discontinuity between human reason and God, there is no point in using the former to gain a hold on the latter. Because God does not have to obey the laws of logic, the laws of logic cannot reveal anything about God as He is in Himself. It follows that theological speculation about the nature of God is fruitless. Faced with infinite power we cannot understand, there is only one alternative. According to Descartes: "I consider only what I can conceive and what I cannot conceive."[43] If science is limited to what we can conceive, there is no possibility of a science of God.[44] Nor is there any possibility of referring to God for the purpose of advancing a scientific demonstration. He is beyond the sphere of what science can grasp. It follows that what we believe about God is one thing, what we can prove scientifically, another.

To take a specific example, it may be true that God can make a square with a diagonal equal to the side. But there is no scientific use to which this proposition can be put. We cannot use it in mathematics because mathematics is limited to what we are capable of understanding. We cannot use it as the foundation of a rational theology because God resists all our attempts to know His essence. After admitting that God's power is limitless, there is very little we can do except go about our business in the normal way, provided, of course, that we are not in the business of natural theology.

On my reading, the positions discussed so far share this much: they are both opposed to theological dogmatism. Maimonides has essentially two opponents: (1) those who think that God possesses attributes in the way finite substances do, and (2) those who think that the principles that explain phenomena in the sublunary realm also explain phenomena in the heavens. Descartes' position is more

extreme but appears to be motivated by similar concerns. His enemies are those who think that what we regard as necessary imposes
any kind of restriction on God. Both want to resist the tendency to
think that God can be grasped by principles which arise out of human experience. Again, I do not think Maimonides carried his position as far as he could have. The skepticism he expresses in regard
to Aristotelian metaphysics seems to vanish when it comes to logic
and mathematics. But in one respect, even Descartes did not carry
the argument as far as it could be taken. For that we must finally
turn to Kant.

6. Kant and the Practical Turn

Both Maimonides and Descartes prevent us from saying that
we can know God's essence. But if we cannot know *what* He is or
comprehend the power He wields, we can at least know *that* He is.
For Descartes, this means that adherence to the laws of logic requires the conclusion that God exists. Since God need not follow
the laws of logic, there is the possibility that He might will Himself
out of existence and render these arguments false. As far as human
understanding is concerned, this possibility makes no sense. We
cannot conceive of a universe in which God does not exist. Therefore we have no choice but to accept the argument that proves that
He does.

There is a respect in which Kant goes further than Descartes
and a respect in which he does not. With practical interests of his
own, Kant does not take seriously the possibility that God can contravene the laws of logic. Indeed, Kant believes that our idea of God
is nothing more or less than what is required by the moral law.[45]
Since the moral law is an imperative arising from my conception of
myself as a rational agent, my idea of God is neatly circumscribed
by the limits of practical reason. But there is a respect in which Kant
thinks that even Descartes was not skeptical enough. God's existence cannot be known with certainty. As far as theoretical reason is
concerned, I can deny God's existence and still be coherent.

This denial does not involve anything as radical as conceiving
of a God who could will Himself out of existence. All I have to do is
recognize that existential judgments are synthetic. Thus existence is
not the sort of thing that can be contained in or implied by essence.
Put otherwise, it is impossible to demonstrate the existence of anything from concepts alone (*Critique of Practical Reason* 139).[46] In order
to get to existence, I have to move beyond concepts to intuition. But

as a supersensuous being, God cannot be given in intuition. If I cannot show that God's existence is implied by His essence, neither can I show that His existence follows from empirical judgments about the world. In order to move from a judgment about the world to knowledge of God, I would have to know that this world is the best possible. If it were less than the best possible, it would not imply the existence of an all-perfect Creator. To know that this world is the best possible, I would have to compare it to every other possible world. But to complete this infinite series of comparisons, I would have to be omniscient.

In some ways Kant's criticism of metaphysics is a familiar theme. The categories that define human understanding cannot be applied to things outside the scope of that understanding and yield knowledge. If Maimonides showed that God is outside the scope of physics, and Descartes that He is outside the scope of logic, Kant's point is that He is outside the scope of anything whose existence is given in experience and that can be known as a matter of fact. To put this a different way, the idea of God is possible in the sense that it does not involve a contradiction. But this idea has no constitutive role to play because there is no intuition whose understanding requires it. It follows that thinking this idea cannot provide us with knowledge of a corresponding object. Nor can it provide us with a causal understanding of a natural phenomenon. Kant does insist that the idea of God plays a regulative role in science. Although "God willed it" is never an explanation for why something happens, it may help us in our understanding of natural phenomena to assume that the world has been fashioned by an intelligent Creator. But this is an assumption only, not a proven fact.

As far as metaphysics is concerned, the thrust of Kant's philosophy is, like that of Maimonides, negative. Nothing we assert of God can be brought to bear on spatial/temporal phenomena. By the same token, nothing that arises in space and time can be applied directly to God. To do otherwise is to succumb to anthropomorphism. In the *Critique of Practical Reason* (137–38), Kant insists that if we were to remove all empirical content from the attributes that the natural theologians apply to God, we would see that nothing remains but empty words. We can imagine Maimonides applauding.

Still, if we cannot reach God with concepts derived from experience, we can, according to Kant, reach Him with concepts derived from morality. This argument may be abbreviated as follows. We have a duty under the moral law to seek the highest good. Therefore the highest good must be possible. As Kant frequently points out, *ought* implies *can*. If the highest good is possible, a cause capable of bringing it about must be postulated. The highest good implies a connection between happiness and those *worthy* of happiness. A cause capable of bringing about such a connection would have to effect a harmony between nature (happiness) and freedom (moral worth). Since no human being is the author of nature, no human being can effect this harmony. We must therefore postulate the existence of a being who is the cause of nature and who can furnish the ground of this connection. Such a being is God.

This is a difficult, and, I think, not altogether satisfactory argument.[47] What concerns me is not the detail of Kant's position as much as the strategy he employs to get to it. God's existence is established on practical rather than theoretical grounds. Based as they are on physics or metaphysics, the standard arguments are misconceived. For even if they did prove the existence of something, that being would be far less than what our idea of God requires. In the *Critique of Pure Reason* (A818/B846), Kant concludes:

> It was the moral ideas that gave rise to that concept of the Divine Being which we now hold to be correct—and we so regard it not because speculative reason convinces us of its correctness, but because it completely harmonizes with the moral principles of reason. Thus it is always only to pure reason, though only in its practical employment, that we must finally ascribe the merit of having connected with our highest interest a knowledge which reason can think only, and cannot establish, and of having thereby shown it to be, not indeed a demonstrated dogma, but a postulate which is absolutely necessary in view of what are reason's own most essential ends.

Theology, then, is a moral rather than a physical or metaphysical enterprise. If God is to be found at all, it is not behind nature but behind the moral law.

Another way to see this is to recognize that, for Kant, morality is pure; it has no empirical content. Therefore, as long as we use morality as the basis of our understanding of God, we cannot be accused of anthropomorphism. Anything given in experience is limited or conditioned. To the degree that we employ such concepts to understand God, we are not thinking of God but of a superlatively qualified human being. It is only when we move beyond experience to the rational concepts of morality that we have any hope of understanding perfection. So once again, theology cannot take nature as its point of departure. Kant is, and admits to being, within the Platonic tradition.[48]

It could be argued that Kant's stress on the priority of moral reason as a way of understanding God is an extension of Maimonides' claim that God is known through His acts. For Kant the only content that can legitimately be ascribed to our idea of God is that of a moral agent who insures the connection between virtue and happiness. That is, God, as author of the universe, insures the possibility that those worthy of happiness will achieve it. Beyond the predicates needed to define God as a moral agent, there is nothing of a positive nature we can say about Him.

On the question of analogy, Kant maintains a deliberate ambiguity. On the one hand, he grants the negative theologians the majority of what they want. God's knowledge and will are not just stronger versions of the knowledge and will we possess. Human understanding is discursive and dependent on external objects given in sense. God's understanding is intuitive and independent of any kind of representation. God knows everything at once, not as an external object which affects Him from without, but as a way of knowing Himself. Kant is clear that *we* cannot form any concept of a purely intuitive understanding.[49] Similar considerations apply to the will. The will of man is intermittent, directed to objects external to itself, and capable of being determined by sensible motives. The will of God is completely self-sufficient and inscrutable. In the *Critique of Teleological Judgment* (90, n.1), he even points out that we cannot infer properties in God by analogy. The causality that God exercises over the world is nothing like that which we exercise over external objects. Human causality cannot be transferred to "a being which has no generic conception in common with man beyond that of a thing in the abstract." Again, we can imagine Maimonides applauding.

Yet, having said this much, Kant retains the notion of analogy, albeit in the weakened sense. In the passage from the *Critique of Teleological Judgment* referred to above, he maintains that while I cannot *infer* properties in God by analogy, I can *think* them by analogy.[50] God's authorship of the world is conceived on the analogy of the human creation of artifacts. But, again, Kant is careful not to imply that God is like a grand carpenter or watchmaker. The comparison is not between the watchmaker and God, which is the standard way of interpreting analogy, but between the watchmaker's relation to his product and God's relation to the world. As Kant puts it: "Such knowledge is knowledge *by analogy*, which means not, as the word is commonly taken, an imperfect similarity of two things, but a perfect similarity of two relations between quite dissimilar things."[51] The difference is significant because it allows Kant to uphold something close to Maimonides' position. According to Kant, it is not God Himself that I think by analogy but His role as creator. The divine nature remains inscrutable.[52] When I think about God, what I focus on is not His essence, what He *is*, as much as His authorship, what He *does*. Put otherwise, God is understood not as the subject of predicates but as an agent with a purpose. It is as true for Kant as it was for Maimonides that "the place of being is taken by action."

To be sure, God's creation of the world is not the same as our creation of artifacts. It is therefore misleading to say that there is a *perfect* similarity of the two relations. Kant admits this in the *Critique of Teleological Judgment* when he claims that our causality is sensuously conditioned and therefore cannot be transferred to a being that has no generic conception in common with humans. So the analogy or proportion is a weak one at best. We do not create watches or cabinets ex nihilo. It may be said, therefore, that while Kant invokes the notion of analogy, he does nothing to hide his misgivings. A tight analogy between God and humans would lead right back to the dogmatism Kant hopes to avoid.

Yet even a weakened analogy is not without problems. The Kantian categories apply only to objects of experience. But in the *Critique of Practical Reason* and Kant's other religious writings, possibility, actuality, necessity, causality, and unity are applied to God. Kant was aware of this but argues that the use to which these concepts are put in moral reasoning is different from that required by theoretical reason.[53] A full discussion of this problem, including the neo-Kantian solutions, is beyond the scope of the current inquiry.[54] The nature of the problem, however, is clear. It is the familiar one we have encountered since the beginning of this chapter. If God is unique, He cannot be characterized by ideas that arise in human experience. But if He cannot be characterized by such ideas, how can He be characterized at all? The negative theologian claims that, in an important sense, He cannot be. The question is how far to press the claim that God is unknowable.

We have seen that Maimonides allowed some positive assertions about God provided they have to do with His consequences or effects. Yet here, too, problems developed. We can take the Cartesian option of saying that God is so unknowable that we cannot even say He is rational. In place of reason, we get what Frankfurt terms "sheer unconstrained will or power" at the source of the universe. Kant is much closer to Maimonides in this debate, but as a result, Kant is faced with what he himself terms "the enigma of critical philosophy"—namely, how he can renounce the application of the categories to supersensible reality in speculation but make use of them in morals.[55] If God were completely unknowable, this problem would vanish only to be replaced by another: how can God be a necessary postulate of moral reason if nothing of a positive nature can be said of Him? We are back to the question of whether negative theology implies total skepticism about God or whether it implies what we might call a critical attitude. Descartes opts for the first, Maimonides and Kant for the second.

7. Contemporary Reflections

The most obvious contribution of negative theology is the extent to which it forces us to take the limits of human reason seriously. Not one of the figures discussed is an atheist or an absolute skeptic. All put a great deal of trust in the sciences and made original contributions there. But the general tendency of their thought is to distinguish between the causes and principles that operate in the sciences and the things we can say about God. If Maimonides refuted the Aristotelians by showing that God is not known as a substance with an essential form, Descartes showed that neither can He be known as the repository of eternal truth. With the benefit of two thousand years of theological debate and the assistance of David Hume, Kant sought to show that the only area where we have any hope of comprehending God is ethics. In spirit, Kant's position is thoroughly Jewish. The prophets did not seek God by engaging in cosmological speculation or by reflecting on the certainty of the Pythagorean Theorem. Cohen writes:

> The prophet knows nothing of science. Not even in Babylonia did he come under its spell, and in Palestine he certainly felt no inclination to lift its veil. The host of stars is of interest to him only because of the God who brought them into being, counted, and named them. Nature, by the same token, exists for him only as God's creation. . . . Unconcerned with science, it [the prophetic mind] is equally unconcerned with the problem of cognitive knowledge.[56]

Kant's own position with respect to science and cognitive knowledge could hardly be described as unconcern. But in arguing that our only mode of access to God is through practical reason, he gave new life to the prophetic tradition.

In keeping with that tradition, I wish to affirm agnosticism on creation and the status of the eternal truths. We have no idea what it is like to bring whole galaxies into existence or even to create a single atom out of nothing. For all we know, a being who could do this might be able to make a square with a diagonal less than the side. But this fact, if it is one, will not take us very far. All we have to say with respect to creation is that God is a moral agent and has dominion over the world. Everything having to do with how or when the world came into existence is, as Maimonides insisted, beyond the limits of human reason. The same is true of the capabilities of the being who produced it. The only thing which matters is that the consequences of God's action are good.

It will be objected that we cannot even know *this* much if we remain consistent with negative theology. Recall the principle which has guided this discussion: only a conditioned object can resemble another conditioned object; hence no conditioned object can resemble God. If this is true, on what grounds can we make the minimal claim that God is a moral agent? Why not say that, like knowledge and power, His moral status is a total mystery? The answer is that if there were a respect in which *human* existence is unconditioned, there would be a basis for affirming an analogy with God.

According to Kant, morality affords such a perspective. It is here, and here alone, that I view myself as a being of infinite worth. Whatever the limits of my theoretical knowledge or physical power, from the standpoint of morality, I am a rational agent and therefore an end in myself. My dignity is, as Kant indicated, unconditioned and incomparable. By this he means that it is incomparable with anything in nature. The command to preserve my life and respect its dignity applies categorically. According to Kant, my status as a moral agent can only be expressed by the word *reverence*.[57] In religious terms, this means that I revere myself to the degree that I bear a mark of the Creator's perfection. According to Jewish tradition, every human being is created in God's image. Therefore, every human life is sacred and irreplaceable.

My contention is that the infinite dignity of human life affords the only basis for an analogy with God: both God and I are rational agents capable of acting for the sake of the moral law. If God transcends the spatio-temporal world, to the degree that I view myself as a rational agent, I do as well. It should be stressed that if my idea of God has no constitutive employment, neither does my idea of myself as being of infinite worth. I cannot know that either of them is true. All I can say is that both God and I are moral agents if (a) I am under an obligation to behave in certain ways, and (b) there is a possibility that those who fulfill their obligations will achieve happiness.

The positive contribution of negative theology is that the only content we can ascribe to our idea of God is moral. I offer this as a modern rendering of Maimonides' claim that God is known through His acts. My own position has less to do with the problem of applying multiple attributes to God than it does with the way I understand myself. It is only as a being capable of moral action that I can rise above my finitude and assert an analogy with God. In a way, we are back to Gersonides: I have inferred something about God based on my conception of myself. The difference is that while Gersonides' example of analogous predication is reason *per se*, my example is reason in its practical employment. It is not as a thinker of thoughts that God is intelligible to me but as an agent who acts for a purpose.

Notes

1. Alexander Altmann, "The Divine Attributes: An Historical Survey of the Jewish Discussion," *Judaism* 15 (1966), 40–60. For further discussion, see Harry Austryn Wolfson, "Maimonides on Negative Attributes," and "Maimonides and Gersonides on Divine Attributes as Ambiguous Terms," both in Twersky and Williams (eds.), *Studies in the History of Philosophy and Religion*, vol. 2 (Cambridge: Harvard University Press, 1977), chaps. 5 and 6.

2. Cohen, *Religion of Reason*, 35.

3. This thesis is challenged by Fred Sommers in "What We Can Say About God," *Judaism* 15 (1966), 64–66. Sommers offers two examples of things in different categories that have the same predicates. The first is the fact that Sally Jones is interested in men and in mathematics. Thus two different things, men and numbers, share the predicate "interests Sally." The second is that sand remains in the top part of an hourglass as long as Lincoln's Gettysburg address. Thus two different things, an event and a material object, can be compared with respect to duration and share the predicate "lasted an hour." I do not find either example convincing. Surely

Aristotle's thesis is not meant to apply to intentional predicates. If it did, it could easily be reduced to absurdity, because I can think about things in any category whatever. In regard to the second example, it seems clear that what is being compared is two events, not an event and a material object. What lasts for an hour is not the sand itself but the presence of the sand in a container.

4. Wolfson, "The Knowability and Describability of God in Plato and Aristotle," in Twersky and Williams (eds.), *Studies*, vol. 1, 107–8.

5. The best account of this is Joseph Owens, *The Doctrine of Being in the Aristotelian Metaphysics*, 2d edition (Toronto: Pontifical Institute, 1963), 107 ff. A less technical account can be found in Owens, *An Elementary Christian Metaphysics* (Milwaukee: Bruce Publishing Co., 1963), 86–93.

6. Owens, *Being*, 124–25.

7. *Politics* 1457b16–18, *Eth. Nic.* 1131a30–b4.

8. For an English translation and commentary, see N. Samuelson, *Gersonides on God's Knowledge* (Toronto: Pontifical Institute of Medieval Studies, 1977), 185–224, or the translation of Seymour Feldman excerpted in Hyman and Walsh (eds.), *Philosophy in the Middle Ages*, 2d edition (Indianapolis: Hackett Publishing, 1973), 429–31.

9. Isaac Franck, "Maimonides and Aquinas on Man's Knowledge of God: A Twentieth Century Perspective," *Review of Metaphysics* 38 (1985), 606–8. The mystical significance of Maimonides' position is explored by David R. Blumenthal in "Maimonides' Intellectual Mysticism and the Superiority of the Prophecy of Moses," *Studies in Medieval Culture* 10 (1977), 51–67. But notice how rational such "mysticism" has become. My own position is much closer to that of Alexander Altmann, "Maimonides' Attitude toward Jewish Mysticism," in Alfred Jospe (ed.), *Studies in Jewish Thought* (Detroit: Wayne State University Press, 1981), 200–219.

10. For Maimonides' relation to classical skepticism, see Josef Stern, "Skeptical Themes in the Guide of the Perplexed," unpublished manuscript. Stern is here extending the argument of Shlomo Pines as found in "The Limitations of Human Knowledge according to Al-Farabi, ibn Bajja, and Maimonides," in I. Twersky (ed.), *Studies in Medieval Jewish History and Literature* (Cambridge: Harvard University Press, 1979), 82–109. With respect to creation, see Sarah Klein-Braslavy, "Maimonides' Interpretation of the Verb 'Bara' and the Question of the Beginning of the World," *Da'at* 16 (1986).

11. Maimonides' position is anticipated by ibn Daud in *ha-Emunah ha-Ramah* 131a–b. For an English translation, see *The Exalted Faith*, trans. N. Samuelson (Rutherford, N.J.: Farleigh Dickinson University Press, 1986),

148. For further discussion of this point in scholastic philosophy, see Wolfson, "St. Thomas on Divine Attributes," in J. I. Deinstag (ed.), *Studies in Maimonides and St. Thomas Aquinas* (New York: KTAV Publishing, 1975), 1–6.

12. Cf. Zevi Diesendruck, "The Philosophy of Maimonides," *Central Conference of American Rabbis Yearbook* 65 (1935), 355–68. For further discussion, see Norbert Samuelson, "Judaism and God-Talk," address given to the Academy of Jewish Philosophy, 1968. For difficulties in reconciling Kant's position on infinite judgments with Aristotle's, see Wolfson, "Infinite and Privative Judgements in Aristotle, Averroes, and Kant," *Philosophy and Phenomenological Research* 8 (1947), 173–87.

13. According to Pines, "The Limitations of Human Knowledge According to Al-Farabi, ibn Bajja, and Maimonides," in Twersky, *Studies in Medieval Jewish History and Literature* (Cambridge: Harvard University Press, 1979), 82–109, Maimonides' position derives from Al-Farabi's lost commentary on the *Nicomachean Ethics*. Apparently Al-Farabi's position was that it is impossible for a being who is a composite of matter and form to know a being who is pure form. In short, all we can know is forms which originate in the senses or the imagination. It follows that there is no possibility of knowing God or the separate intellects. Cf. ibn Daud, *ha-Emunah ha-Ramah* 133a10–16.

14. See Pines, "Introduction," in *The Guide of the Perplexed*, lxxi, cxi.

15. Maimonides is here referring to Al-Farabi's treatise "On the Intellect." For an English translation, see A. Hyman and J. J. Walsh (eds.), *Philosophy in the Middle Ages*, 2d edition (Indianapolis: Hackett Publishing, 1973), 215–21.

16. For a perceptive discussion of the relation between Maimonides and Kant, see Majid Fakhry, "The 'Antinomy' of the Eternity of the World in Averroes, Maimonides and Aquinas," in J. I. Deinstag (ed.), *Studies*, 107–23.

17. The leader of this school is, of course, Strauss. But see, in addition, W. Z. Harvey, "A Third Approach to Maimonides' Cosmogony-Prophetology Puzzle," *Harvard Theological Review* 74 (1981), 287–301.

18. These arguments will be taken up in greater detail in the next chapter.

19. This does not mean that Maimonides has a causal theory of predication, although that is how some scholastics interpreted him. On this point, see Wolfson, "St. Thomas on Divine Attributes," and Seymour Feldman, "A Scholastic Misinterpretation of Maimonides' Doctrine of Divine Attributes," in Deinstag, *Studies*, 58–74.

20. On this point, see Cohen, *Religion of Reason*, 95.

21. Arthur Hyman, "Maimonides on Religious Language," in Samuelson, *Studies*, 362.

22. Gersonides, *Wars of the Lord* 133–35 and Aquinas, *Disputed Questions on the Power of God*, q. 7, a. 5.

23. Cf. Wolfson, "Maimonides on Negative Attributes," in Twersky and Williams (eds.), *Studies*. "The term corporeality, by its mere sound and irrespective of its meaning, carries with it the implication of an imperfection in God."

24. On this principle, see David S. Shapiro, "The Doctrine of the Image of God and the *imitatio Dei*," *Judaism* 12 (1963), 57–77.

25. Maimonides' strategy for proving God's existence seems to be: (1) the world is either eternal or created; (2) if it is eternal, then by demonstration God exists; (3) if it is created, then by definition God exists; therefore, (4) God exists. But Strauss, "Study of the Guide," 1ii, has a decisive objection: the argument equivocates on what is meant by "God." The conception of God established by assuming the world is eternal does not include free will. The conception of God established by assuming creation does. So all that is proved is that we have to accept *some* conception of divinity. Which one is open to discussion. As far as the text is concerned, sometimes Maimonides implies that God's existence is demonstrable (*Guide* 1.71, 2.33, 3.28), but sometimes he implies that it is not (2.25, according to Pines's reading). Rather than accuse Maimonides of inconsistency, we can interpret him as referring to the two senses of proof mentioned above. That is, if all one wants to show is that some conception of God is inevitable, then convincing arguments exist. But if one wants to show that the biblical conception is inevitable, there is no demonstration because it cannot be known for certain that the world was created. We can say that it is impossible to account for the Torah and an acceptable theory of human perfection without the biblical conception of God, but this does not amount to a demonstration. What is more, even if "God exists" is true, the existence we attribute to God bears no relation to the existence we attribute to ourselves.

26. Pines, "Introduction," cxxii. Cf. Strauss, *Persecution*, 92.

27. Ibid., cxvi, n. 96.

28. Ibid., cxxviii, cf. xcvii–xcviii. Strauss, too, finds a secret doctrine of analogy, "Study of the *Guide*," 1i.

29. See *Metaphysics* 10072b21–23, 1075a3–5, *De Anima* 425b25–31, 430a2–9. For Pines's discussion of this issue, see "Introduction," xcvii–xcix. Throughout his discussion, Pines tries to argue that Maimonides was working toward a position like Spinoza's. This claim was effectively refuted by Wolfson in *The Philosophy of Spinoza* vol. 2 (1934; rpt. New York: Schocken

Books, 1969), 25–27. Note that Wolfson never treats Maimonides' negative theology as a smokescreen.

30. Pines, "Limits."

31. On this point, see J. Stern, "Skeptical Themes."

32. On the subject of Socrates' religious views, see my *Dialogue and Discovery* (Albany: SUNY Press, 1987), chapter 4. For a very different view of Maimonides' Platonism, see Leo Strauss, *Philosophy of Law*, trans. F. Baumann (Philadelphia: Jewish Publication Society, 1987), 105 ff. According to Strauss, Maimonides' Platonism is to be explained by the fact that he conceived of the prophet along the lines of Plato's lawgiver. Both Plato and Aristotle teach that contemplation is the highest human perfection. But they take different stands toward it. Aristotle frees it; Plato insists that the philosopher cannot linger in a contemplative state but must return to the cave to help his fellow prisoners. According to Strauss (110): "What Plato *required*—that philosophy stand under a higher court, under the state, under the *Law*—is *fulfilled* in an era that believes in revelation." But Strauss never really considers the possibility that the contemplation Maimonides is talking about is critical rather than speculative—in short, that Maimonides has replaced the Aristotelian understanding of divine science with something different. Strauss does consider Cohen's position as expressed in "Charakteristik," but rejects it on the grounds that Cohen confuses his own view with "historical actuality."

33. Isadore Twersky, *Introduction to the Code of Maimonides* (New Haven: Yale University Press, 1980), 511 n. 390. For further discussion, see Shubert Spero, "Is the God of Maimonides Truly Unknowable?" *Judaism* 22 (1973), 72 ff., as well as Steven S. Schwarzschild, "Moral and 'Middlingness' in the Ethics of Maimonides," *Studies in Medieval Culture* 11 (1977), 65–94. For a departing view, i.e., that knowledge of God is not practical, see Hartman, *Maimonides*, 202–4. Notice, however, that throughout his study, Hartman assumes that philosophic knowledge is speculative rather than critical.

34. See Anthony Kenny, *Descartes: Philosophical Letters* (Oxford: Clarendon Press, 1970), 18–19.

35. Kenny, *Descartes*, 15. From a letter to Mersenne dated May 6, 1630.

36. Harry Frankfurt, "Descartes on the Creation of the Eternal Truths," *The Philosophical Review* 86 (1977), 44–45. My debt to Frankfurt is obvious. One difficulty with Frankfurt's article is his tendency to talk about "scholasticism" without identifying which scholastics he has in mind. Suarez and Aquinas are mentioned on page 39, but in a very general way. In fact, there were anticipations of Descartes' position in scholasticism:

Ockham, to take one example, and the more extreme forms of negative theology, to take another. For further discussion on Descartes' relation to Aquinas, see N. J. Well, "Descartes and the Scholastics Briefly Revisited," *New Scholasticism* 35 (1961). Frankfurt's position is criticized by E. M. Curley, "Descartes on the Creation of the Eternal Truths," *The Philosophical Review* 93 (1984), 569–97. Curley takes Frankfurt to mean that the eternal truths are merely possible. Curley's position is that the eternal truths are necessary, but for some of them, this is a contingent fact. There are two problems with Curley's interpretation. First, it is not clear what it means to say that a proposition is contingently necessary; in fact, Curley must introduce a number of controversial modal propositions to give this thesis a clear sense. Secondly, in the end, there may not be much difference in saying that the eternal truths are only possible and that they are contingently necessary.

37. Kenny, *Descartes*, 236–37. The letter is dated July 29, 1648.

38. Ibid., 151. The letter is dated May 2, 1644.

39. In addition to Maimonides, see Saadia, *Beliefs and Opinions* 2.13 and Albo, *Ikkarim*, 1. 22.

40. Cf. Frankfurt, "Descartes," 53–54.

41. To say that God has given us a mind that cannot conceive His denial is to raise the famous question of whether God is a deceiver. In the Fourth Meditation, Descartes tries to show that because God cannot be a deceiver, He would not endow us with a mind that would be led into error when used properly. Therefore, everything I clearly and distinctly understand must be true. Does this not show that God understands the necessary truths as we do? For if He endowed us with a mind which is compelled to accept propositions that are false, He would be a deceiver. I agree with Frankfurt that nothing of the sort is implied. All that the Fourth Meditation shows is that *we* cannot understand how God could be a deceiver, so that within the confines of rationality we have no choice but to believe that clear and distinct ideas are true. According to Frankfurt (52), "the proof that God is not a deceiver, like any rational demonstration, can establish for Descartes nothing more than that its conclusion is required by the principles of human reason." It does not establish what is true "absolutely speaking" or "in God's eyes." Although we do not see how God could deceive us, this possibility, like any other, remains open to Him.

42. Frankfurt, "Descartes," 40–41.

43. Kenny, 241. From a letter to More dated February 5, 1649.

44. For an extended treatment of this point, see J. L. Marion, *Sur la théologie blanche de Descartes* (Paris: Presses Universitaires de France, 1981).

45. *Critique of Practical Reason*, 137.

46. Cf. *Critique of Pure Reason* A47, A597/B625.

47. The standard objection is that the moral law commands us to seek virtue without any regard for the likelihood of achieving happiness. Suppose, for example, that I had reason to believe that God does not exist so that there is nothing but a chance connection between virtue and happiness. Might I not still feel under an obligation to tell the truth? For further discussion, see Lewis White Beck, *A Commentary on Kant's Critique of Practical Reason* (Chicago: University of Chicago Press, 1960), 274–77.

48. See *Critique of Pure Reason* A312/B369 ff.

49. See *Lectures on Philosophical Theology,* trans. Allen W. Wood and Gertrude M. Clark (Ithaca: Cornell University Press, 1978), 85.

50. Notice Kant's use of analogical reasoning at *Lectures* 83–84. And notice his use of a disreputable medieval argument: if God is the cause of X, then God possesses X to an infinite degree. On the history of this argument, see Feldman, "A Scholastic Misinterpretation," ibid.

51. *Prolegomena*, 357.

52. *Prolegomena*, 359.

53. *Critique of Practical Reason*, 5.

54. For a more detailed discussion, see Gottfried Martin, *Kant's Metaphysics and Theory of Science*, trans. P. G. Lucas (Manchester: Manchester University Press, 1955), 158–70.

55. Again, see *Critique of Practical Reason*, 5.

56. Cohen, H. "The Social Ideal as Seen by Plato and the Prophets," in *Reason and Hope*, trans. and ed. E. Jospe (New York: W. W. Norton, 1971), 68–69.

57. Kant, *Groundwork*, 436.

Chapter Three

Miracles and Creation

1. Foundation or Stumbling Block

In the *Star of Redemption*, Rosenzweig maintains that what was once the firmest and ultimate line of defense for theology—the claim that it is rooted in history—has turned out to be one of its worst embarrassments.[1] In this connection, it is noteworthy that the central ideas of Judaism are not set forth in logical order but in chronological: creation, the flood, the covenant with Abraham, the exodus from Egypt, revelation at Sinai, and so forth. In fact, one might say, as Yehezkel Kaufmann does, that in the Bible, historical claims are offered as proof that YHWH is God and that there is none else.[2]

But what kind of proof is this? According to the Bible, the Israelites were rescued from certain death when God parted the Red Sea. There is, however, no independent evidence that this event took place. So believing in it is not like believing in the French Revolution or the American Civil War. The Bible claims, as no standard history book does, that its story is sacred: it is the record of divine involvement in human affairs. To talk about divine involvement, however, is to talk about the signs and wonders that form the backbone of the biblical narrative; in short, it is to talk about miracles. The formative events in the history of Judaism are often ones which defy human or mechanical explanation. That is why they are said to offer proof that YHWH is God.

Since the Enlightenment, such "proof" may have turned into a stumbling block. It is not merely that the events in the Bible are not corroborated by other sources. According to arguments offered by Spinoza and Hume, it is irrational to believe that any such events occurred. If, as Maimonides insisted, Judaism does not contain anything abhorrent to reason, how can it encompass the miraculous? In one respect, Maimonides prefigured the Enlightenment's skepticism. As a rationalist, he wants people to obey the commandments because they convey true opinions and promote human welfare, not because they were handed down in extraordinary circumstances.

71

Along these lines, he warns that we should not expect the messiah to be a miracle worker. And when it comes to specific accounts of miracles in the Bible, he often looks for naturalistic explanations.[3] Still, he cannot dismiss miracles altogether, because for him, miracles and creation go hand in hand. If God created the world, He is free to do with it what He wants. Thus (*Guide* 2.19): "He who designed all things may change them if He changes His design." Behind Maimonides' belief in miracles is the following argument: If miracles occur, God is a free agent. If God is a free agent, creation is possible. If creation is possible, so are revelation, providence, and the rest of the biblical worldview. The question is how Maimonides can reconcile belief in miracles with an equally strong belief in an orderly world.

To defend his position, Maimonides must oppose two extremes. The first is cosmic determinism and is associated with Aristotle; the second is a form of voluntarism usually associated with the Mutakallimun. If one denies the possibility of miracles, the second overemphasizes their importance. In one case, God is powerless to affect the course of events; in the other, He affects it all the time. According to the determinist view, God is a necessary and eternal being. The world exists by emanation from God. What emanates from a necessary and eternal being is itself necessary and eternal. Maimonides concludes that according to the Aristotelians, God does not have free will and cannot intervene in the world— even to alter the size of a fly's wing (*Guide* 2.22). It is clear that if the world were not ruled by an agent with free will, the Bible would require massive reinterpretation. At *Guide* 2.25, Maimonides indicates that such reinterpretation could be done if there were a demonstration that the world is eternal. We have seen that there is a group of scholars who believe that despite his stated preference for creation, Maimonides was committed in secret to a belief in eternity. The rationale for this interpretation is that the doctrine of eternity was the standard view among philosophers in the Aristotelian tradition; Maimonides supposedly was committed to the standard view but could not say so in public.[4] Notice, however, that if Maimonides believed in an eternal world, he would have to be given more than the usual pedagogic license: he would be seeking to establish a position which, by his own admission, undermines the foundation of the law (*Guide* 2.25).

Another reason people think Maimonides believed in an eternal world is that his arguments on behalf of creation are not decisive. As noted earlier, they do no more than tip the scales (*Guide*

2.16). This first argument claims that the motions of the heavenly bodies are too chaotic to support the theory that everything emanated from a necessary being. According to medieval astronomy, the heavenly bodies are carried along on their paths by spheres. But if the spheres are made of a common material substance, and emanated from a common source, how can it be that some rotate in one direction while others rotate in another? And how can it be that some rotate faster than others? Maimonides claims that the best explanation for this diversity is that the spheres were set in motion by an agent with free will. This argument leaves open the possibility that future research might establish that the apparent disorder is in fact a tightly constructed system which could have emanated from an eternal and necessary being.

The second argument is that if the world were eternal, the matter of the heavenly bodies should be constantly shedding one form and taking on another, which experience indicates is not the case. Since the spheres are made of the same matter, what is to prevent one sphere from shedding its form and receiving another? And if it does, what is to prevent the sphere from changing direction or speed before our eyes? Again, Maimonides claims the best explanation is that a free agent has assigned each sphere its specific form. This argument is even more speculative than the first. The bulk of what Maimonides says about creation is polemical: the arguments of the Aristotelians *against* it are not persuasive. But this hardly amounts to a demonstration of his own view.

The third argument is based on the principle: it is impossible for anything but a simple thing to come from a simple thing (*Guide* 2.22). In other words, if God is simple, and if everything proceeds from Him by necessity, there would be no way to account for any diversity in the universe at all. Since Maimonides believes that God is simple, and that the universe does emanate from Him, he concludes that the universe must emanate from a free will—in this case, a will that chooses to have a universe with metaphysical complexity.

The most interesting aspect of this discussion is what Maimonides does *not* say. In view of the connection between creation and miracles, he could have said that miracles offer irrefutable evidence that the world is governed by a free agent. But since he never maintains that belief in creation is certain, he could not have regarded the evidence for miracles as certain either. Put otherwise, he does not argue from the historical accuracy of the Bible to the truth of creation. As Alfred Ivry suggests, Maimonides attempts to show that God *could* have created the world, not that He *has* done so.[5] Creation, and therefore miracles, too, remain within the realm of what it is rational to believe in, not what historical evidence forces us to accept. Maimonides is no dogmatist. But as we shall see, the claim that it is rational to believe in miracles and creation is still controversial.

According to the Mutakallimun, the world has no permanent order (*Guide* 1.71). All events are brought about by a single cause: the will of God. Since God is free to will whatever He wants, anything imaginable can happen.[6] The reason Maimonides cannot accept this position is that when it comes to the physics of the sublunary realm, he sides with Aristotle. Aristotle may have been wrong about the heavens and creation; but Maimonides never supposes he is wrong about the orderly flow of events in the material world. What is more, voluntarism has moral consequences which Maimonides cannot accept: it leads to a conception of God which makes Him inferior to humans (*Guide* 3.25 & 31). If ethical behavior in humans requires a will which listens to the dictates of reason, then, it would seem, ethical behavior in God requires nothing less. For my purposes, it is significant that positions similar to the ones Maimonides opposes were advocated by Spinoza and Descartes. Before looking at their arguments, however, we must ask what is meant by saying that an event is miraculous.

2. The Problem of Definition

What does it mean to say that God has wrought a miracle? According to the standard medieval definition, a miracle is a change in a thing's internal nature. But as Richard Swinburne pointed out, that definition is anachronistic and should be modified to read: violation of a law of nature.[7] Unfortunately the law-of-nature formula is also problematic. Nature, according to a long and distinguished tradition, is a system of mechanical processes governed by unalterable laws. On this view, a miracle occurs when God interferes with one of these processes and brings about an effect that, but for His interference, would not happen. It is in this sense that a *violation* has occurred. Yet not any violation can qualify. No religious significance could be claimed if tomorrow water were observed to boil at 213 degrees. To have a miracle, we need a violation of natural law that serves a moral or religious purpose. If a modern-day Elijah predicted that water would boil at 213 degrees in order to show that the "priests" of mechanical determinism are wrong, then we would have a miracle. The assumption is that left to its own devices, nature is indifferent to human purposes, so that divine intervention is needed to compensate.

Here is a case where philosophy is forced to take account of an alternate conceptual framework. The biblical view of the world does not include mechanical determinism. This does not mean that it takes no notice of natural regularities but that its explanation of them is quite different from that of an eighteenth-century scientist. After the flood, God makes a covenant with every living creature that guarantees that: "So long as the earth endures, seedtime and harvest, cold and heat, summer and winter, day and night, shall not cease."[8] By the same token, Jeremiah tells us that it is the Lord "who giveth the sun for light by day, and the ordinances of the moon and of the stars for a light by night, who stirreth up the sea, that the waves thereof roar."[9] There are regularities, but the explanation for them is not to be found in the blind succession of cause and effect. It is to be found in the constancy of God's will. Note two things: (1) on this view, nature is not an impersonal mechanism which stands over and against God, and (2) for precisely that reason, nature is not indifferent to human purposes; it was fashioned by the same Creator who watches over human beings and therefore can be expected to assist them in various ways. Thus it is misleading to say that according to the Bible, God *violated* nature when He parted the Red Sea. It would be better to say, with J. P. Ross, that in our sense of the term, miracles are unknown in the Bible.[10]

According to Midrashic literature, during creation God made an arrangement with the sea so that it would divide to allow the children of Israel to pass through.[11] I will have more to say on this passage in a bit. For the present, note that it does not describe the sea as a mechanical body with which God must interfere in order to accomplish His purpose. It is not as if He has fashioned a machine and must, at some propitious moment, pull the plug. It is rather that the machine will stop of its own accord because it is God's will that the children of Israel be saved. Put otherwise, nature is not blind; like everything else, it conforms to God's providence. What looks like interference is really what Wolfson called a preestablished *dis*harmony: for one instant in history, the sea will do something out of character.[12]

The difference between the biblical view of nature and our own leads to another difference in the respective conceptions of miracle. To stay with Ross, there is a clear sense in which we would view a miracle with horror. Whether it is a violation of an unbreakable law or of a well-established probability, a miracle would be disruptive for us because it would cast doubt on a wide area of knowledge. If water were found to boil at 213 degrees, a number of theories about the physical world would have to be revised. But so far from disrupting the biblical worldview, the extraordinary events wrought by God confirm it. That is because the biblical worldview is fundamentally moral in its outlook. The parting of the Red Sea was awe-inspiring, even incomprehensible, to those who witnessed it. Yet we are projecting our own assumptions onto the text if we describe it as anomalous. In watching the waters recede, biblical actors saw proof, not disconfirmation. The same applies to Elijah's "experiment" on Mount Carmel. It may be significant, therefore, that when Josephus talks about miracles, he rarely uses the term *paradoxon* (which implies something contrary to expectation) and uses instead *semeion* (which refers to a sign or signal).[13] In the Septuagint, *semeion* is the usual rendering of the Hebrew *ot*, and *teras* the usual rendering of *mofet*. Neither set of terms needs imply a violation. In both cases, the essential idea is not disruption but communication.

Following Kant, we can conceive of a miracle as *either* something woven into the fabric of the natural order *or* something done in an extraordinary way.[14] And, following Leibniz, we do not have to conceive of a miracle as a one-time-only occurrence.[15] There is no reason why a miracle cannot be repeated indefinitely. It is clear that if Leibniz and Kant are right, we can view the creation of the universe as a miracle that God repeats in every second of the world's history. In short, the miracle of creation implies the process of constant renewal.[16]

3. Pre-Established Disharmony

In biblical times, divine agency was invoked more than it is today. But the notion that God might do something extraordinary presented a problem. If God is the source of regularity in nature, then there is a tension between His faithfulness and His willingness to perform dramatic acts. A person might argue that so far from constituting proof of God's greatness, such acts testify to the opposite: a disorderly world in which there is constant need of makeshift solutions. This is part of Spinoza's argument *against* miracles in the *Theologico-Political Treatise*. On the other hand a person might say that if God does not perform dramatic acts, then He is too distant from human concerns and, more importantly for our purposes, the theory of creation lacks credibility.

If my suspicion is correct, this is precisely the problem the Midrash addressed. God entered into an agreement with the sea so it would allow the children of Israel to pass through, with the sun and moon so they would stand still for Joshua, with the ravens so they would feed Elijah, with fire so it would not harm Hananiah, Mishael, and Azariah, with the lions so they would not harm Daniel, and with the fish so it would cough up Jonah—all during the first six days of Creation. This passage parallels one in the *Mishnah* (*Pirke Abot* 5.6), according to which ten things were created on the eve of the first Sabbath: the mouth of the earth, the mouth of the well, the mouth of the ass, the rainbow, manna, the rod, the shamir, the shape of written letters, the writing and the tablets of stone.

The midrashic view was the standard one among Jewish philosophers in the Middle Ages and versions of it can be found in Philo, Judah Halevi, and Maimonides.[17] It asserts that miracles were prearranged and are part of the natural order rather than violations of it. On this view, nature contains hidden powers or virtues. It was inherent in the nature of the sea that it would recede, in the rock that it would gush water, in the sun that it would stand still, and so on. Putting aside the question of empirical confirmation, the important point is that the midrashic view represents a compromise. Miracles are not last-minute attempts to rectify the course of nature. God made provision for them at the beginning of time, and if we knew more about nature, we would see that they are rooted in the overall scheme of things. In this way, the wondrous acts described in the Bible are compatible with a faithful God and an orderly world.

Another way of looking at the midrashic view is to say that miracles leave natural laws intact. In cases where a naturalistic explanation of a dramatic event is available, there is no problem. In cases where a naturalistic explanation is not available, we still would assume that the event falls under a law. This law accounts for both the original law and the supposed violation. How is the new law known? Maimonides answers with reference to prophecy. The prophet does not deny the scientific view of the world; what he claims is that his account contains everything natural science does plus some. So while miracles may give the scientist pause, their irregularity is only apparent. They show that the scientific understanding of the world is corrigible or incomplete but not that God has acted in an arbitrary fashion. In principle, they, too, are capable of explanation. In this sense, the midrashic view opens the door to rationalism. Although nature may surprise us from time to time, we do not have an arbitrary God in need of makeshift solutions. The world follows a pattern—even if we do not know, or do not *yet* know, everything it contains.

The midrashic view is attractive for another reason. Maimonides argues that miracles and creation imply each other. If provision for miracles was made *during* creation, if, as Kant suggested, they are woven into the fabric of the natural order, then to talk about miracles and to talk about creation is to talk about the same thing. Creation is the setting in motion of an order which contains surprising events. It implies that God has free will. But we can attribute free will to God without assuming that He changes His mind from one moment to the next. A single free act is enough to refute fatalism and justify the biblical worldview. Multiple exercises are possible, but once we allow the first, the victory is secured.[18]

It should now be clear why the midrashic view appealed to Maimonides: it attempts to reconcile the freedom of the creator with the orderliness of His creation. But the freedom of the creator still presents a problem. According to Maimonides (*Guide* 3.13), belief in creation implies belief that ". . . what exists, its causes, and its effects, could be different from what they are." Does this mean that God could have created a different world but, having chosen this one, can no longer alter the course of events? Or, does it mean that having created the world, God can alter it at any time? At *Guide* 2.19, and again at 2.29, Maimonides tells us that all things exist as a result of design, not merely of necessity, and that He who designed them may change them if it suits His purpose.[19] Having brought the world into existence, God could alter it, even annihilate it. Maimonides is convinced that God will not annihilate the world; but as long as the possibility is present, the existence of the world over time implies that God could bring about a sequence of events different from that which actually obtains. The question is how far Maimonides' limited voluntarism extends. Maimonides clouds the issue by saying that God *could* change the world but has promised He *will* not (*Guide* 2.27–8).

4. The Objections of Spinoza
and Descartes

For Spinoza, the duality of Maimonides' position is unimportant. Any ascription of free will to God is mistaken. We can see this in either of two ways. Since God is one, His intellect and will are identical.[20] Thus God wills all that and only that which His intellect apprehends. There are no possibilities known to God which He has not decreed and no decrees which are not known to Him.

If God's understanding is what it is by strict necessity, then His will is what it is by strict necessity. Therefore the order of the world follows from the necessity of the divine nature:

> Nothing, then, comes to pass in nature in contravention to her universal laws, nay, everything agrees with them and follows from them, for whatsoever comes to pass, comes to pass by the will and eternal decree of God; that is, as I have just pointed out, whatever comes to pass, comes to pass according to laws and rules which involve eternal necessity and truth; nature, therefore, always observes laws and rules which involve eternal necessity and truth, although they may not all be known to us, and therefore she keeps a fixed and immutable order.[21]

It follows that the actual world is the only one possible. Creation and miracles are totally excluded.

Another way to see this is to consider what would happen if God exercised His power to bring about a sequence of events other than that which now obtains. If God decreed an order different from the actual one, He would possess a different will from that which He has and, by implication, a different intellect. But if God's intellect and will were different, His essence would be different.

> All the philosophers whom I have read admit that God's intellect is entirely actual, and not at all potential; as they also admit that God's intellect, and God's will, and God's essence are identical, it follows that, if God had had a different actual intellect and a different will, his essence would also have been different; and thus, as I concluded at first, if things had been brought into being by God in a different way from that which has obtained, God's intellect and will, that is (as is admitted) his essence would perforce have been different, which is absurd.[22]

In the language of scholasticism, this objection goes as follows. If God is entirely actual, He cannot move from potency to act. Thus God cannot be subject to change over time. If so, it makes no sense to suppose that He can alter the course of the world at a future date or that He was free to create a different world at the beginning.

According to Spinoza, God is free in the sense that there is no external cause to which He is subject. But it is not true that God is endowed with free *will* as we normally understand the term.[23] Intellect and will are modes of the attribute of thought. As such, both are determined by thought and are what they are by necessity. It makes no sense to suppose that God can change His mind or can will something other than what is determined by His nature. This position stands in direct contrast to that of Maimonides, where *will* is defined as ability to will and not to will (*Guide* 2.18).[24] Pines glosses over this problem by saying that "out of public spirit, Maimonides chose to aid and abet the faithful adherents of religion through the act of will" but really belonged to the fatalist camp.[25]

It is interesting to note that Descartes attacks the scholastic understanding of God from the opposite perspective. Here the identity of intellect and will implies a voluntarism more radical than most scholastics envisioned. If God's intellect and will are identical, it makes no sense to suppose that God deliberated *prior* to issuing His decrees. Thus God's understanding cannot influence His will in one direction or another. The divine will is subject to no constraint or direction at all. As Descartes tells us,

> it is self-contradictory that the will of God should not have been from eternity indifferent to all that has come to pass or that ever will occur, because we can form no conception of anything good or true, of anything to be believed or to be performed or to be omitted, the idea of which existed in the divine understanding before God's will determined Him so to act as to bring it to pass. Nor do I here speak of priority of time; I mean that it was not even prior in order, or in nature, or in reasoned relation, as they say in the schools, so that that idea of good impelled God to choose one thing rather than another. Thus, to illustrate, God did not will to create the world in time because he saw that it would be better thus than if he created it from all eternity; nor did he will the three angles of a triangle to be equal to two right angles because he knew that they could not be otherwise. On the contrary, because he worked to create the world in time it is for that reason better than if he had created it from all eternity; and it is because he willed the three angles of a triangle to be necessarily equal to two right angles that this is true and cannot be

otherwise; and so on in other cases. And though it may be said that it is the merit of the saints which is the cause of their obtaining eternal life, this causes no difficulty; for their merits are not causes of their obtaining this in the sense that they determine God to will anything; they are merely the cause of an effect of which God wished them from all eternity to be the cause. Thus that supreme indifference in God is the supreme proof of his omnipotence.[26]

I follow Frankfurt in taking Descartes to mean that from the standpoint of possible essences or eternal truths, God's will is purely arbitrary.[27] It is as if the unity of God's will and intellect causes the former to swallow up the latter: at the bottom of things is, once again, sheer unconstrained will. For Spinoza, it is the opposite. If a possible essence or eternal truth is contained in God's understanding from eternity, then it is willed from eternity in precisely the form in which it is understood. One thinker interprets the unity of will and understanding to imply that anything is possible, the other that nothing but the actual is possible.

Maimonides opposes both for reasons which bear on ethics. At *Guide* 3.25, he argues that God's will is consequent upon His wisdom:

> For while we believe that the world has been produced in time, none of our scholars and none of our men of knowledge believe that this came about through the will and nothing else. For they say that His wisdom . . . obligatorily necessitated the existence of this world as a whole at the moment when it came into existence. . . .

Maimonides' fear is that belief in an arbitrary God will cause people to think there is no rationale for the commandments. Asked why God wants us to do X rather than Y, a person would have no answer except "He willed it so." Such a response is an abdication of intellectual responsibility with which Maimonides has little patience. But in making will *consequent* upon wisdom, he falls into Descartes' trap by speaking of them as if they were two.

The opposite tack is taken with respect to fatalism. Here Maimonides speaks as if wisdom were consequent upon will. Should God change His design for the world, He would be free to change the things in it. Maimonides agrees that God is a being who is always in action. But for that very reason, the principles that govern

His behavior are different from the principles that govern ours. In a corporeal being, changes of will are brought about by changes in environment. As new circumstances present themselves, a person devises new responses. If God were affected by external causes, Spinoza would be right: a change in will would imply movement from potency to act. In a being who is purely actual, however, the fact that the will decrees one thing today and a different thing tomorrow "does not call for another cause"—that is, an external cause. The idea is that the only cause for a change in God's will is the will itself. Since God's will determines its own course, it is never the recipient of action and thus never moves from potency into act.[28] By the same token, a change in God's will, and therefore a change in His intellect, does not imply a change in essential nature (*Guide* 2.18). A change in will forced on God by something else would be an absurdity. But as long as God determines His own actions, any changes are already "in" the will which means that the will is eternal.

We are left with the following situation. Maimonides, Spinoza, and Descartes all claim to respect the unity of intellect and will in God. But all come up with very different accounts of divine causation. This fact supports Maimonides' insistence on the limits of human reason. Clearly there is no *inference* from the unity of intellect and will in God to knowledge of the natural world. But Maimonides' position is only a qualified success. His purpose is to recommend a view of God compatible with biblical morality. An arbitrary God with an unconstrained will would undermine the principle of *imitatio Dei* and put us on the doorstep of *Fear and Trembling*. A fatalistic God would require a serious reinterpretation of divine commandments.[29] Maimonides' solution is to say that intellect and will are one in God but that we do not know how (*Guide* 1.69). Again, *intellect* and *will* are homonyms. From the standpoint of Descartes and Spinoza, Maimonides' insistence on the limits of human knowledge is nothing but a way of covering up the limits of his own theory.[30] His explanation of purposive action in God clearly suggests that the intellect is prior to the will. That is his answer to divine indifference. But his explanation of creation often implies that the will is prior to the intellect. That is his answer to fatalism. The crux of Maimonides' position is that neither the arbitrary nor the fatalistic God is a necessity. When it comes to the specifics of the biblical God, however, he takes refuge in skepticism. God is purely actual and does not admit of plurality. Yet he brought the world into existence by a free choice and is free to change the world if it suits Him.

The problem has nothing to do with satisfying different audiences. Maimonides is searching for a conception of God, the details of which are not yet in focus. He is right in thinking that self-determined behavior is not analogous to behavior produced by external causes. When it comes to freedom, purpose, and changes of will, he has scattered insights but no consistent theory. In the Enlightenment, the job of opposing Descartes and Spinoza was taken up by Leibniz. This world is only one of many possible worlds which God could have created. The decision to create the best of all possible worlds was made on the basis of reasons which incline but do not necessitate.[31] God chose to create the best possible world, but His choice, though rational, was free. Once again, we may ask how intellect and will can be one if the latter is consequent on the former. For Leibniz, too, there are frequent claims of duplicity. It may be said, therefore, that the problem did not reach a stable conclusion until Kant.

5. Kant on the Unity of Intellect and Will in God

From a historical standpoint, Kant's *Lectures on Philosophical Theology* are important because they give the lie to the notion that he was an unrelenting critic of scholastic philosophy. According to Allen Wood:

> Kant is fundamentally unable to conceive of the human situation except theistically, and unable to conceive of God in any terms except those of the scholastic-rationalist tradition. Kant's criticism of the tradition is not intended by the philosopher himself to crush its intellectual world, or to destroy its kingdom of thoughts. Kant no more considered wandering outside its intellectual world than he did of leaving the vicinity of his native Königsberg. And his philosophy, viewed integrally and as a whole, actually leaves the traditional kingdom of thought pretty much intact. For Kant's real aim is not to destroy theology, but to replace a dogmatic theology with a critical one: to transform rational theology from a complacent speculative science into a critical examination of the inevitable but perpetu-

ally insoluble problems of human reason, and a vehicle for the expression of our moral aspirations under the guidance of an autonomous reason.[32]

If the foregoing discussion of Maimonides has shown anything, it is that prominent scholastics were just as "critical" as Kant and just as willing to view theology as a vehicle of expression for moral aspirations.

Like Maimonides, Kant never doubts that morality requires "a *living* God who has produced the world through knowledge and by means of His free will."[33] And he readily admits there is no proof to show that knowledge is compatible with other divine perfections.[34] On the other hand, neither is there a proof that knowledge is *in*-compatible with them. To repeat: God is an idea that can be thought but cannot be known. Although reason presents no obstacle to the idea of a perfect being, and in some cases urges us to assume it, reason cannot show that the idea is logically necessary. The concept of God remains a possibility, a hypothesis.

We have seen that Kant depicts God's knowledge as purely intuitive. To this it should be added that the intuition involved is a priori. Since God cannot be affected by external objects, He has no sensory representations. On the contrary, because God is the source of all existence, He knows all things by knowing Himself. This is another way of saying that God's relation to what He knows is always active. For Him, knowledge of an object is identical with self-reflection; there is no element of receptivity in God. It follows that God's knowledge is *free*, since the object known has no independent status and depends for its existence on the knower. For humans confronting an external world, the object of knowledge is given, which means that we must adapt ourselves to something external. But to the degree that God knows Himself as the source of all existence, His knowledge of the world is spontaneous. There is no force or factor He must take into account, nothing to stand between Him and the immediate intuition of what He knows.

If God's knowledge is different from ours, so is His causal activity. God's knowledge is efficacious. According to Kant (*Lectures*, 89), "the divine knowledge of all things is nothing but the knowledge God has of Himself as an effective power." Because God knows Himself as the source of all existence, His knowledge is the cause of what He knows. The object owes its existence to the fact that God represents it to Himself. If so, then will, which Kant defines as the faculty of causing objects by means of their representation, and intellect are the same in God. Put otherwise, God's representing something to Himself and acting on that representation are the same. But there is nothing that God confronts as a given. In this sense, He is always in an active relation to the world. There are no impulses or inclinations to interfere with His will; no obstacles for it to encounter.

For Maimonides, too, God is in an active relation to the world. But Maimonides is not sufficiently clear on what this involves. He retains the idea that freedom is ability to will or not will and concludes that God must be able to change the world (*Guide* 2.19, 2.29, 3.22). It is this conception of freedom that Kant calls into question. According to Kant, freedom has nothing to do with the contingency of the act—as if freedom in God implies that He is capable of evil—but with the spontaneous appropriation of a law.[35] Maimonides touches on the idea of spontaneity at *Guide* 2.18, but his discussion is abbreviated. The Kantian position is best understood by seeing that there are two aspects to freedom. The first is the one Maimonides and other scholastics accept: God is not affected by external causes. His freedom consists in the fact that He is always the instigator of causal chains, never an occupant within them. The problem is that this definition is incomplete. For all we know, God's decision to instigate this causal chain rather than that one is arbitrary.

In the *Groundwork*, Kant goes further. Freedom is not just spontaneous action but a spontaneous act of a particular kind: self-legislation. Put otherwise, God's will is not arbitrary; it can be subsumed under a law. But the law is not the kind that obtains in the realm of nature. It is not a matter of external compulsion but of the agent's understanding of Himself. The agent acts according to His *idea* of law, and in that respect is the source of His own regularity. If the second part of Kant's definition is right, freedom has nothing to do with ability to change one's mind. On the contrary, a being who is susceptible to changes of opinion is one who is affected by impulse. God's freedom is pure autonomy or, as Kant describes it in the *Lectures* (104), ability to will a priori. It follows that God cannot do otherwise than act as morality requires. That is why it is misleading to suggest that God considers a variety of options before making a decision. Against Leibniz, Kant argues that we cannot know whether there is one possible world or many (*Critique of Pure Reason* A232/B284). All we can say is that the origin of the world is a moral act and therefore a voluntary (*willkürliche*) one. From a historical perspective, Kant has given full expression to the sense of freedom invoked by Plato. Plato argued that while the tyrant does everything he wants, he never does what he wishes and, in that respect, has less freedom than anyone in the city.[36] The point is that freedom is not opposed to law but to a kind of folly.

Although Kant goes well beyond Maimonides, the position he defends is similar to the one defended in the *Guide*. Both want to find a middle ground between voluntarism and fatalism. Against Descartes, Kant would point out that rational activity does not imply that the intellect *precedes* the will, either logically or temporally. At bottom, both are names for the same thing: God's spontaneous act of representing the world to Himself. But there is no inference from God's spontaneity to the possibility of realizing logical absurdities. Kant agrees it is presumptuous for us to say that God cannot create something (*Lectures*, 79). But he insists it is equally presumptuous for us to picture Him as an arbitrary despot. Again, freedom does not imply lawlessness. We do not separate God from the Fates and the Styx by imputing to Him the possibility of arbitrary behavior. In the *Groundwork* (446), Kant argues that far from being a mark of perfection, arbitrariness, in the sense of following no law whatever, is an absurdity (*Unding*). It is open for a Cartesian to argue that God *is* absurd, but there is nothing in this view which is compelling. Why accept it if we can account for divine transcendence without it?

Against Spinoza, Kant would argue for the converse; from the fact that God cannot do otherwise than He does, it does not follow that He is subject to some sort of internal necessity. Like Kant, Spinoza rejects the liberty of indifference as an explanation of freedom. In the *Ethics* (1.1), he connects freedom with the idea of being self-caused: "That thing is called free, which exists solely by the necessity of its own nature, and of which the action is determined by itself alone." So God is free but not in the sense that He exercises volition or acts for a purpose. As we have seen, God's will is a modification of the attribute of thought. Kant objects that if God is not subject to external causes, neither is He subject to internal. In other words, it is not enough to say that God's actions are self-caused if that means His will is determined by an inner ground or prior principle. Not only is this condition not worthy of the name *freedom*, according to Kant, it is not even worthy of the name *self-determination*. In one place, he suggests that *predetermination* is the best description of it.[37]

The point at issue between Spinoza and Kant is volition: whether God chooses to act as He does or whether His actions are a logical consequence of His essence. One must always add that Kant has no proof that the will is free and therefore no proof that the will of *God* is free. In the last analysis, the only "evidence" he can adduce in support of his understanding of freedom is practical: the experience of obligation one feels when presented with a moral choice.[38] The necessity of complying with the moral law cannot be explained by natural causes; it is the recognition that we are subject to a law that is valid whether or not it is obeyed. The only way we can be subject to this law is if we are capable of determining ourselves to act in accord with it: in short, if we are free. If there were a determining ground anterior to this freedom, so that the will were a consequence of some prior cause, we would not be free, and the law which commands us to behave in a certain way would lose its binding force. This is another way of saying that the will, if free, must be the ultimate ground of its own behavior. According to Kant, no contradiction arises in supposing that this freedom applies to God (*Lectures*, 105). It follows that insofar as human reason requires an idea of the highest perfection to serve as a standard, that idea must be of an agent who wills the moral law without internal or external compulsion. So Kant's "proof" is that the idea of God would have no moral validity if it lacked the element of choice.

To return to miracles, if God's will is ultimate, it cannot be limited by physical causality. In the *Lectures* (154), Kant writes:

> God's extraordinary direction consists in the fact that he sometimes determines in accordance with his aims that individual events should not correspond to the order of nature. It is not at all impossible that in even the best world the powers of nature may sometimes require the immediate cooperation of God in order to bring about certain great purposes.

This does not mean we can determine in any individual case whether God has acted. Nor does it mean we can please God by persuading ourselves that He has. Kant is adamant that the only thing we can do to please God is answer the call of duty. For this miracles are superfluous. By allowing for the possibility of "extraordinary direction," all Kant has done is stress the transcendence of the moral order over the natural. It follows that the only positive content we can attach to the idea of a miracle is that the world was brought into existence by a moral agent.[39] Once we go beyond this idea and attempt to introduce miracles into the day-to-day practice of religion, reason is crippled and the result is superstition.[40]

6. The Objection of Hume

Until now, the discussion has concentrated on philosophers in the rationalist tradition. Since no treatment of miracles would be complete without mention of Hume, it is to his essay that we now turn. Although Hume supposes throughout that a miracle has to be a violation of nature, his objection to believing in such events raises a number of important issues. Unlike Spinoza, he does not challenge the claim that miracles are possible; what he challenges is the far different claim that we could have adequate evidence for believing that a specific event qualifies as an instance of one:

> There is not to be found, in all history, any miracle attested by a sufficient number of men, of such unquestioned good-sense, education, and learning, as to secure us against all delusion in themselves; of such undoubted integrity, as to place them beyond all suspicion of any design to deceive others; of such credit and reputation in the eyes of mankind, as to have a great deal to lose in case of their being detected in any falsehood.[41]

According to this passage, the key issue is evidence. Since those who wrote biblical history were interested parties, since there is a tendency for people to enjoy the telling and hearing of exotic exploits—"the usual propensity of mankind towards the marvelous"—and since the Israelites were a primitive people, their testimony cannot be considered authoritative. Testimony that can might contain astonishing facts, but it could not contain anything miraculous. If it did, we would be justified in concluding that the witnesses were not describing what really happened.

If we take seriously the notion that observation is theory-laden, we can challenge the suggestion that there is any neutral account of "what really happened." Kaufmann discusses this issue in regard to the biblical account of the conquest of Palestine:

> It was not the priests or the people who parted the waters of the Jordan or laid flat the walls of Jericho. They did what God ordered and at the appointed time God's word came to pass. This idea was not superimposed on the legends by a late literary redaction. It is part of their original warp; it is the fountain-head of their creation. This idea in Israel shaped the narratives of the real events even as they came into being, at

the earliest stage of their oral creation, from the moment when the happenings were formed into a *story* in the mouth of those who had lived them. There never was a "realistic" account of the events. The account of the events was "idealistic," "legendary," right from the start. Every warrior who came from the battle-line to the camp and told his story to the women and children related "legendary" things, "idealistic" history stamped with the idea of the miraculous sign.[42]

It might be said, therefore, that biblical observers did not see lightning, hear thunder, and *then* interpret them as divine signs. As N. R. Hanson once wrote, the interpretation was "there" in the seeing from the outset.[43]

It is wrong, then, to suggest that the key issue is evidence—or evidence conceived in a simple way. The participants did the best job they could of describing the facts. The problem is not so much that they were given to flights of fancy as that the categories at their disposal were different from ours. As we have seen, what is for us a disconfirming experience is for them the opposite. A modern observer would not describe the conquest of Palestine in the way it is described in the Bible. But it does not follow that the account given in the Bible is "mythical" and that in reading it we should be on guard for a propensity toward the marvelous. Rather than evidence itself, we must consider the categories that allow us to view it *as* evidence in the first place. In a biblical context, one cannot make sense of things like war, famine, or national liberation without seeing the hand of God. It follows that divine agency is not necessarily an embellishment, a literary device, or an epiphenomenon; it is the basis of the biblical worldview.

Hume could answer this point in a straightforward way. If divine agency is the only way biblical observers could make sense of what was happening, if lacking a meteorology or sociology, they found the hand of God in everything of substance, then *we* have been given no reason to accept miracles. We must take the Bible for what it is: the historical record of a primitive people. The problem is that the theory-ladenness of observation cuts two ways. In the words of Ross, it transfers events from the category of the miraculous to that of "digestible history."[44] But in making the Bible "digestible" do we not rob it of its sacred character? And if we do, does it not follow that if modern observers had witnessed the conquest of Palestine, they would not have reported anything that contradicts the uniformity of experience *as presently understood?* Thus

Hume could admit that observation is theory-laden and still advance his objection. He could agree that biblical observers were not *deliberately* misrepresenting the facts but insist that their accounts should not be taken at face value.

Against whom is Hume arguing? He cannot be arguing against a position like Maimonides', because that position holds only that miracles are possible; it does not hold that we have sufficient historical evidence to be certain that one has occurred. When it comes to this or that miraculous event, Maimonides, too, is skeptical and claims we cannot always read the Bible literally. It would seem, therefore, that Hume's opponents are not medieval rationalists but empirically based fundamentalists. But here we find that Hume's own position is subject to crucial ambiguity. Is his claim: (a) that no evidence to date supports belief in miracles, or (b) that no evidence could ever support it?

The passage quoted above suggests that (a) is all Hume has in mind. Since miracles violate the uniformity of experience, and since we are all inclined to believe the uniformity of experience, an account of a miraculous event would have to surmount a formidable level of skeptical doubt. In such a case, a reasonable person would ask: "Is it more likely that the uniformity of experience has been overturned or that the witnesses to this event are not giving an acceptable report?" On the weaker interpretation of Hume, it would take considerable testimony to make us reject the uniformity of experience and believe the witnesses. Yet, it is possible we might.

But Hume goes on to suggest that we can *never* believe the report of a miracle; it is "not only [that] the miracle destroys the credit of testimony, but the testimony destroys itself."[45] There *could not* be a miracle attested to by a sufficient number of people of unquestioned good sense because even if a blue-ribbon panel were to report that a miracle occurred, it would always be more reasonable to conclude that they were mistaken than that nature had been irregular.[46] In short, the fact that the blue-ribbon panel reported a miracle would immediately disqualify it as a blue-ribbon panel. At this point, Hume quotes the old proverb, "I should not believe such a story were it told me by Cato," and concludes that the incredibility of the fact would be reason enough to invalidate the authority.[47]

To put this a different way, the reason we believe the testimony of others is not that we perceive an a priori connection between such testimony and reality; it is rather that experience has accustomed us to expect that such a connection holds. If so, we cannot accept this testimony without believing in the uniformity of experience. But in the case of a miracle, the testimony claims that the uniformity of experience has been violated, thereby calling into question the principle on which its credibility rests. That is why the testimony necessarily defeats itself:

> Upon the whole, then, it appears that no testimony for any kind of miracle has ever amounted to a probability, much less to a proof; and that, even supposing it amounted to a proof, it would be opposed by another proof; derived from the very nature of the fact, which it would endeavor to establish. It is experience only, which gives authority to human testimony; and it is the same experience, which assures us of the laws of nature. When, therefore, these two kinds of experience are contrary, we have nothing to do but subtract the one from the other, and embrace an opinion, either on one side or the other, with that assurance which arises from the remainder. But according to the principle here explained, this subtraction, with regard to all popular religions, amounts to an entire annihilation; and therefore we may establish it as a maxim, that no human testimony can have such force as to prove a miracle, and make it a just foundation for any such system of religion.[48]

What first seemed like an empirical claim—*in fact* no testimony has been strong enough to persuade us that a miracle has happened—has now become a conceptual one: there is no *possibility* of testimony convincing us that a miracle has happened. Leaving aside primitive peoples, Hume concludes that he would not believe in a major violation of the laws of nature even if all of the historians of England should agree to it.

To the extent that he has shifted from an empirical to a conceptual claim, Hume damages his case. As long as his claim is empirical, he forces his opponents to produce evidence and evaluate testimony. But once he goes beyond this, he allows his opponents the luxury of merely *conceiving* of a case in which the testimony would be strong enough to convince us that the regularity of nature had been violated. And here Hume's opponents are bound to win, for our understanding of what constitutes a natural regularity is corrigible—a fact Hume himself admits.[49] Science discovers anomalies and irregularities all the time. According to Thomas Kuhn: "Discovery commences with the awareness of anomaly, i.e., with the recognition that nature has somehow violated the paradigm-induced expectations that govern normal science."[50] We would require reliable testimony from several observers to be persuaded that such an anomaly had in fact occurred. But it is simply not true that there are *no* circumstances in which it would be reasonable to accept it—that we should not believe it even if it were told to us by Cato.

To take Hume's own example, suppose a person were pronounced dead and, after a reasonable length of time, came back to life. Our first reaction is and ought to be disbelief. But we cannot rule out the possibility that our current understanding of death is flawed, so that a witness who reported such an event may be telling the truth. Unfortunately Hume's normal skepticism in regard to science seems to vanish at this point. He admits he simply could not believe "so signal a violation of the laws of nature."

The question is not "Can we believe the report of an anomalous event?" but "What significance would we attach to it?" If we take the anomalous event to show that our current understanding of nature is flawed, no problem arises. There is a problem only if we assume our understanding of nature is *not* flawed and therefore the event represents divine incursion into human affairs. What sort of evidence could persuade us of the latter? It is on this point that, so far from opposing the rationalist tradition, Hume supports it. For there is no evidence that ever could prove we have a case of "extraordinary direction." As F. R. Tennant put it, "No testimony can reach the divine."[51]

7. Signs, Wonders, and the Moral Law

Recall Kant's claim that if an event cannot be subsumed under a law, reason is crippled. By this he means that reason is not instructed with respect to any religious doctrine. We can say that *if* God has acted, it must be for the good; but whether God has acted in any individual case is known only to God. To return to the Bible and Yehezkel Kaufmann, there can be no empirical proof that YHWH is God. Since God is supremely perfect, no display of signs and wonders can justify the inference that He has acted. To justify that inference we would have to show that, whether anomalous or otherwise, the events in question are the best possible. The only way we can argue for this is moral: by establishing that the action springs from a good will. The problem is that the idea of a good will is beyond the scope of empirical evidence. It is noteworthy that the Bible itself (Deuteronomy 13.26) warns against the practice of identifying prophets on the basis of miraculous deeds. According to the Talmud, even three anomalous events in succession cannot decide a legal argument.[52]

If there is a lesson to be learned from this discussion, it is that the question raised by miracles does not concern extraordinary events in the world's history as much as it does the God who created it. Simply put, belief in miracles is nothing more than belief in divine transcendence: If God created the world, He can transform it; if He can transform it, He is not identical with it. The ethical implications are obvious. If God is not identical with the world, then the world is not ultimate. If the world is not ultimate, we do not have to accept it as it is. The only thing that is ultimate is a will that always answers the call of duty. It follows that in determining the course of behavior, we should not look to the world but to our sense of obligation. It is from this argument that we derive the notion of a philosophy that is *messianic* in a broad sense of the term, a philosophy that sees the purpose of human action not as integration into an existing order but as an effort to construct a new one. Again, it is noteworthy how many Bible stories contain an element of upheaval; either the younger son comes to dominate the older, or slaves dominate their masters, or prophets dominate kings. Once we grant that the present constitution of the world is not ultimate but is ruled by a rational agent who sits as its judge, the signs and wonders mentioned in the Bible are so many parables designed to communicate a fundamental truth.

Notes

1. Rosenzweig, *The Star*, 93.

2. Kaufmann, Y., *The Religion of Ancient Israel*, trans. M. Greenberg (1960; rpt. New York: Schocken Books, 1972), 132.

3. See *Guide* 2.35 as well as 2.42.

4. According to Herbert Davidson, "Maimonides' Secret Position on Creation," in I. Twersky (ed.), *Studies*, 16–40, the evidence for a "secret" position on creation suggests that Maimonides is closer to the Platonic account than the Aristotelian. See *Guide* 2.25, where Maimonides admits that Plato's account of creation may not be that different from the one in Genesis. Davidson's position is challenged by W. Z. Harvey, "A Third Approach to Maimonides' Cosmogony-Prophetology Puzzle," *ibid*. In addition to Davidson's account, there is the classic article by Wolfson, "The Meaning of *Ex Nihilo* in the Church Fathers, Arabic and Hebrew Philosophy, and St. Thom-

as," in Twersky and Williams (eds.), *Studies,* vol. 1, 207–21. Wolfson's point is that *ex nihilo* (*to me on*) can mean either "what is not" in the sense of nonexistence or "what is not something" in the sense of not having an identifiable nature. According to the latter meaning, creation *ex nihilo* would be creation out of an indeterminate matter that is in a state of extreme privation but that nonetheless exists (cf. Aristotle, *Physics* 192a6–7). How does Maimonides understand the term? As he presents the "Platonic" account of creation, God cannot create the world out of absolute nonexistence because it is self-contradictory for anything to be produced from nothing. Therefore there must be a preexisting but indeterminate substrate if the doctrine of creation is to be logically coherent. Does Maimonides accept this? He obviously accepts the claim that God cannot contravene the laws of logic. Now if, according to the traditional Jewish view, God created the world "not from a thing" then this might mean that He created it from proto-matter that was not yet a *determinate* thing. In other words, the traditional view could be interpreted to be compatible with the Platonic view. For an excellent discussion of this point, one which ascribes a neo-Platonic interpretation to Maimonides, see Alfred Ivry, "Maimonides on Creation," in D. Novak and N. Samuelson (eds.), *Creation and the End of Days* (Lanham, Md.: University Press of America, 1986), 185–213.

5. Alfred Ivry, "Revelation, Reason & Authority in Maimonides' *Guide of the Perplexed*," in N. Samuelson (ed.), *Studies in Jewish Philosophy* (Lanham, Md.: University Press of America, 1987), 335.

6. For further discussion, see Pines, "Introduction," cxxiv–vi.

7. Richard Swinburne, *The Concept of Miracle* (London: Macmillan & Company, 1970), chapter 1. Notice that while Swinburne accepts the violation-of-nature formula, he raises a number of good objections against it. For a discussion of this problem from a Jewish point of view, see David Bleich, *Contemporary Halakhic Problems* (New York: KTAV Publishing Co., 1983), chapter 10. Bleich argues that as far as the recitation of *hallel* is concerned, a miracle has to involve suspension of the laws of nature; providential or fortuitous events occurring through natural causes do not count. But (1) What is his understanding of natural law? (2) Can seemingly unnatural events be part of nature if we believe that God made provision for them at the creation? And (3) there was no violation of natural law in the story of Purim, but we do say "who has performed miracles for our fathers in those days at this season." In response to (3), Bleich claims that Ahasuerus did not exercise free will in complying with the requests of Esther and that deprivation of free will is an interference in the natural order. Perhaps, but look what has happened to the concept *law of nature* if it is extended to include acts of free will, and why is there no mention of this act of interference in the text?

8. Genesis 8.22.

9. Jeremiah 31.35, cf. 33.20–21.

10. "Some Notes on Miracles in the Old Testament," in C. F. D. Moule (ed.), *Miracles* (London: A. R. Mowbray, 1965), 45–60.

11. *Genesis Rabbah*, 5.5.

12. H. Wolfson, *Philo*, vol. 1 (Cambridge: Harvard University Press, 1962), 351–52, n.24.

13. See G. MacRae, "Miracle in The Antiquities of Josephus," in Moule, *Miracles*, 142–47.

14. *Lectures on Philosophical Theology*, 155.

15. Leibniz, *Correspondence with Clarke*, 4.43.

16. See Cohen, *Religion of Reason*, 67–70.

17. For Philo, see *Moses* 1, 33, 38, 185, 210–11; for Judah Halevi, see *Kuzari* 3.73; for Maimonides, see *Commentary on Mishnah Abot* 5.6, as well as *Guide* 2.29. There is a long-standing controversy on whether two texts of Maimonides are consistent. In the *Commentary on Mishnah Avot*, Maimonides accepts the view that all miracles were foreordained. To some people, this view implies that once having created the world, God cannot now interfere with it. In the passage from the *Guide*, however, Maimonides stresses that God could make radical changes in His design for the world, even to the point of destroying it. He there quotes the view of *Mishnah Avot* in a way which raises questions, whether he still accepts it. I agree with Guttmann, *Philosophies*, 192–93, that it is difficult to determine whether Maimonides has changed his position in the *Guide* or simply refined it. The problem is that even in the *Guide*, while it is true that God *could* make radical changes in the world, it is also true that he *will* not. More on this point below. For further discussion of the issue of inconsistency, see Joseph Heller, "Maimonides' Theory of Miracles," in Alexander Altmann (ed.), *Between East and West* (London: East and West Library, n.d.), 112–27. To the degree that Maimonides' overriding concern is to refute fatalism, it matters little whether God exercised one free act or many.

18. Cf. Hartman, *Maimonides*, 158: "Once an individual admits that miracles are possible, as Maimonides does by accepting the doctrine of creation, then, from a strictly logical perspective, it makes no difference whether he admits one or one thousand miracles."

19. But, again, God cannot change the laws of logic.

20. Spinoza, *A Theological-Political Treatise*, chapter 6. For a modern defense of Spinoza's position, see E. M. Curley, "Spinoza on Miracles," in E. Giancotti (ed.), *Proceedings of the First Italian International Congress on*

Spinoza (Naples: Biblipolis, 1985), 421–38. Notice that Curley's proposition (4—"God's nature is what it is by strict necessity") would be disputed by Maimonides—at least the interpretation put on it by Curley and Spinoza. For Maimonides, God's essence is what it is by necessity; but that does not mean that God cannot will today what He does not will tomorrow (*Guide* 2.28). For further discussion of the difference between Maimonides and Spinoza, see Wolfson, *Spinoza*, vol. 1, 308–19, 400–22. For Kant's position, see *Lectures*, 105–6 and my discussion in the next section.

21. Spinoza, *A Theological-Political Treatise*, trans. R. H. M. Elwes (1883; rpt. New York, Dover: 1951), 83. Cf. *Ethics* 1.33.2.

22. Spinoza, *Ethics*, 1.32, Elwes translation.

23. At *Ethics* 1.17.2, Spinoza sees that if Maimonides is right, if intellect and will pertain to the essence of God and are not just modes, they would have nothing in common with the *human* intellect and will. Maimonides would agree and regard this as one of the advantages of his position. If Maimonides had nothing further to say, there would be no problem. But he discusses God's will throughout the *Guide* suggesting that the claim of nothing in common is not entirely true.

24. Cf. Crescas, *Light of the Lord*, 2.5.3.

25. Pines, "Introduction," cxxviii–cxxix.

26. "Reply to Objections VI," in *The Philosophical Works of Descartes*, vol. 2, trans. Haldane and Ross (Cambridge: University Press, 1967), 248. Note that in this passage, Descartes *does* perceive a difference between our mind and God's. The words quoted are preceded by: "As to freedom of the will, a very different account must be given of it as it exists in God and as it exists in us." But unlike Maimonides, Descartes seems to think the difference leads to relative certainty about God. Note how the next sentence begins: "For it is self-contradictory . . ."

27. Frankfurt, *Descartes*, 40–41.

28. For further discussion, see Wolfson, *Spinoza*, vol. 1, 412 ff.

29. See, for example, *A Theological-Political Treatise*, 62–68, where Spinoza tries to show that the decrees of God are to be understood as necessary truths rather than as moral laws. This is in direct opposition to the position expressed by Maimonides at *Guide* 3.20: "[T]he whole of religious legislation, the commandments, and the prohibitions, goes back to this principle: namely, that His knowledge concerning what will happen does not make this possible thing quit its nature [as possible]."

30. Cf. Wolfson, *Spinoza*, vol. 1, 419.

31. See my essay, "Moral Necessity," *New Scholasticism* 51 (1977), 90–101.

32. Wood, A., *Kant's Rational Theology* (Ithaca: Cornell University Press, 1978), 17.

33. *Lectures*, 30.

34. *Lectures*, 83: "Thus we cannot prove with apodictic certainty that the reality of a faculty of knowledge does not cancel any of the other realities when put together with them. But neither can any man ever prove the contrary. . . ."

35. *Religion Within the Limits of Reason Alone*, trans. T. M. Greene and H. H. Hudson (1934, rpt. New York: Harper & Row, 1960), 45, n.3.

36. *Gorgias* 467a, *Republic* 577e. For further discussion, see my *Dialogue and Discovery*, 136–9.

37. *Religion Within the Limits*, 45.

38. *Critique of Practical Reason*, 92. For further discussion, see Beck, *A Commentary*, 195–97.

39. *Religion Within the Limits*, 81.

40. *Religion Within the Limits*, 48.

41. Hume, *Enquiries*, 2d edition, ed. L. A. Selby-Bigge (Oxford: Clarendon Press, 1966), 116.

42. Kaufmann, Y. *The Biblical Account of the Conquest of Palestine*, trans. M. Dugat (Jerusalem: 1953), 74–75. Cf. Buber, *Moses*, 74–79.

43. Hanson, N. R., *Patterns of Discovery* (Cambridge: Cambridge University Press, 1965), 10.

44. Ross, *Notes*, 60.

45. Hume, *Enquiries*, 121.

46. Ibid., 128. Hume does allow for the possibility that nature may be in a process of decay or dissolution. For further discussion of the theological consequences of this possibility, see H. G. Alexander's introduction to *The Leibniz-Clarke Correspondence* (Manchester: Manchester University Press, 1956), xvi–xviii.

47. Ibid., 113.

48. Ibid., 127.

49. He seems to recognize this in his discussion of the Indian prince, ibid., 114, n.1.

50. Kuhn, T. S., *The Structure of Scientific Revolutions* (Chicago: University of Chicago Press, 1962), 52–53.

51. F. R. Tennant, *Miracle and its Philosophical Presupposition* (Cambridge: Cambridge University Press, 1925), 68.

52. *Baba Metzia*, 59b.

Chapter Four

Revelation

1. The Rationalist's Perspective

Revelation, or as it is known in Jewish tradition, the giving of the law (*matan Torah*), is often considered the miracle *par excellence*. Emil Fackenheim writes:

> The core of both the Jewish and the Christian faiths is the belief that a God who is other than the world nevertheless enters into the world; that He enters into the world because He enters into the life of man. The Jewish and Christian God descends to meet man, and "a man does not pass, from the moment of supreme meeting, the same being as he entered into it." Judaism and Christianity, or groups within either faith, may differ as to what, more specifically, revelation is; they may also differ as to when it has taken place. But they agree that God *can* reveal Himself and that, in the entire history of man, He has done so at least once.[1]

Both Judaism and Christianity profess monotheism. Fackenheim is right in saying that traditional monotheism posits a God who is other than the world. But it is not clear what Fackenheim means when he says that God enters *into* it. Judaism cannot accept an incarnate God. Thus Cohen maintains that God never reveals Himself *in* something but *to* something.[2] And the something to which God reveals Himself can only be a human being. It follows that revelation is the relationship which exists between the divine and the human.

As early as the twelfth century, Maimonides tried to play down the miraculous nature of this relationship. In his discussion of prophecy (*Guide* 2.32), he rejects the idea that God can choose anyone at all to be a prophet. Instead he offers what he describes as "the opinion of the Law." This opinion states that prophecy is a perfection of human nature. To be specific, it is the perfection of the rational and imaginative faculties, an overflow from the Agent Intellect that we might describe as a kind of *illumination*. The nature of the illumination is such that discursive or theoretical knowledge is combined with intuitive: the prophet not only understands an important truth but has a vision of it. I follow Strauss in concluding that the model at work in Maimonides' account of prophecy is that of the escaped prisoner in Plato's cave.[3] To the objection that he has made prophecy a natural phenomenon like genius, Maimonides replies that extraordinary mental ability is only a necessary condition for obtaining the rank of prophet. Although God cannot make anyone a prophet, He can *deny* prophecy to someone who, on mental criteria alone, would be worthy of it. In this way, prophecy involves *both* extraordinary ability *and* the concurrence of God. It is well known that Maimonides creates problems for himself by adopting this position.[4] What concerns me is the degree to which he has reduced the supernatural component of prophecy to a minimum. If Maimonides is right, the relation between God and the prophet is almost entirely intellectual.

The same is true for Kant. We have seen that he is open to the possibility of divine incursions into the normal order of things. He therefore allows for the possibility of *external* revelation, by which he means revelation through works or words.[5] But he points out that external revelation presupposes *internal* revelation: God's revelation to us through reason. The logic is straightforward. Even if we assume that the earth moves, the sky opens, and a voice is heard, we must ask whether the external revelation so received is really from God. As we saw in the previous chapter, no testimony can insure us that it is. If God is perfect, the only way we can decide whether He is the author of the message is to ask about its content. Is the content consistent with our idea of an autonomous will? We cannot derive our concept of God from the lightning, thunder, and trembling earth. To do so is to succumb to paganism. It is only by thinking of God as a moral agent, as a being worthy of respect, that our concept of Him can represent perfection. It follows that external revelation presupposes consciousness of the moral law. If the voice which addressed us commands acceptable behavior, we can believe it is the voice of God. If not, no amount of thunder and lightning ought to persuade us that we are in the presence of the Divine. Kant extends this claim to both oral and written communication. In the *Groundwork* (408), he claims that "even the Holy One of the gospel" must first be compared with our idea of moral perfection before we can recognize Him as such. In either case, internal revelation, which is another name for the development of moral reason, must precede external revelation and serve as a yardstick (*Lectures*, 162).

Cohen's discussion of revelation in *Religion of Reason* is a further development of the Kantian position. According to Cohen, the significance of Sinai is not the *fact* of revelation but the *content* (*Religion of Reason*, 78). Put otherwise, we should not think of revelation as the cause of moral reason but as its precondition or ground (*Ursprung*). In moving from temporal to logical priority, Cohen strives to eliminate the supernatural component altogether. Like Maimonides, he insists that the relation between the divine and the human is an intellectual one. Cohen calls it *correlation* (*Religion of Reason*, 82):

> By now the relation between God and man proves itself to be a *correlation*. The uniqueness of God determines his relation to man's reason. And man's reason, as God's creation, determines man's relation to God as a rational relation, and therefore determines also the consummation of this rational relation in revelation, which together with the creation establishes the correlation of man and God.

It should be understood that in this and similar passages, Cohen is not talking about the relation between God and an individual person. If he were, the focus of the discussion would be shifted from the content of revelation back to the fact. Rather, he is talking about God conceived as a moral archetype and humanity conceived as a moral agent. Again from *Religion of Reason* (79): "Man, not the people and not Moses: man, as rational being, is the correlate to the God of revelation." As Cohen argues in a later chapter (*Religion of Reason*, 161), the love of humanity for God is nothing but the love of the moral ideal.

It follows that correlation is not a mystical relation, nor a spatio-temporal one, nor even a relation between God and the historical Moses. It is the relationship in which a person comes to recognize his or her moral duty and the progressive task of fulfilling it. In Cohen's terms, it is an *idealized* relation, which is to say a relation which connects the essence of one term (God) to the essence of the other (humanity). Schwarzschild writes:

> What was done typically in the history of neo-Platonism by way of ontological claims—namely, to build new, additional rungs into the ladder of emanations in order to keep spirit and

matter as far apart as possible and yet to relate them—is here done in conceptual terms: God is now . . . the regulative idea of ethical reason. . . .[6]

As a regulative idea, God is not an existent thing in the way that material objects are. He remains radically "other"—an otherness that Cohen captures by taking God out of the realm of the ontological and putting Him in the realm of the normative.

Much of Cohen's task in chapter 4 of *Religion of Reason* is an attempt to show that already, in the Book of Deuteronomy, the process of idealizing revelation had begun. At Deuteronomy 4.6, we read: "This is your wisdom and your understanding in the sight of the peoples, that, when they hear all these statutes, shall say: 'Surely this great nation is a wise and understanding people.' " Cohen takes these verses to mean that the uniqueness of God is confirmed through the wisdom of His laws (*Religion of Reason*, 413). He is not just the God who reveals but the *God who reveals laws which reason grasps as valid*. Again, Cohen follows in the footsteps of Maimonides. Unless the content of revelation makes sense to rational people of every nation, it does nothing to exult Israel. According to this approach, there are no principles or insights unique to Jews. Nor are there extrarational modes of access to God. Cohen also quotes the famous passage at Deuteronomy 30.11–14:

> This commandment which I command thee this day, it is not
>   too hard for thee, neither is it far off.
> It is not in the heavens, that thou should say: "Who shall go
>   up for us to heaven, and bring it unto us, and make
>   us to hear it, that we may do it?"
> Neither is it beyond the sea, that thou should say: "Who will
>   go over the sea for us, and bring it unto us, and make
>   us hear it, that we may do it?"
> But the word is very near unto thee, in thy mouth, and in thy
>   heart, that thou may do it.

According to Cohen, the content of revelation is not in heaven but written in the heart of every person, which is to say: accessible to reason. It follows that revelation is not a one-time-only event. It occurs whenever a person acknowledges the demands of autonomy.

Cohen offers this understanding of revelation as an extension of Maimonides' claim that God is known through His acts. Overall he sees himself as continuing the fight against anthropomorphism.

The thunder and lightning have been pushed to the margins. Instead we have the concept of a moral archetype, which means we are back to the principle of *imitatio Dei*. In *Religion of Reason* (162), Cohen cites the same verses cited by Maimonides in support of this idea. So Schwarzschild is right: Cohen's understanding of revelation does no more than establish the priority of practical reason.

2. The Existentialist Response

Against this rationalism, the existentialists protested that Cohen's idea of God is too abstract to capture the flavor of religious experience and that what is needed is a return to a personal God. The normal way of expressing this point is to say that we must reject "the God of the philosophers" and reorient ourselves to "the God of Abraham, Isaac, and Jacob." Although the historical precedent for this shift is as old as Judah Halevi, it was and still is an important part of Jewish thought in the twentieth century.[7] In a memorial lecture to Cohen delivered in 1969, Fackenheim pronounced it "quite certain . . . that the Jew of today can put far less trust in Cohen's God-Idea than in the ancient God of Israel."[8] Why is this certain? Fackenheim continues: "For the Jewish philosophy of today to stay with the God-Idea would be to reduce it to a necessary thought only, divorced from history and therefore impotent."

Let me reconstruct the idea Fackenheim is rejecting. According to Cohen, morality confronts us with an infinite task—that of realizing the moral law in the material world. As creator of the material world and moral archetype, God is the ground of both. He is presupposed any time someone takes a step toward the goal of making the world a better place. Without God, there is no way to insure that the task can be completed. The world might thwart our attempts to improve it or perish in the interim. This does not mean that God will see to it that human action is successful, only that He is needed to guarantee the *possibility* of such success. We have to assume the world was created by a moral agent to explain why the categorical imperative can be realized in principle—even if it is not realized in fact.

As we saw above, grounding is a logical rather than an empirical relation. To say that God is presupposed by morality and the existence of the material world is not to say that God is the *historical* cause of either.[9] Already in Plato's Academy, people talking about creation distinguished logical from temporal priority.[10] Cohen is simply following in Plato's footsteps. That is what prompts Facken-heim's charge that Cohen's God is impotent. Such a God is reached by reflection. He is an idea, not in the way that a unicorn is an idea, but in the way that Plato's form of the Good is: an eternal, transcen-dental principle.[11] As Fackenheim points out, the ancient God acts in history both in commanding people to prepare the way for the Messianic kingdom and in helping to bring about that kingdom Himself. Cohen's God affects history only to the degree that He guarantees the possibility that the empirical world can be brought into harmony with the moral. In this respect, Cohen is more of a rationalist than Kant. Kant allowed for God's "extraordinary direc-tion," Cohen does not. The question is whether the return to the ancient conception of God is really an illusion.

Behind Fackenheim's charge of impotence lurk Rosenzweig and Buber. It was Rosenzweig, in his introduction to Cohen's *Jewish Writings*, who originated the view that Cohen became dissatisfied with the God-Idea and, in his later years, attempted to "break through the circle of idealism."[12] The truth is, however, that while Rosenzweig himself attempted such a break, it is far from clear that Cohen did. As late as *Religion of Reason* (160), Cohen is still very much in the Kantian tradition:

> The unique God can have no actuality. For actuality is a con-cept relating thought to sensation. This relation to sensation is, however, excluded from the concept of God.

Buber argues that while Cohen *tried* to preserve the unique status of God by denying existence or actuality (*Dasein*), he failed. According to Buber (*Eclipse of God*, 79), "though Cohen indeed thought of God as an idea, Cohen too loved Him as—God." Since Buber's work is better known than Rosenzweig's, I shall concentrate on Buber.

Throughout *Eclipse of God*, Buber argues that the God of the philosophers is "accessible only to reason, not to the whole of man as he lives his concrete life."[13] It ignores "the existential reality of the I and of the Thou." Insofar as philosophers try to abstract from the concrete reality of the living person, their investigation is bound to fail: "The concrete, from which all philosophizing starts, cannot again be reached by way of philosophical abstraction."[14] This is as true for the Cartesian *ego* as it is for Cohen's God-Idea. Both ignore the dialogical nature of human existence, what Buber calls "face to face being."

Buber's stress on the concrete offers another instance of historical irony. Suppose someone were to ask: What makes an experience concrete? Although it is true that Cohen's idea of God is accessible only to reason, Cohen never tired of underscoring the importance of action. Morality can become actual only by being put into practice. As Cohen himself says (*Religion of Reason*, 160): "Action establishes the realm of morality." And again: "The archetypes have no worth of their own unless they are models for the actions of reasonable beings." Let us recall that Cohen had a social program, a theory of culture, and a lifelong interest in jurisprudence. On the other hand, it is well known that Buber's work is infused with mysticism. The man who insisted on concreteness in *Eclipse of God* could write the following passage in *I and Thou*:

> Spirit in its human manifestation is a response of man to his *Thou*. Man speaks with many tongues, tongues of language, of art, of action; but the spirit is one, the response to the *Thou* which appears and addresses him out of the mystery. Spirit is the word. And just as talk in a language may well first take the form of words in the brain of the man, and then sound in his throat, and yet both are merely refractions of the true event, for in actuality speech does not abide in man, but man takes his stand in speech and talks from there; so with every word and every spirit. Spirit is not in the *I*, but between *I* and *Thou*. It is not like the blood that circulates in you, but like the air in which you breathe. Man lives in the spirit, if he is able to respond to his *Thou*. He is able to, if he enters into relation with his whole being. Only in virtue of his power to enter into relation is he able to live in the spirit.[15]

What is concrete and what is abstract? To understand Buber's criticism, we must look closely at his concept of revelation.

His most succinct statement on revelation is also from *Eclipse of God* (135):

> It must be mentioned here, for the sake of full clarity, that my own belief in revelation, which is not mixed up with any "orthodoxy," does not mean that I believe that finished statements about God were handed down from Heaven to earth. Rather it means that the human substance is melted by the spiritual fire which visits it, and there now breaks forth from it a word, a statement, which is human in its meaning and form, human

conception and human speech, and yet witnesses to Him, who stimulated it and to His will. We are revealed to ourselves— and cannot express it otherwise than as something revealed.

Revelation is an experience in which a person is visited by God, not an image, or an idea, or a psychological urge. The record of this visitation, the laws and beliefs which comprise the backbone of traditional religion, is human in its meaning and form. According to Buber, no written code can be an authoritative statement of the will of God. The encounter between God and a person is not one in which God forces on that person an established doctrine; it is rather one in which the person freely responds to the Divine presence. This response may lead to the production of a legal code or body of dogma, but if it does, the code is the result of human reflection and modification. In *I and Thou* (117), Buber insists that revelation does not "pour itself into the world through him who receives it as through a funnel." The prophet always puts something of himself or herself into the message attributed to God.

The crux of Buber's position, then, is a distinction between the immediate experience of God and the verbal account which comes later. As soon as the prophet formulates a code or dogma, what we have is not God Himself but the prophet's reflection *on* God. This does not mean that the prophet's account can be disregarded, only that we should not confuse the encounter with its aftermath. Religion demands an openness to God, a willingness to confront the eternal Thou and be transformed by the experience. A legal code or body of dogma would interfere with this openness and therefore with the possibility of revelation *if* it prevented the believer from going beyond the written word to the experience that inspired it. In a word, religion asks that we reach beyond commandments to the One who commands. To do so, we must put aside fixed rules or logical constructs and recognize that each encounter with God is unique. Each encounter is a revelation to, and correspondingly, a transformation of, a different individual. In *I and Thou*, Buber writes: "The meaning that has been received can be proved true by each man only in the singleness of his being and the singleness of his life. . . ."[16] The attempt to approach God through a set of prescriptions or theological generalities is not, as Fackenheim points out, to respond to revelation but, on the contrary, to flee from it.[17] So the focal point of revelation is not a content but a meeting. According to Buber: "Man receives, and he receives not a specific 'content' but a Presence, a Presence as power."[18]

We have seen that, for Cohen, the content *is* the focal point: revelation is humanity's awareness of its duties under the moral law. For Buber, the moral law is no different from any other law: it is a statement that is human in its meaning and form. As he tells us: "An I-Thou knowledge that can be held fast, preserved, factually transmitted does not really exist."[19] It follows that, strictly speaking, revelation has no content at all. It is the disclosure of God, not the transmission of a message about Him. God cannot be reached by way of concepts. Any God occupying a place in a system of thought would be an It rather than a Thou. Such a God would lack the transformative power of which Buber speaks. As Buber reminds us, God, the Eternal Thou, can never become an It. The minute we apply logical categories to the initial encounter, we have lost Him. Revelation is and remains personal.

Viewed by traditional standards, Buber's account is inadequate. As Eliezer Berkovits and Steven Katz have pointed out, the dialogical view of revelation raises questions it cannot answer.[20] How do we know if the One whom we encounter is really God? How do we reidentify Him from one experience to the next? What do we do with statements like "God exists" or "God demands our love?" We cannot deny them and have a credible account of a religious tradition. On the other hand, if we affirm them, we run the risk of approaching God through a system of thought. If Buber is right, this approach is bound to fail. Anything in a system of thought is impersonal, an It. But God is the one Thou who can never become an It. He is beyond concepts or categories. How, then, can He transform me, make me His Thou, without disclosing something of His nature, providence, or will? Or, as Fackenheim puts it, how can revelation call for a response, a unique response, if no content is forthcoming? What am I responding to? Since any answer puts me in the realm of concepts, which is to say the realm of It, Buber's view of revelation leads to an enforced silence. All we can say is that God is found in the realm of the personal and that the personal is destroyed once philosophic questions are put to it.

Clearly Buber is no ordinary philosopher. It is true, as Katz charges, that his writings presuppose philosophic sophistication. A person ignorant of Plato, Spinoza, Kant, Hegel, or Nietzsche could make no sense of *Eclipse of God*. But it does not follow that Buber thinks of himself as the last name in the series.[21] Like Dewey, Wittgenstein, and Heidegger, he was a philosopher unsympathetic with philosophy. If these thinkers showed us how to disengage from Hegel, Russell, and Husserl, Buber showed us how to disengage from Cohen: make God personal rather than universal. Buber would admit that God exists. He would only point out that existence should not be understood as an abstract category. To be meaningful, it must be lived; to be lived, it must arise in the particularity of the relation between an I and a Thou. By its very nature, philosophy distorts this relation. It presents God under a description—creator of the world, redeemer of Israel, and so on—but for that very reason, philosophy presents me with a fixed mode of access to Him. It is not that such descriptions are false. We can interpret them for what they are—human statements, records of past encounters—provided we do not make the mistake of thinking that they set the parameters for future ones. There are no criteria for identifying or reidentifying the personal God. Each experience is momentary, each unique. At one place, Buber argues that the most philosophy can do is *point* to God, not deal with Him.[22] Philosophy can lead us to God only if, at the moment when God is about to disclose Himself, it recognizes its inherent limitations and moves out of the way. As Buber puts it (*Eclipse of God*, 69):

> This means that the philosopher would be compelled to recognize and admit the fact that his idea of the Absolute was dissolving at the point where the Absolute *lives*; that it was dissolving at the point where the Absolute is loved; because at that point the Absolute is no longer the 'Absolute' about which one may philosophize, but God.

What is a philosopher to make of this? The best answer is offered by Fackenheim: Buber should not be read as a philosopher but as a sage. How else can one deal with someone who is systematically unsystematic, who claims a mode of awareness "higher than reason?"

Such an answer is not without risks. Hume once remarked that while errors in religion are dangerous, those in philosophy are only ridiculous.[23] In moving from philosopher to sage, Buber may not have to answer epistemological questions, but he takes on a heavy burden in regard to moral ones. A personal God can be a frightening thing in the wrong hands. What is for Buber a way of going *beyond* the critical spirit of philosophy can become for the fanatic a way of avoiding it. To his credit, Buber is aware of this danger and refuses to carry the notion of a personal God to its logical conclusion. Before considering his hesitation, however, we must return to his argument with Cohen.

3. Love of a Person, Love of an Idea

Needless to say, Cohen is very much a philosopher. How, then, can the dispute between Buber and Cohen be resolved? I suggest that the battleground concerns religious love. It is here that Buber is most strident in his criticism. According to Buber, one cannot love an idea and certainly cannot be loved *by* one. The relations of loving and being loved are irreducibly personal. Personality is revealed in dialogue. In the culmination of his attack on Cohen, he writes (*Eclipse of God*, 81):

> He who loves God loves the ideal and loves God more than the ideal. He knows himself to be loved by God, not by the ideal, not by an idea, but even by Him whom ideality cannot grasp, namely, by that *absolute personality* we call God. Can this be taken to mean that God "is" a personality? The absolute character of His personality, that paradox of paradoxes, prohibits any such statement. It only means that God loves as a personality and that He wishes to be loved like a personality.

To this charge, Cohen would reply that we should not fall into the trap of thinking that the meaning of religious love, either God's love for us or our love for Him, is self-evident. Surely love in a monotheistic religion is different from that found in mythology. The same could be said for personality. I can use the word *person* in a purely descriptive way to distinguish human beings from inanimate objects. But often the word carries an evaluative force. When we say that someone lacks personality or did not treat a subordinate *as a person*, we are calling attention to a moral shortcoming. It is not uncommon to hear people say, with Buber, that they believe in a personal God. The question is: What does it mean to ascribe personality to God?[24] And what does it mean to love this personality?

It is worth noting that Buber is not a religious empiricist. He does not discuss God's disclosure of Himself in terms of lightning, thunder, and heavenly voices. With Cohen, he wants to downplay the miraculous component of revelation. If God cannot be reached by analysis of concepts, neither can He be reached by causal connections leading from phenomena to their source. Both approaches destroy spontaneity and therefore the possibility of dialogue. Both turn God into an It. How do we reach God? And what does Buber mean when he says that the experience of reaching Him must be *concrete*?

The problem is that for all of his distrust of written codes and universal laws, Buber is still a moralist at heart. There can be no dialogue without honesty, humility, and respect for the other person. Buber deplores circumstances in which the other person is treated as an It. Such a relation is not only damaging to the other person, it is damaging to me: the I of I-Thou is not the same as the I of I-It. So if I treat the other person as an It, I prevent myself from achieving the openness of genuine interaction. He deplores anything which smacks of domination, exploitation, or loss of personal integrity. Although Buber does not usually employ Kantian terminology, there is little doubt that both partners of the I-Thou relation are autonomous individuals and therefore ends in themselves. No exchange value can be put on an I-Thou relationship. Neither one's partner nor oneself can be viewed as a causally determined organism. The difference is that Kant thinks one respects the other person's dignity by treating that person according to universal rules, while Buber does not. Buber insists that the individual must be considered *in his or her individuality.* Each person must be allowed to fulfill the unique purpose for which he or she was created.

This difference does not obscure the fact that the I-Thou encounter is normative. Although not categorical in Kant's sense, it is as idealized a picture of human interaction as Kant's kingdom of ends. In *Between Man and Man* (25), Buber writes:

> He who lives the life of dialogue knows a lived unity: the unity of *life*, as that which once truly won is no more torn by any changes, not ripped asunder into the everyday creaturely life and the "deified" exalted hours; the unity of unbroken, raptureless perseverance in concreteness, in which the word is heard and a stammering answer dared.[25]

To this it should be added that Buber never tires of talking about *transformation*. The person who is open to someone else, and eventually to God, emerges from the encounter a different person, what Buber sometimes calls a *real* person. Here, too, Buber's moralism is evident. The concept of personality is infused with the distinction between right and wrong. In *Eclipse of God* (125–26), he tells us:

> We find the ethical in its purity only where the human person confronts himself with his own potentiality and distinguishes and decides in this confrontation without asking anything other than what is right and wrong in this his own situation.

The criterion by which this distinction and decision is made may be a traditional one, or it may be one perceived by or revealed to the individual himself. What is important is that the critical flame shoot up ever again out of the depths, first illuminating, then burning and purifying. The truest source of this is a fundamental awareness inherent in all men, though in the most varied strengths and degrees of consciousness, and for the most part stifled by them. It is the individual's awareness of what he is "in truth," of what in his unique and non-repeatable created existence he is intended to be. From this awareness, when it is fully present, the comparison between what one actually is and what one is intended to be can emerge. What is found is measured against the image, no so-called ideal image, nor anything imagined by man, but an image arising out of that mystery of being itself that we call the person.

Against Cohen, he has replaced the notion of an ideal image with that of "the mystery of being itself." But the distinction between the "is" and the "ought" is still crucial. When I confront another person, or aspect of personality in myself, I am not confronting a simple matter of fact. To understand the other person, I must understand the person he or she is *meant* to be.[26] Unless I recognize the distinction between the actual person and the person he or she could become, I take away the person's autonomy, and therefore the person's sense of self-worth. In this way, to treat someone as a person is already to make a judgment about the future: what is not but could be realized. So the concept of personality is inseparable from the concept of the "ought."

On the issue of love, Cohen anticipates Buber's criticism. Asked how it is possible to love an idea, he replied that it is impossible to love anything *but* an idea (*Religion of Reason*, 160). According to Cohen, even in sensual love, it is the idealized person, not the empirically conditioned one, who is the object of my affection.[27] Again Cohen is not saying that love is directed to a mental image. Nor is he denigrating the importance of the individual with whom I am involved. All he is claiming is that love is not an ontological relation, that is, a relation which takes place totally within the realm of what is. By its very nature, love is normative, directed to the future, respectful of the other person's freedom. To put this in a different way, love always involves an aspiration, both in regard to myself and in regard to the loved one. For Cohen, this means that it is a relationship between noumenal entities. In one sense Buber would agree. Freedom and aspiration are as much a part of his world as they are of Cohen's. And Buber would also agree with Cohen's contention that: "Selfhood is the result of an unending relation of I and Thou as well as its abiding ideal."[28] Buber would insist, however, that the I and the Thou must be concrete. In short, what Buber wants is a concrete noumenon. He wants to bring together the Kantian emphasis on freedom with the existentialist preference for lived reality. So while Cohen's I and Thou are understood as archetypes, Buber's are understood as "real" individuals. Buber would point out that while I can reflect on an archetype, I cannot *encounter* one, cannot deal with it "face-to-face."

4. Face-to-Face with God

Buber's attack on idealism was part of a historical phenomenon which extended far beyond religion. By the beginning of the twentieth century, many people concluded that philosophy had become too removed from experience and that the only way to reestablish vitality was to return to fundamentals. To Russell and Moore this meant sense data and logical simples; to Husserl, the phenomenon; to Heidegger and Sartre, facticity; to Buber, the immediacy of human interaction. In any case, Buber's stress on "face-to-face" encounter was in keeping with his time. Notice how similar in spirit Russell's call for a "robust sense of reality" is to Buber's "actual lived concreteness." Both were objecting to the same thing: the notion that we cannot "break through the circle of ideas" and establish contact with things themselves. Both offer a mode of awareness that is immediate, spontaneous, and irreducible, an experience in which we confront the world without the burden of a philosophic system. In both cases, the things we confront do not yet fall under a description; they are simply *present*. But if this mode of awareness is to have any validity, Hanson must be wrong: one must find no element of interpretation "there" in the initial seeing. For if there is any element of interpretation, we are not confronting reality "face-to-face"—only reality as understood by a system of thought.

There is a respect in which Buber would welcome the idea that experience is theory-laden. Remember that any *account* of a divine/human encounter is human in its meaning and form. The prophet is not a funnel through which God pours a message. Yet somehow we must get beyond an account of God's presence to that presence itself. An account puts me in the realm of ideas and constructions. There is nothing wrong with ideas and constructions as long as we do not confuse them with God Himself. The question is: How do we get to God? Mindful of Buber's status as a sage, let us put aside the epistemological objections that overwhelmed Russell's notion of direct acquaintance. The proper comparison is not between Buber and Russell but between Buber and Kierkegaard. And the proper question is: Can we encounter God apart from the moral law or is our experience of Him so bound up with morality that the two are inseparable? Unless Buber can separate them, all the references to "lived experience" and "concrete reality" will not help. The moral law is a universal truth well within the realm of "theory." According to Cohen, it is the pinnacle of the realm of theory, much as Goodness is the pinnacle of Plato's realm of ideas.

Kierkegaard has no problem making such a separation. Faith requires an absolute duty toward God. Such a duty precludes mediation, in particular the mediation afforded by the moral law. The knight of faith regards a personal relation with God as higher than a moral relation to the rest of humanity: the particular is higher than the universal. It is this relation that transforms an act of murder into an act of piety. On the question of how God is to be identified, Kierkegaard is clear: He cannot be. If the particular stands above the universal, criteria are of no help. That is why the knight of faith is not intelligible to others—even to another knight of faith. Because a relation to God is absolute, *any* reference to theories or constructs, any attempt at mediation, is ruled out; the knight of faith does everything by virtue of the absurd. It could be said, therefore, that absurdity is the price the knight pays for immediacy. Nothing, not even the fundamental rules of logic, stands between the knight of faith and God.

Buber is no knight of faith. He admires Kierkegaard and approves of the idea that an authentic relation with God transcends ethical laws. But when he sees people around him suspending the ethical with impunity, he shudders.[29] According to Manfred Vogel, Buber has a twofold reaction: he wants to retain the notion of absolute personality but reject that of ethical indifference.[30] In the last analysis, the latter tendency carries the day. He cannot get himself to say that killing, torture, or loss of personal integrity are ways of achieving a higher end, much less ways of pleasing God. The notion that cruelty can be "transformed" into piety by divine decree is too much for him to bear. Here he abandons the role of sage and raises a standard philosophic objection, the one raised by Kant:

How do you know if the voice which addresses you belongs to God or to Moloch? According to Buber, the problematics of faith are preceded by the problematics of hearing. If the voice we hearken to is Moloch's, then the "leap of faith" is really an act of idolatry. How, then, do we make the crucial decision? Buber relies on the words of Micah 6.9: "It has been told thee, Oh man, what is good, and what the Lord requires of thee: Only to do justice, to love mercy, and to walk humbly with thy God." Buber concludes that what God demands of us is "not much more than the fundamental ethical."

If all God demands of us is righteous behavior, God and righteousness are inseparable. To love God, even to love Him as a person, is to renounce murder, torture, and loss of personal integrity. The moment one tries to find God *beyond* the sphere of the ethical, she must ask whether the person whose presence is felt is not really Moloch. If it is, the attempt to put systematic considerations aside and confront God "face-to-face" is a failure. No matter how "concrete" our experience of Him may be, the God to whom we bow our heads must present Himself under a description. And that description can only be one that reduces to morality. This is as true for Cohen's God-Idea as it is for "the ancient God of Israel." As Isaiah put it (5.16, cf. Psalms 11.7, 97.2): "The Lord of hosts is exalted through justice [*mishpat*], and God the Holy One sanctified through righteousness [*tzedakah*]."

Forced to choose between Kierkegaard and the prophets, Buber opts for the latter, which is the traditional Jewish response. No abstract system builder himself, Elie Wiesel admits: "I have never really been able to accept the idea that inhumanity could be one more way for man to move closer to God. Kierkegaard's too convenient theory of occasional 'ethical suspension' never appealed to me."[31] Nor, in the last analysis, does it appeal to Buber. What, then, becomes of Buber's existentialism? He can still walk under the existentialist banner by pointing out that Micah's formula is a generalization. It may be true that God demands justice, mercy, and humility and cannot be met except on these terms. Still, the question of what I am supposed to do in the next moment of my life remains open.[32] It is a long way from justice as a moral ideal to the specific situation in which I find myself. How do I realize justice in everyday life? Here Buber can hold that God speaks to me in my individuality. Even the most explicit guidelines leave open a degree of personal discretion. It is within the realm of such discretion that Buber can espouse situational ethics. In *Between Man and Man* (114), he writes: "No responsible person remains a stranger to norms. But the command inherent in a genuine norm never becomes a maxim and the fulfillment of it never a habit." Yet once he admits the existence of norms and invokes the authority of Micah, he concedes a great deal to Cohen. By loving God, I love someone who wills the moral law. If so, it is not true that the philosophic idea of the absolute dissolves at the point where God lives. Unless we follow Kierkegaard, there is no way to distinguish them. Again from Vogel, the ethical is "built into" the religious.[33]

5. God as Person

Belief in a personal God is vacuous unless one has something to say about the *sort* of person God is. If God wills the moral law, then to respond to Him as a person, I have no choice but to will it myself. Conversely, for God to respond to *me* as a person is to demand that I devote myself to its empirical fulfillment. Such is the sum and substance of revelation. If this is what one means by a personal God, no one was more committed to this belief than Cohen. Insofar as personality is a normative concept and concerns what ought to be, God is the personality *par excellence*. The question that concerns the existentialists—Is it the law or the law-giver?—is therefore of secondary importance. Even if we opt for the latter, our conception of God's personality is all that and only that which is needed to conceive of a morally perfect individual. We can attribute mercy, justice, and forgiveness to God only because these qualities are praiseworthy in us. Take away the moral law and we have thunder and lightning but no personality.

On the other hand, if, by a personal God, one means that there is a way of putting oneself in God's good graces without respecting the dignity of one's fellow human beings, Cohen would insist, with Kant, that a personal God is nothing but another name for human vanity.[34] In other words, Cohen would deny that any encounter with God can be immediate. Recall that according to Maimonides, even Moses could not get beyond God's consequences or effects. So I cannot encounter God as a living person if that means confronting Him in the way I confront my wife. Cohen insists that Maimonides destroyed this type of analogy once and for all (*Religion of Reason*, 160). Rather than being present as a concrete fact, God is known to us through the process of construction, a process that looks to the Bible, its commentaries, the philosophic tradition, and everything else which informs our religious experience.

Because God is an archetype, He stands at the limits of human experience. We can encounter Him only to the degree that we have clarified our duties as moral agents. Encountering God is therefore a long and potentially infinite project. But there is no reason why the commitment to it cannot be passionate, even awe-inspiring. Against this idea, Buber maintains (*Eclipse of God*, 84) that "when man learns to love God, he senses an actuality which rises above the idea." We have seen, however, that the attempt to rise above the idea is fraught with risk; a risk that, in the end, Buber is not willing to take. If absurdity is the price one pays for immediacy, Buber has to forgo immediacy. That raises the question of what to say to someone who is willing to take the risk. In many ways, the controversy between Buber and Cohen is based on the more decisive controversy between Kierkegaard and Kant. It is to that subject that we now turn.

Notes

1. Fackenheim, E., "Martin Buber's Concept of Revelation," in P. Schilpp (ed.), *The Philosophy of Martin Buber* (LaSalle, Ill.: Open Court Press, 1967), 294.

2. Cohen, *Religion of Reason*, 71.

3. Strauss, *Philosophy and Law*, 53–58, 102–5, 107–10.

4. The problems are: (1) If God prevents someone from being a prophet who otherwise deserves it, it seems that God would be acting in an arbitrary fashion; (2) if God prevents a person from achieving prophecy, then he prevents a person from having a good that person might otherwise obtain. Both run contrary to the spirit of Maimonides' rationalism. Notice, however, that these objections are applicable only if Maimonides adopts the compromise position. To the degree that prophecy is purely natural, they are met. But if it is purely natural, another objection applies: Why can there not be another prophet of the stature of Moses or prophets after the destruction of the Second Temple in the year 70?

5. Kant, *Lectures* 160–61. Cf. *Religion Within the Limits*, 157, footnote: "[I]n whatever manner a being has been made known to him by another and described as God, yea, even if such a being had appeared to him (if this is possible), he must first of all compare this representation with his ideal in order to judge whether he is entitled to regard it and to honor it as a divinity. Hence there can be no religion springing from revelation alone, i.e., without *first* positing that concept, in its purity, as a touchstone. Without this all reverence for God would be *idolatry*."

6. Schwarzschild, "The Title of Hermann Cohen's 'Religion of Reason out of the Sources of Judaism' " in J. Edelheit (ed.), *The Life of Covenant: Essays in Honor of Herman E. Schaalman* (Chicago: Spertus College of Judaica Press, 1986), 211.

7. Halevi, *Kuzari* 1.4, 1.11–25.

8. Fackenheim, "Hermann Cohen—After Fifty Years," *Leo Baeck Memorial Lecture*, 12 (1969), 20.

9. See Cohen, *Religion of Reason*, 10, and Schwarzschild, "The Title," in Edelheit, *Life of Covenant*.

10. Aristotle, *On the Heavens*, 279b.

11. Cf. Rosenzweig's introduction to Cohen's *Jüdische Schriften*, xxxii: "Eine Idee für Cohen nicht, nur eine Idee ist. . . ."

12. Rosenzweig, ibid., xiii–lxiv. Cf. Nathan Rotenstreich, *Jewish Philosophy in Modern Times* (New York: Holt, Rinehart & Winston, 1968), 64. For a different view, one to which I am sympathetic, see Guttmann, *Philosophies of Judaism*, 415. If God were an existent entity that humans confront by some kind of moral intuition, Cohen would be abandoning the entire spirit of the Critical Philosophy. Ethics would no longer involve choice or self-legislation. We would confront our moral duties as we confront objects of perception. Instead of a religion of *reason*, we would have a modern version of religious dogmatism.

13. Buber, *Eclipse of God*, trans. M. S. Friedman (New York: Harper & Row, 1952), 28.

14. Ibid., 55–56.

15. Buber, *I and Thou*, 2d edition, trans. R. G. Smith (New York: Charles Scribner's Sons, 1953), 39.

16. *I and Thou*, 111.

17. Fackenheim, "Martin Buber's Concept of Revelation," 285.

18. Buber, *I and Thou*, 110.

19. Buber, "Reply to My Critics," in Schilpp (ed.), 692.

20. Eliezer Berkovits, *Major Themes in Modern Philosophies of Judaism* (New York: KTAV Publishing, 1974), 72–75, and Steven T. Katz, *Post-Holocaust Dialogues* (New York: New York University Press, 1983), 1–51. For a defense of Buber, see Maurice S. Friedman, *Martin Buber* (1955; rpt., New York: Harper & Row, 1960), 161–75.

21. In a personal letter to Maurice Friedman, Buber once wrote: "I have no inclination to systematizing, but I am of course and by necessity a philosophizing man." See Friedman, *Martin Buber,* 161. Unfortunately, this quote leaves Buber's status as ambiguous as ever.

22. Buber, *Eclipse of God,* 69.

23. Hume, *A Treatise of Human Nature* 1.4.7.

24. For a modern existentialist answer to this question, see Wyschogrod, *Body of Faith,* chapter 3. Notice, however, that Wyschogrod's attempt to ascribe personality to God goes far beyond Buber's.

25. Buber, *Between Man and God,* trans. R. G. Smith (London: Kegan Paul, 1947).

26. Buber, *Good and Evil,* trans. R. G. Smith (New York: Charles Scribner's Sons, 1952), 142.

27. Cohen, *Religion of Reason,* 160. For Buber's reply, see *Eclipse of God,* 80.

28. Taken from "I and Thou: Selfhood Through Ethical Action," in *Reason and Hope: Selections from the Jewish Writings of Hermann Cohen,* trans. Eva Jospe (New York: W. W. Norton, 1971), 218.

29. See Buber, *Eclipse of God,* 149–56.

30. Manfred Vogel, "Kierkegaard's Teleological Suspension of the Ethical—Some Reflections from a Jewish Perspective," in R. Porreco (ed.), *The Georgetown Symposium on Ethics: Essays in Honor of Henry Babcock Veatch* (New York: University Press of America, 1985), 26.

31. Elie Wiesel, *Messengers of God* (New York: Random House, 1976), 90.

32. Buber takes a position like this one in answer to Marvin Fox. See "Reply to My Critics," in Schilpp, 719–20.

33. Vogel, "Kierkegaard's Teleological Suspension of the Ethical," 32.

34. Cf. Kant, *Religion Within the Limits,* 47.

Chapter Five

Suspending the Ethical

1. The Rationalist's Dilemma

From Plato to Cohen, the crux of the rationalist's understanding of God is that the relation between God and humans is never immediate. The possibility of the particular standing *above* the universal does not exist. All judgments about particulars presuppose universal criteria. In order to know whether the voice we hear is God's, we must first ask whether it is worthy of the respect owed a perfect being. But in order to do that, we must compare the content of the message we receive to our idea of perfection. Until such a comparison is made, the voice is nothing but an auditory representation which may originate with God as easily as with Moloch. According to Kant:

> If God should really speak to man, men could still never *know* that it was God speaking. It is quite impossible for man to apprehend the infinite by his senses, distinguish it from sensible beings, and *recognize* it as such. But in some cases man can be sure that the voice he hears is *not* God's; for if the voice commands him to do something contrary to the moral law, then no matter how majestic the apparition may be, and no matter how it may seem to surpass the whole of nature, he must consider it an illusion.[1]

To the rationalist, the only way to answer the question "God or Moloch?" is to appeal to moral criteria. There is nothing in the auditory representation itself which can supply the answer.

The appeal to criteria has at least one important consequence. If the voice commands something for which no rational justification can be found, we have no grounds for thinking the voice is God's. In other words, the rationalist assumes that God never acts in an arbitrary fashion. The only authentic commands are those for which reason can discern some purpose. Thus Kant rejects as superstitious

119

any attempt to please God through acts of worship which circumvent the moral law.[2] It is a corruption of true religion—what Kant terms "self-incurred perversity"—to think that God can be reached through expiations that imply no improvement in character.

Although not as extreme as Kant, Maimonides advocates a similar position. At *Guide* 3.31 (cf. 3.26), he deems it a sickness to think that some commandments have nothing to recommend them but divine decree:

> There is a group of human beings who consider it a grievous thing that causes should be given for any law; what would please them most is that the intellect would not find a meaning for the commandments and prohibitions. What compels them to feel thus is a sickness that they find in their souls, a sickness to which they are unable to give utterance and of which they cannot furnish a satisfactory account. For they think that if those laws were useful in this existence and had been given to us for this or that reason, it would be as if they derived from the reflection and the understanding of some intelligent being. If, however, there is a thing for which the intellect could not find any meaning at all and that does not lead to something useful, it indubitably derives from God; for the reflection of man would not lead to such a thing. It is as if, according to these people of weak intellects, man were more perfect than his Maker; for man speaks and acts in a manner that leads to some intended end, whereas the deity does not act thus, but commands us to do things that are not useful to us and forbids us to do things that are not harmful to us. But He is far exalted above this; the contrary is the case—the whole purpose consisting in what is useful for us, as we have explained on the basis of its dictum: *For our good always, that He might preserve us alive, as it is at this day.* And it says: *Which shall hear all these statutes [hukkim] and say: surely this great community is a wise and understanding people.* Thus it states explicitly that even all the *statutes [hukkim]* will show to all the nations that they have been given with *wisdom and understanding.* Now if there is a thing for which no reason is known and that does not either procure something useful or ward off something harmful, why should one say of one who believes in it or practices it that he is *wise and understanding* and of great worth? And why should the religious communities think it a wonder?[3]

The passage Maimonides refers to is one we have encountered before: Deuteronomy 4.6–8. According to the standard interpretation, God's revelation consists of two kinds of commands: ordinances (*mishpatim*), which it would be proper (*din*) to add even if God had not commanded them, and statutes (*hukkim*), which must be followed even if no reason is apparent.[4] An example of the former is the prohibition against murder; of the latter, the prohibition against mixing fibers. Notice, however, that Maimonides departs from the traditional view by arguing that there must be reasons for the statutes as well. Nothing God commands is arbitrary. If something were, God would be less perfect than humans, and the principle of *imitatio Dei* would make no sense.

To some, the statutes are important precisely because we *cannot* find a plausible justification. It is easy to obey commands that recommend themselves to human reason. According to this view, however, God wants to see if we are willing to obey Him even when the intellect is stymied. Maimonides objects that the statutes are not inducements to blind obedience but, as Twersky put it, "messages which must be deciphered and decoded."[5] Nor did Maimonides think that the decoding of the statutes is beyond present intellectual capacity. It requires rigorous study but not superhuman modes of awareness. The fruits of such study will reveal to the people of every nation that the Torah reflects a superior understanding of human perfection. There is, of course, a danger in trying to seek explanations for the statutes: either (1) people who reject the explanations will reject the commandments, or (2) people who see the reason for the commandments will think that the practice in question can be dispensed with. Mindful of these dangers, Maimonides still insists that the search for universally valid reasons must go forward. Maimonides qualifies his view in two ways. First, he allows that the specific features of a statute may elude us even though the general ones do not. For example, there were good reasons for the laws regarding sacrifice of animals, but no one will ever know why a ram is needed here and a lamb there (*Guide* 3.26). Second, he admits that the human race cannot go from idolatry and superstition to monotheism all at once. Certain laws are needed to facilitate this transition (*Guide* 3.31). If so, there may be practices that served a purpose in ancient times but do not appear to serve one in the present. We can agree with Josef Stern that Maimonides is not recommending that these commandments be dropped.[6] It would be better to say that, having understood their original justification, the worshiper must now look for a different one. A practice may serve as a reminder of what had to be done to weaken the appeal of idolatry. Or there may be jurisprudential considerations that favor legal stability. But while the justifications of different commandments will achieve different levels of certainty, the need for justification is ever present.

Within the scope of rationalism, there is a difference of opinion on what counts as a justification. For Kant, all ethical judgments are a priori, which is to say necessary and universal. It is certain that truth telling and respect for human life are moral obligations. But on this issue, Maimonides parts company with Kant. Early in the *Guide* (1.2), he introduces a distinction between truth and falsity, which are known to the intellect, and fine and bad, which are not known to the intellect but are "generally accepted things."[7] This distinction is in keeping with his contention that there are two categories of commandment: those whose purpose is to instill truth and those whose purpose is to produce social conditions that enable people to pursue truth (*Guide* 3.27). At *Guide* 2.35, he maintains that with respect to the existence and unity of God, in essence the first two commandments, there is no difference between the prophet and the person of superior intelligence. The reason there is no difference is that these truths can be known by reason alone.[8] But with respect to all the other commandments, we leave the realm of necessity and enter that of convention. I follow David Novak in claiming that all the other commandments presuppose a social context.[9] Therefore all the other commandments, including the prohibitions against murder and lying, are means of achieving the conditions necessary to realize the first two. The ethical commandments are needed to achieve the commandments that assert the existence and radical transcendence of God. Yet as soon as we start talking about means to an end, we lose a measure of certainty. Maimonides does not claim that the ethical commandments can be known by reason alone. On the other hand, we have just seen that all commandments have a rationale. The only way to make him consistent is to say that the rationale for the ethical commandments is one level removed from that of the intellectual ones. With respect to the former, Maimonides does not talk about necessity but about arguments which recommend themselves to reason or to which reason is inclined.[10] In short, there are reasons for convention, too.

The difference between Maimonides and Kant is that Kant insists on the unconditional necessity of the moral law. That is why Kant argues that if there is to be a universal moral religion, it will have to rid itself of historically conditioned practices. In *Religion Within the Limits of Reason Alone* (112) he imagines a time when "religion will gradually be freed from all empirical determining grounds and from all statutes which rest on history . . . and thus at last the pure religion of reason will rule over all. . . ." For an individual worshiper, this view is problematic because one can always ask whether we should start eliminating historically conditioned practices in the present or whether we still need them to continue working toward the ideal Kant envisions. A person could agree with the norm Kant has established but point out that the human race is nowhere near the point where it can be fulfilled. As Cohen notes (*Religion of Reason*, 346), the moral law may be the supreme principle of human conduct but it need not be the immediate one. People require symbols and reminders in order to have a realistic chance of following the moral law. Kant himself recognizes the need for an ecclesiastical or statutory religion provided it is "in harmony with" the true, moral one. We may conclude that, even for Kant, there are justifications for historically conditioned statutes. In effect, these justifications are concessions to human fallibility. Some practices, though not deducible from the moral law, are needed for its empirical realization. If the human race developed greater understanding than it now has, if idolatry were no longer a temptation and people did not need to have their moral sensibilities aroused from time to time, then, like the Marxist state, the need for historically conditioned statutes would wither away. Ecclesiastical religion would be transformed into a purely rational faith. But it is perfectly in keeping with Kantian principles to say that this transformation, though always a possibility, will be completed only at the end of time.[11]

Another difference between Maimonides and Kant is that the former does not think of freedom as self-legislation. He insists that human beings are free and have an obligation to understand the reasons behind the law. In the same way, he depicts God as a free agent but a constant and purposeful one. In chapter 3 we saw that Maimonides stresses the negative aspect of God's freedom, that is, freedom from external causes, but has little to say about the positive side. For Kant, the necessity of the moral law is not something opposed to God's will but that will itself understood as the author of its own legislation. The fact that God cannot do otherwise than will the moral law does not show that God is constrained but exactly the opposite. In short, autonomy or self-legislation is the only way to make freedom and constancy compatible. But this insight is part of

Kant's Copernican Revolution. It is not an explicit part of Maimonides' understanding of God and certainly not a part of his understanding of human beings.

For present purposes, however, we can put aside these differences and formulate a general description of the rationalist position. God is not arbitrary. He is a rational agent who wants His children to develop their own powers of reason to the fullest extent. We do not flatter God or demonstrate loyalty to Him by obeying commands that have no justification. On the contrary, it demeans God to obey Him in an obsequious manner. This does not mean that every command must have the same force as the prohibition against murder. Some may be symbolic. Some may serve as reminders. Some may be needed to establish identity in a religious community *provided* that community dedicates itself to the improvement of the human race. As Cohen puts it (*Religion of Reason*, 345), what is not the moral law is to be thought of as a means to the promotion *of*, or education *in*, the moral law. So we can admit the distinction between universal and statutory commands but still hold that there is a reason for everything God asks. The danger of obeying commands for which there is no reason is that the religion we practice will have no moral truths supporting it—only the claim that God wants something done. Lacking support, this claim will have to be accepted on faith alone. Although we get a commanding God, it is a God who does nothing *but* command, which is to say a God who commands without educating. There is little question that the God of Deuteronomy, who stressed the wisdom of His law, did both.

So characterized, the rationalist position leads to a problem. If God is morally perfect, and if there is a reason for everything He asks, then, following Kant, the only way we can assure ourselves that God has spoken is to compare the command to our conception of morality. But if there is no way of identifying God apart from morality, what need is there of God? Why not simply obey our moral obligations and forget about heavenly pronouncements altogether? For even if these pronouncements are divine in origin, they can neither add to nor subtract from the obligations we impose upon ourselves as rational agents. From the standpoint of morality, the question of authorship—Is it really *God* who addresses us?—is speculative. As we saw in a previous chapter, no empirical testimony can reach the divine. To take an obvious example, we can conclude with certainty that murder is wrong. Should a heavenly voice ask us to commit murder, we would never be justified in sacrificing our conviction that murder is immoral for the probability that the heavenly voice is genuine.

There is at least one passage where Maimonides seems to be aware of this difficulty. In the *Mishneh Torah* (14.8.10–11), he claims it is not enough for a righteous gentile to obey the commandments on the basis of a rational argument. Such a person must obey because God commanded them and made them known to Moses. Some have argued that in this passage, Maimonides is trying to reestablish the notion that morality is a system of divine commands. But a better interpretation has been offered by David Novak.[12] A gentile who obeys these commandments because they are necessary for the preservation of human society may have fulfilled his or her legal requirements but has not grasped the full philosophical perspective from which a justification of the commandments can be given. In any case, if revelation is understood as an intellectual relationship rather than a miraculous one, Maimonides cannot avoid the question of how we know that something is commanded. At *Guide* 2.40, he argues that truth is a primary criterion. It could be argued that if our knowledge of divine commands is consequent upon truth, that is, what can be established by rational argument, Maimonides undermines the imperatival dimension of morality and opens himself up to the same problem that plagues Kant. So Maimonides is not as clear as we might like.

Textbooks in the history of philosophy often portray existentialism as a reaction to Hegel. But we can agree with Alasdair MacIntyre that it is really Kant who is the target of their invective.[13] If the source of the command is no longer important, then from an existentialist perspective, the command has lost all religious significance. Rationalism is but another instance of the eclipse of God. We can see this by turning to Kierkegaard. If I perform my duty to my neighbor, then it is my neighbor with whom I come in contact, not God.[14] To say that performance of this duty constitutes love of God is to utter a platitude. If my only access to God is through duties to the rest of humanity, then: "God becomes an invisible vanishing point." To bring God out of the shadow, we must reestablish the notion of heavenly authority. To do this, we must put morality aside and emphasize the notion of *commanding presence*. The correlate of commanding presence is the religiously authentic individual who is free to accept that presence or not. According to Fackenheim,

the Divine manifests itself as *commanding*, and in order to do so it requires real human freedom. And since the Divine is *presence* as well as commanding, the required human freedom cannot be merely conditional—it must be unconditional and absolute. Finally, this unconditional and absolute freedom

must be more even than the freedom to accept or reject specific commandments for their own sake, for there are as yet no
such commandments. The freedom required in the pristine
moment of the divine commanding Presence, then, is nothing
less than the freedom to accept or reject the divine commanding Presence as a whole, and for its own sake—that is, for no
other reason than it is that Presence. It is such freedom that
the prophet displays when he responds, "Here I am, send
me"; or that the people as a whole display when they respond, "We shall do and hearken."[15]

The moment Fackenheim describes is one in which the prophet accepts God's authority merely because it is God's. Thus the reference
to Exodus 24.7: "We shall do and [then] hearken." His point is that
the question of authorship is prior to the question of content. The
commanding presence of God is accepted immediately; the question
of *what* God commands is derivative. This order is the reverse of
Kant's. The existentialist's claim is that only by putting authorship
before content can we prevent God from disappearing.

The rationalist's dilemma is clear: either (a) God is superior to
the moral law, in which case suspension of the ethical is legitimate;
or (b) God is the upholder of the moral law, in which case the authorship of the commandments is secondary. As far as Kant is concerned, there is no dilemma at all. In one respect, it is true that
God has been eclipsed: authorship is subordinate to content. But
the God who vanishes is not the God who is worthy of adoration.
On the contrary, it is the "god" of superstition—the one who
makes arbitrary commands and responds to special pleading. The
fact that this god has been eclipsed is only a sign that religion is
making progress. To use Cohen's term, it is a sign that the relation
between God and humans has been *idealized*. Who, then, is guilty of
idolatry—the person who bows before the moral law or the person
who emphasizes commandment ahead of what is commanded?

2. The Knight of Faith

Enter Abraham. On Kierkegaard's interpretation, the dilemma
is solved at Genesis 22, when Abraham is asked to sacrifice Isaac.
From a moral standpoint, the command is shocking. I can never
satisfy an obligation to X by committing an immoral act against Y.
But, says Kierkegaard, the obligation to God is absolute, from which
it follows that obligations to the rest of humanity are relative. Un-

less this is true, Abraham is no better than a common criminal. It is only by recognizing that God stands above our obligations to the rest of humanity that Abraham's behavior can be seen as a test of faith. Faith, then, is the paradox capable of transforming a murder into a way of pleasing God. According to Kierkegaard (*Fear and Trembling*, 41):

> If Faith does not make it a holy act to be willing to murder one's son, then let the same condemnation be pronounced upon Abraham as upon every other man. . . . The ethical expression for what Abraham did is, that he would murder Isaac; the religious expression is, that he would sacrifice Isaac; but precisely in this contradiction consists the dread which can well make a man sleepless, and yet Abraham is not what he is without this dread.

Behind Kierkegaard's position is an assumption he shares with Descartes. Monotheism demands a God who is completely transcendent. Complete transcendence implies that logic has no purchase on God. Although *we* may not understand how a merciful God can demand such an action of a devoted servant like Abraham, this is simply a fact about us. To stand in relation to the absolute, we have to put aside anything connected with human values or expectations. As Kierkegaard points out (*Fear and Trembling*, 54): "Spiritually speaking, everything is possible, but in the world of the finite there is much which is not possible"—or, more appropriately, which cannot be asked.

If everything is possible, it is possible that a merciful God could ask His servant to commit human sacrifice. The rationalist's response to this is simple. Relying on a conception of what is possible and what not, a rationalist like Kant would conclude that the request did not originate with God.[16] From Kierkegaard's perspective, the rationalist never leaves the realm of the finite. If a husband asked a wife to forgo her obligations to other members of the family in order to demonstrate love for him, then, in Kierkegaard's opinion, the husband would be demonstrating stupidity.[17] The love of one person for another is not analogous to the love of a person for God. It is only when we come to God that the commitment must be absolute. And it is only the person willing to shut his or her eyes and plunge into the absurd who has made such a commitment.

Note the reference to absurdity. It is important that Kierkegaard's position not be confused with what is commonly referred to as divine command theory.[18] The divine command theorist argues that right and wrong are objective, nonnatural facts properly understood as agreement or disagreement with the will of God. On this view, if God commands something whose justification eludes us, we have no choice but to obey. Other than God's will, there is no standard we can consult, no body of natural law. God's will is expressed in commandments to which everyone has access. Although justifications for these commandments, such as the statutes of the Mosaic code, may not be available, they are not for that reason absurd. Kierkegaard, on the other hand, is not asking for a commitment *beyond* reason as much as a commitment *despite* it. The command to sacrifice Isaac is given to Abraham alone and is unintelligible to other people—even in what Kierkegaard describes as "the great ages of faith." In *Fear and Trembling* (57), he insists that "the absurd is not one of the factors which can be discriminated within the proper compass of the understanding: it is not identical with the improbable, the unexpected, or the unforeseen." The improbable, the unexpected, and the unforeseen are the sort of obstacles which beset other heroes in the Bible. But Kierkegaard has eyes only for Abraham. In Abraham and Abraham alone do we have someone willing to swallow a patent contradiction: that the same God who said he would be blessed through Isaac is now asking him to offer Isaac as a sacrifice. In this way, Abraham makes the double movement characteristic of faith: he resigns himself to the sacrifice at the same time that he believes he will get Isaac back.

From Kierkegaard's perspective, divine command theory is another form of rationalism. Insofar as the divine command theorist thinks that publicly expressed commandments are the ultimate expression of God's will, the divine command theorist, too, never leaves the realm of the finite. Only if the divine command theorist allows for a private relation with God can he or she make room for the knight of faith. To see this in a different way, the divine command theorist still operates within a religious tradition. The Bible is taken as an authoritative statement of God's will. For the divine command theorist, God's will can be communicated from one person to another. So the divine command theorist does not put the particular above the universal. Faced with a command to do something out of the ordinary, for example, to spit at a sacred symbol, the divine command theorist could retreat into a position similar to Kant's: How do I know that the voice which addressed me is God's? My tradition is an authoritative guide to what God wills. Therefore if the voice that addresses me demands a radical departure from tradition, it cannot be God's.

Another possibility for the divine command theorist is to follow the rabbinic interpretation of Deuteronomy 30.12 ("Torah is not in the heavens").[19] According to this alternative, God has already made His will known. There is no body of unrevealed commandments to be communicated at a future date. Once this principle is accepted, the voice from heaven is no longer authoritative—particularly if it asks one to change the content of Mosaic legislation. On either interpretation, the divine command theorist opts for a mediated relation with God. For Kant, the mediating factor is the moral law; for the divine command theorist, the body of religious law. For the knight of faith, however, there is no mediation at all. Ordered to spit, the knight would approach the symbol with fear and trembling but spit nonetheless.

A standard way of attacking Kierkegaard is to point out that human sacrifice was common in the ancient Near East. Hence: (1) Abraham could have believed without absurdity that the command to sacrifice Isaac came from God; and (2) the point of the story is not that Abraham was willing to sacrifice Isaac but that, in the end, God did not want him to. In short, the story rests on its happy ending: God does not demand that innocent blood be shed on His behalf. Unfortunately there are a number of problems with this interpretation. A prohibition against murder is issued at Genesis 9.6, long before Abraham comes on the scene. If the purpose of the story were to end the practice of human sacrifice, then, as Nahum Sarna maintains, we would expect the story to end with an unequivocal rejection of this practice.[20] In fact, the story ends with words of praise for Abraham. Since the entire episode is described as a "test," it is reasonable to conclude, with Sarna, that "the demand of God is presented as something extraordinary, something that a man would not dream of doing on his own initiative, and something that tries the believer to the utmost so that his response is by no means predictable." Although Sarna does not mention Kierkegaard, he lends support to the existentialist reading by bringing in the notion of dread. Unless God's command is perceived as shocking, the literary value of the passage is greatly diminished. The question is: Can we preserve the literary value of the story without invoking the concept of absurdity?

3. The Knight and His God

To preserve the literary value of the story, Kierkegaard himself ignores other episodes in Abraham's life. When God promises him that he will be blessed through his posterity, he is skeptical (Genesis 15.3) and at one point laughs at the whole idea (Genesis 17.17).[21] According to Maimonides, Abraham interrupts his encounter with God at 18.3 in order to show hospitality to his guests.[22] It seems, therefore, he puts his duty to his neighbor above his relation to God. More important, when Abraham thinks that divine judgment on Sodom and Gomorrah is too harsh, he protests without hesitation (Genesis 18.25):

> Far be it from You to do such a thing, to bring death upon the innocent as well as the guilty, so that innocent and guilty fare alike. Far be it from You! Shall not the judge of all the earth deal justly?

Kierkegaard interprets this speech as an entreaty (*Fear and Trembling*, 35), but the text indicates it is much stronger: Abraham is holding God to account—and doing so in the name of morality.

As for the trial itself, Abraham's victory is a costly one. Twice the text claims that he and Isaac went to the mountain *together* (Genesis 22, 6 & 8). The repetition of this word is meant to convey an image of familial harmony. But after the attempted sacrifice, we are not told where Isaac is. All we know is that father and son never speak to each other after this episode. In any case, Kierkegaard's suggestion that Abraham found it easy to be joyful again with Isaac is misleading. Then there is the matter of Sarah. It is not just that Abraham does not confide in her but that the very next thing we hear about her is that she has died. In a biblical context, such proximity usually implies cause and effect: she died out of grief at the thought that Abraham might have murdered their only son. So the ending of the story is not as happy as it first appears. There is also the question of why God never speaks to Abraham after he has come down from the mountain. The close relation established in the earlier chapters ends suddenly. Abraham passes the test by not withholding anything from God. He is completely unselfish. But did God want him to protest as he had done earlier for the people of Sodom and Gomorrah—protest not on his own behalf but on that of Isaac and Sarah?[23] Or, did God think that the moment Abraham agreed to do His will, further communication was unnecessary?

We shall never know. The same man who challenged God at one point in his life agreed to perform a human sacrifice at another. All we can say is that the text does not present a religious fanatic ready to plunge into the absurd: the characterization of Abraham, and the events following the trial, paint a much subtler picture.

When it comes to heroes, the Hebrew Bible fights a constant war against just the sort of thing Kierkegaard engages in: the glorification of an individual. It wants us to admire the prophets and patriarchs but not so much that we lose sight of God. The result is that all of the biblical heroes are flawed. Aside from Abraham, Jacob is deceitful, Moses impetuous, David lustful. The Bible does not want a hero to become a demigod.

It is noteworthy that in *Fear and Trembling*, Kierkegaard has much more to say about Abraham than about the God he is serving. If we inquire into Kierkegaard's conception of God, disturbing questions arise. This God is beyond moral rules, logical rules, or anything else which would allow those who believe in Him to make themselves intelligible. He is distinguished not by mercy or justice but by the infinite freedom of His will, a will we can neither question nor understand. Called to service by such a deity, the knight of faith can only shut his eyes and leap into the abyss. We can say that this is a sign of love since the knight of faith has surrendered everything to God. But like Kierkegaard's swain who falls in love with a beautiful princess, the knight must love God from afar. *Fear and Trembling* never discusses how human love is returned. We are told that the knight of faith has an absolute relation to God, but for all we know, the relation is never reciprocated. We must close our minds and shut out the rest of humanity or else his relation to God is not absolute. God, in turn, is indifferent to, even contemptuous of, human concerns. The usual way of bringing God and humans together—morality—has been suspended.

It may be argued that the knight of faith does not suspend the ethical as much as widen its application.[24] The knight acts for a purpose but not one which can be reduced to universal laws. But the purpose is still an irrational one. The knight never receives an explanation of *why* the general rules do not apply and how his action will remedy the situation. As committed a rationalist as Aristotle believed that ethical judgments apply only to typical cases.[25] So it is conceivable we might want to suspend our judgment if extraordinary circumstances arise. But Aristotle's suspension is based on a considered judgment; Kierkegaard's is not. At the point where the knight of faith suspends the ethical, intelligibility comes to an end.

The problem with *Fear and Trembling* is that humans and God are presented as adversaries. As long as God is characterized by the infinite freedom of His will, any person who possesses a will of his or her own must appear as a rival. If humans retain any degree of autonomy, they must do so at God's expense. Once this assumption is granted, it is impossible to view God's commands as expressions of love. Instead of helping humans, God is here engaged in a cosmic test of wills. The more absurd the command, the lower we must bow to fulfill it. On the question of whether God teaches as well as commands, Kierkegaard is clear (*Fear and Trembling*, 90): "The true knight of faith is a witness, never a teacher, and therein lies his deep humanity, which is worth a good deal more than this silly participation in others' weal and woe which is honored by the name of sympathy, whereas in fact it is nothing but vanity." The true knight of faith does not even take an interest in other knights of faith because (*Fear and Trembling*, 82) "in these regions partnership is unthinkable." The people to whom God speaks are His personal servants; the second they develop an interest in helping others, their relation to God dissolves. To love the absolute absolutely, one cannot love anything else.

4. Worship of the Absurd

It is well to remember that throughout *Fear and Trembling*, Kierkegaard insists *he* is not a knight of faith. He can think himself into the role of tragic hero because the tragic hero remains within the realm of the ethical. But when it comes to Abraham, all of Kierkegaard's powers of imagination fail (44): "I fall down, for what I encounter there is the paradox." The knight of faith is a rare person, a prodigy. At one point (45), Kierkegaard wonders whether anyone in his generation is capable of making the movements of faith. At another (49), he claims he has never come across a reliable example of a true knight—though he admits that "every second man may be such an example." It is this admission which worries Buber. For in one respect, Kierkegaard is surely wrong: personal relations with the absolute are commonplace. Buber writes (*Eclipse of God*, 154):

> Ours is an age in which the suspension of the ethical fills the world in a caricaturized form. The apes of the Absolute, to be sure, have always in the past bustled about on earth. Ever and ever again men are commanded from out of the darkness to sacrifice their Isaac. *Here* the sentence is valid, "That which the Single One is to understand by Isaac, can be decided only by and for himself." But stored away in men's hearts, there were in all those times images of the Absolute, partly pallid, partly crude, altogether false and yet true, fleeting as an image in a dream yet verified in eternity. Inadequate as this presence cer-

tainly was, insofar as one bore it concretely in mind one only needed to call on it in order not to succumb to the deception of the voices.

Two qualifications should be noted. First, Buber is talking about *our* age. As Vogel points out, Buber does not say anything about biblical times or the possibility of a messianic future.[26] Second, Buber is talking about suspension of the ethical in a *caricaturized* form. His concern is not Abraham but Abraham's imitators. For the latter, Kierkegaard too would have nothing but contempt.

The problem is, however, that there is no way to tell the original from the copies. We cannot consult a religious tradition because that would imply mediation. We cannot ask questions because, to repeat, the knight of faith is not intelligible. We cannot look to behavior because not even the most heinous crime or pointless act would disqualify someone. It is hardly surprising, then, that Kierkegaard picked a literary example to make his point. But here he, too, runs the risk of mediation. If Kierkegaard is right, there is no way to generalize from the actions of one knight of faith to those of another. Each one has a personal relation with the absolute. But since the absolute is bound by nothing, one knight of faith may receive a command at odds with another. For all we know, the local preacher might be a knight of faith, or the local criminal, or the local sheriff. And if we cannot tell whether someone is a knight of faith, whether a person is answering the call of the Absolute or one of its apes, neither can the knight of faith. To the question "God or Moloch?" the knight of faith has no certain answer—only faith. In doing as the voice commands, the knight is taking an infinite risk. Unless there is a real possibility the knight is serving Moloch, or acting on a subconscious desire to destroy what he loves, or going mad, the action would be based on calculation. The knight would be applying rationality rather than leaping beyond it. Faith neither has nor requires a guarantee.

Yet it is one thing to say that a person has no guarantee he or she is answering the call of God, another to say that the relation between humans and God resists any characterization. God's will is infinite. The knight of faith has an absolute commitment to this will. An absolute commitment to an infinite will is at once everything and nothing—the former because no possibility is ruled out, the latter because no content is conveyed. There is nothing to prevent subjective, even disgusting practices, from being transformed into divine commands. In the end, the question "God or Moloch?"

will be settled by default: Moloch. In stressing the transcendence of God *against* the integrity of humans, Kierkegaard has turned God into an It. There is no dialogue—in Buber's sense or anyone else's. Partnership with others is impossible and anything but total servility impious. The great irony is that in Kierkegaard's understanding of faith, there is no personal dimension. It is not enough to say that the particular stands above the universal if the dignity of the particular has been surrendered. Between the knight of faith and God, there is no I and no Thou, only the abyss of absurdity. Kierkegaard has turned the absurd into an absolute.

Does this constitute idolatry? Normally idolatry involves the worship of a finite object like a piece of clay or a clap of thunder. In one respect, Kierkegaard's God is unconditioned: He does not fall within the scope of the understanding. In His hands, anything is possible. But if we have to forgo all traces of rationality to approach Him, for all we know, we might be approaching an impersonal force or idol. Nor will it do to point out that faith always requires a measure of risk. For unless ethical considerations have some hold on God, unless He has something to answer for, we will have not the risk but the certainty of debasing ourselves as a way of finding favor with "the absolute." Kant goes further. By suspending the ethical, we do not open the way to a higher plane. On the contrary, we put ourselves at the mercy of the demonic.[27] It is not just that our sensuous nature will take control but that we will give expression to a perverse desire to corrupt ourselves. And this desire will not just be expressed, it will become the object of worship and adoration. The result is what Kant terms *radical evil*.[28]

5. Abraham in Historical Perspective

Still, Kierkegaard has this much in his favor. Abraham is a hero. The story does show him attempting to sacrifice his son. From a moral standpoint, there is no way to make sense of his behavior. Since the history of his life reveals someone of sterling character, there is no question of perversity. God only tempts the righteous.[29] Does the story not imply, then, that Abraham rose *above* the ethical by doing God's will? And if it does, can we not conclude that God's will is superior to the moral law? One side of this debate argues that there are no constraints on God's will. The other argues that the moral law is the highest expression of any will so that if, *per impossible*, God violated the moral law, He would no longer be God.

From a philosophic perspective, it is difficult to decide the matter without begging the question.

It is hardly surprising, therefore, that Jewish tradition does not speak with a consistent voice on how to interpret Abraham's trial. Some have seen in the writings of J. B. Soloveitchik an acceptance of the Kierkegaardian suspension of the ethical.[30] But it is unclear whether Soloveitchik wants to appropriate Kierkegaard's understanding of the absurd or merely the fear and trembling with which the faithful worshiper goes to do God's will. Others have argued that Kierkegaard's interpretation is more Christian than Jewish. Along these lines, Marvin Fox maintains that the absurdity of Abraham's action *is* apparent if one confines one's attention to Genesis 22.[31] But, he continues, Jewish tradition does not admit that Genesis 22 is the whole story. The burden of Fox's article is to show that rabbinic commentators were reluctant to accept the idea that God issued an immoral command and that Abraham plunged into an abyss of absurdity to obey it. According to one view, God tests Abraham in order to answer Satan's charge that Abraham's piety is questionable.[32] Notice how this interpretation makes Abraham's plight similar to Job's. Notice, too, how this interpretation puts Abraham more in Aristotle's camp than in Kierkegaard's. Normally God would not ask for a human sacrifice. But since Satan has issued a challenge, normal conditions no longer apply. Another theme in rabbinic literature is that Isaac knew about the test and agreed to let himself be sacrificed. This would explain: (a) why Abraham did not protest the loss of innocent life, and (b) why Isaac did not protest when his father strapped him to the altar. Instead of an innocent victim, the Isaac of rabbinic commentators is a man in his thirties who not only understands but participates in his father's action. Of course Kierkegaard was under no obligation to read these commentaries. But we have seen that Kierkegaard's Abraham is also something of a creation. Other than Genesis 22, there is nothing to suggest that Abraham embraced the absurd or even contemplated it. By embellishing the story of the sacrifice, the rabbis tried to make this chapter consonant with the rest of Abraham's life. If Satan's accusation goes unanswered, people will think that the other trials in Abraham's life were worthless. Therefore God needs Abraham this one last time to show that the previous trials were genuine.

Christian interpreters, too, claimed that Genesis 22 is only part of the story. According to Paul (Romans 8.32), the near-sacrifice

of Isaac by Abraham prefigures the actual sacrifice of the son by the
father. In this way, the action of Genesis 22 is not consummated
until much later. Judaism sees it the other way around. According to
one rabbinic source, Abraham agreed to sacrifice Isaac provided that
when Isaac's children sin and suffer in future years, God will remember the day when Abraham stood on Mount Moriah and for-
give them.[33] Thus the prayer book for the High Holidays contains
the following invocation:

> Remember unto us, O Lord our God, the covenant and the
> loving kindness and the oath which Thou didst swear on
> Mount Moriah, and may the binding with which our father
> Abraham bound his son Isaac on the altar appear before Thee:
> how he overcame his compassion in order to perform Thy will
> with all his heart.

Far from suspending the ethical, and attempting to disregard what
Kierkegaard refers to as "silly participation in others' weal and
woe," Abraham, on this reading, is insisting on it. The man who
once called God to account over Sodom and Gomorrah now binds
God to an agreement. What are the terms of this agreement? They
are that He will be merciful, that He will confront Abraham's de-
scendants as a Thou rather than an It. It is as if Abraham has challenged God once again: You can make an extraordinary request now
on condition that you promise never to make one again. From this
time forward, there will be no suspension of the ethical or transval-
uation of values. As judge of all earth, you will do exactly as Your
name implies. On the rabbinic interpretation, Genesis 22 does not
prepare the way for future sacrifice, it closes the door.

In one respect, Kant has the better of Kierkegaard. If God is
free to do what He wants, He is free to make a promise and keep it.
Put otherwise, God is free to impose a duty on Himself. This is all
that is meant by describing Him as autonomous. In another respect,
though, Kierkegaard has the better of Kant. By eliciting a promise
from God, Abraham may not have suspended the ethical, but he
has certainly stretched it. Under the moral law, wrongdoing is pro-
hibited categorically. One cannot do a wrong to prevent the occurrence of additional wrongs in the future. So even on the rabbinic
interpretation, Abraham's behavior is out of the ordinary. The reply
is that the rabbinic interpretation is creating a legal fiction. It is not
recommending that people enter into such agreements with God or
anyone else. The prohibition against murder in Judaism is also cat-

egorical. The rabbinic commentators were using the story as a way of making a point: that God is constant rather than arbitrary, so that forgiveness is always a possibility. If there is a concession to Kierkegaard, it is minimal. Once we think of God as making a promise, personal relations with the Absolute are impossible. From that point forward, the promise has the status of a law, and law is the avenue by which the Absolute is approached.

6. The Eclipse of God Revisited

Again it should be understood that Judaism does not speak with a consistent voice on Abraham. Some have argued, against Fox, that the rabbinic texts support a Kierkegaardian interpretation.[34] Still, it is fair to say that Judaism cannot easily appropriate the notion of the absurd. In most Jewish circles, the real debate is not between Kant and Kierkegaard but between Kant and divine command theory. That is why Buber is important. He was a twentieth-century thinker familiar with Kierkegaard, Nietzsche, and the rest of existentialism. He rejected the abstract constructions of Cohen and the fixed rules of traditional Judaism. He wanted to get beyond both to the living God. If any Jewish thinker was prepared to embrace the paradox that the particular is higher than the universal, it was Buber. The problem is that he was willing to embrace it only as long as the particular falls within the scope of some basic rules, which is to say, only as long as the paradox is not really paradoxical. Buber can accept limits to human intelligence but not a violation of it. He is simply not in a position to argue that a personal relation with God supersedes obligations to the rest of humanity. In *Between Man and Man* (179), he admits that a God reached only by renunciation of everything else is a false deity. But in protecting himself from the ethically indifferent God of *Fear and Trembling*, Buber compromises the immediacy of the I-Thou relation and opens himself to attack from the opposite direction. If God does not command anything but "the fundamental ethical," why bother asking whether the voice that addresses us is God's? Why not follow Cohen and evaluate it according to content rather than source?

One feature of this alternative is attractive: to the degree that content is more important than source, the question "God or Moloch?" does not arise. Our only obligation is to realize the moral law. But another feature is fraught with difficulties: God becomes a vanishing point. We have seen that Kant and Cohen would be happy to live with this result. Buber would not. The whole point of *Eclipse of*

God is to prevent it. It follows that Buber must steer a middle course between an indifferent God, on the one hand, and a vanishing one, on the other. He wants the assurance of knowing that God will not call for a human sacrifice but not so much assurance that one's relation to God is free of risk. Mystery remains important to him. Unfortunately, he has no systematic way of identifying a middle ground. His religious intuitions are clearly with the existentialists.[35] He never tires of insisting that the Absolute is personal. Yet the qualification "in our time" suggests that he is worried about the awful possibility articulated by Kant: that evil will be an object of adoration. The history of our time provides ample evidence that Kant's fear is warranted.

Buber envisions a time, unlike ours, in which God will not be in eclipse and people will be able to approach Him without worrying about Moloch. But he does not say much about how to get from here to there. Do we rely on our sense of right and wrong or admit that right and wrong are at most generalizations? On my reading of Buber, the scales are tipped in favor of the former. In his vision of the future (*Eclipse of God*, 155–56), he calls for the development of a "new conscience of men" that will protect them from "the confusion of the relative with the Absolute" and enable them to "penetrate . . . into the false absolute with an incorruptible, probing glance." This is not a call for a leap of faith. To see through false absolutes, we need more than people who witness to the divine presence; we need people who subject false absolutes to rational critique. Without critique, there is no way to prevent Kant's fear from being realized.

Once again we are back to Kant and Cohen. The purpose of the critical philosophy was not to destroy religion but to free it of anything which implies contempt for reason and human dignity. Despite his antiphilosophical rhetoric, Buber has not broken with this tradition as much as he claims. At one point, he invokes the principle of *imitatio Dei* and claims that to the extent God is knowable at all, He is knowable through the moral attributes or *middot*.[36] This principle takes him back to Maimonides and Cohen with a vengeance. So, against his wishes, Buber faces the question of whether the critique of false absolutes will eliminate a personal relation with the true one—in short, the question of content versus source. To discuss this question, we must look at people who thought the critical tradition in philosophy eliminated any need to refer to God or religion at all, people for whom "critical" and "secular" are one and the same.

Notes

1. Kant, *The Conflict of the Faculties*, trans. M. J. Gregor (New York: Abaris Press, 1979), 115. In a footnote to this passage, Kant claims: "Abraham should have replied to this supposedly divine voice: 'That I ought not to kill my good son is quite certain. But that you, this apparition, are God—of that I am not certain, and never can be, not even if this voice rings down to me from (visible) heaven.' "

2. Kant, *Religion Within the Limits*, 162.

3. For a similar reference to the "sickness" of irrationalism, see ibn Pakuda, *Duties of the Heart*, 1.3. Passages like *Guide* 3.26 and 3.31 raise the question of whether Maimonides was a natural law theorist. According to Marvin Fox, "Maimonides and Aquinas on Natural Law," in Dienstag (ed.), *Studies*, 75–106, it is impossible in principle for Judaism to appropriate a natural law theory. If all Fox claimed is that (1) there is no concept of nature in classical Judaism, and (2) there is no question of God's will being determined by natural causes, his position would be unobjectionable. There is no natural necessity that stands apart from the will of God. But it is still possible to argue that God not only wills the moral law but does so necessarily. Unless freedom is to be understood as arbitrariness, free activity must be law-governed. If it is law-governed, the law can only be one that the will imposes on itself. So God cannot but choose the moral law even though, when He chooses it, He does so freely. Judaism recognizes commandments that would have to be written even if God had not commanded them, for example, the prohibitions against murder, idolatry, sodomy, robbery, and blasphemy. These commandments apply not only to Jews but to all people. According to Fox, their rationale can be given only "after the fact" of divine revelation. But where is the evidence for this qualification? According to Cohen (*Religion of Reason*, 123–24), these laws are universal and apply to people by virtue of their humanity alone. The most sustained presentation of a natural law position in Judaism is David Novak, *The Image of the Non-Jew in Judaism*, Toronto Studies in Theology 14 (New York and Toronto: Edwin Mellon Press, 1983). Notice, however, that Novak rejects the Kantian understanding of autonomy. For another defense of natural law, see David Hartman, *A Living Covenant* (New York: The Free Press, 1985), 57–59, 92–101. According to Hartman (98–99), "God's revelation of the ethical is not meant to compensate for a presumed inability of human reason to formulate an ethical system. Maimonides, too, saw no difficulty in accepting the legitimacy of an Aristotelian ethical worldview based upon an understanding of human nature."

4. The Talmudic source for the distinction between ordinances and statutes is *Yoma* 67b. It is a comment on Leviticus 18.5.

5. Twersky, *Introduction to the Code of Maimonides*, 386.

6. Josef Stern, "The Idea of a *Hoq* in Maimonides' Explanation of the Law," in Pines and Yovel (eds.), *Maimonides and Philosophy* (The Hague: Nijhoff, 1986), 124.

7. According to Pines's translation (*Introduction*, 24), the Arabic *al-mashhurat* renders the Greek *endoxa*. For the role of *endoxa* in Aristotle, see *Topics* 100b21 and *Nicomachean Ethics* 1098b27.

8. But again, the usual qualifications apply. To say that they can be known by reason is to say that reason understands them negatively. What is known is the *inability* of the human mind to grasp God as He is in Himself.

9. Novak, *Image of the Non-Jew*, 295–300.

10. For further discussion, see David Novak, "Natural Law, *Halakhah* and the Covenant," *The Jewish Law Annual* 7 (1988), 48 ff. Maimonides appears to side with Aristotle's view of the nature of ethical reasoning. For the Aristotelian references, see *Nicomachean Ethics* 1094b20–25, 1141b23 ff. Notice the references to means/ends at 1144a8.

11. On this point, see Ernst Cassirer, *Kant's Life and Thought*, trans. J. Haden (New Haven: Yale University Press, 1981, 385.

12. For those who want to make Maimonides a divine command theorist, see Fox, "Maimonides and Aquinas on Natural Law," as well as Twersky, *Introduction*, 454–59. For Novak's position, see *The Image*, 275–80.

13. A. MacIntyre, *After Virtue*, 43.

14. Kierkegaard, *Fear and Trembling*, trans. W. Lowrie (Princeton: Princeton University Press, 1941), 78.

15. Emil Fackenheim, "Abraham and the Kantians," in *Encounters between Judaism and the Modern Philosophy* (1973, rpt. New York: Schocken Books, 1980), 46. A trenchant criticism of Fackenheim is that of Norbert Samuelson, "Revealed Morality and Modern Thought," in Kellner (ed.), *Contemporary Jewish Ethics* (New York, 1978), 84–99. For someone more sympathetic to Kierkegaard and Fackenheim see Gene Outka, "Religious and Moral Duty: Notes on *Fear and Trembling*," in Outka and Reeder (eds.), *Religion and Morality* (Garden City, New York: Doubleday & Company, 1973), 204–54. For a position very close to my own, see Lenn Goodman's discussion of the *akedah* in *Monotheism* (Totowa, N.J.: Littlefield, Adams & Co., 1981), 12–20.

16. See Kant's position quoted in note 1 above. Notice, however, that Kant's position is *not* shared by Maimonides. See *Guide* 3.24. On the other hand, I must take issue with Louis Jacobs, "The Problem of the *Akedah* in Jewish Thought," in R. L. Perkins (ed.), *Kierkegaard's Fear and Trembling:*

Critical Appraisals (Tuscaloosa: University of Alabama Press, 1981), 5, who claims that Maimonides' understanding of the *Akedah* "comes very close to Kierkegaard's." Maimonides argues that the love of God is paramount and that the prophet trusts the revelation he receives from God. But where is the evidence that Maimonides was willing to put the particular ahead of the universal? What distinguishes the prophet is not that he has entered into a personal relation with the Absolute but that he understands things that most people are unable to grasp; the prophet does not abandon rationality, he pursues it to its highest level. And Maimonides would be the last to agree that Abraham was not a teacher (cf. *Fear and Trembling*, 90).

17. Kierkegaard, *Fear and Trembling*, 84.

18. For a modern defense of divine command theory, see Philip L. Quinn, *Divine Commands and Moral Requirements* (Oxford, 1978). A modified form of this position is given by Robert M. Adams, *The Virtue of Faith* (New York: Oxford University Press, 1987), 97–122. I agree with Louis Jacobs that the Jewish tradition has not been sympathetic with extreme versions of this position. See "The Relationship between Religion and Ethics in Jewish Thought," in Outka and Reeder, *Religion and Morality*, 155–72. Jacobs' view is criticized by Sid E. Leiman, "Critique of Louis Jacobs," in Kellner, *Contemporary Jewish Ethics*, 58–60. Leiman has succeeded in showing that the Jewish tradition "speaks in many more voices than Jacobs is willing to concede." But he has not, in my opinion, refuted the idea that the *dominant* tendency in Jewish thought is exactly what Jacobs claims it is. On the other hand, there is the view of Marvin Fox, *ibid.* as well as "On the Rational Commandments in Saadia's Philosophy: A Reexamination," in Fox (ed.) *Modern Jewish Ethics* (Columbus: Ohio State University Press, 1976), 174 ff. For another rejection of natural law in Judaism, see Y. Leibowitz, *Yahadut, Am Yehudi Umedinat Yisrael* (Jerusalem: Schocken Books, 1976), 26 ff.

19. *Baba Metzia*, 59b. For an excellent discussion of the rabbinic interpretation and the problems it creates, see J. David Bleich, "Lo Ba-Shamayim Hi," in N. Samuelson (ed.), *Studies*, 463–88. For the existentialist response, see Michael Wyschogrod, *Body of Faith* (New York: Seabury Press, 1983), 207:

> As a legislative body, the rabbis then have God's before-the-fact approval of their decisions in perpetuity. In effect, this abdicates the sovereignty of Hashem [God]. Israel no longer lives under judgment. The logical corollary of this difficulty, as we have seen, is that the rabbis, in making their decisions, have no guidelines to follow. Since they have blanket approval of whatever course of action they decide to follow, there is no longer any particular reason for following one rather than another. The fear and trembling of displeasing Hashem, of forbidding what he wishes permitted or permitting what he wishes forbidden, vanishes and the domain of action shifts completely to the human realm, from which there is no further appeal. At this point a

decisive shift has taken place in Jewish consciousness. The reality of Hashem diminishes. The law as interpreted by men becomes the dominant presence. It is now the Torah that is obeyed, not Hashem. While the Torah is understood as having been given by Hashem, as expressing his will, the Hashem who is behind the Torah becomes less and less distinct until the Jew's personal relationship with Hashem is completely eclipsed by obedience to Torah and not to its giver.

Notice that with a few minor revisions, this criticism could be made of Kant and Cohen.

20. Nahum M. Sarna, *Understanding Genesis* (New York: Schocken Books, 1966), 161–62.

21. For further discussion, see Marvin Fox, "Kierkegaard and Rabbinic Judaism," *Judaism* 2 (1953), 160–69.

22. Maimonides, *Mishneh Torah*, Book 14, Mourning, 14.2. The precedent for his interpretation can be found at *Shabbat* 127a.

23. There is a minority opinion that holds that Abraham may have failed the test. See, for example, Gunther Plaut, *The Torah: A Modern Commentary* (New York: Hebrew Union College Press, 1981), 150. Plaut cites *Genesis Rabbah* 56.8 in support of his point. Against Plaut, see Jacobs, "The Akedah . . . ," 7–8.

24. On this point, see Frederick A. Olafson, *Principles and Persons* (Baltimore: Johns Hopkins University Press, 1970), 28.

25. Aristotle, *Nicomachean Ethics*, 1137b12–27.

26. Vogel, *Quest*, 37ff.

27. Kant, *Religion Within the Limits*, 78. Cf. Goodman, *Monotheism*, 33n. 18.

28. Ibid., 32.

29. Psalms 11.5. Cf. Nachmanides' commentary on Genesis 22.1.

30. See J. B. Soloveitchik, *Halakhic Man*, trans. L. Kaplan (Philadelphia: JPS, 1983), Part One. Notice, however, that he rejects Tertullian's motto: *credo quia absurdum est* at 10–11. For the connection between Soloveitchik and Kierkegaard, see Jacob Agus, *Guideposts in Modern Judaism* (New York: Block Publishing, 1954).

31. Fox, 163. Notice that as outspoken a critic of natural law as Fox still cannot accept a teleological suspension of the ethical.

32. *Sanhedrin* 89b.

33. See discussion by M. Fox, "Kierkegaard," 168.

34. See, for example, Jacob L. Halevi, "Kierkegaard and the Midrash," *Judaism* 4 (1955), 13–28, and "Kierkegaard's Teleological Suspension of the Ethical—Is It Jewish?" *Judaism* 8 (1959), 291–302. The strongest Jewish opponent of this reading is Milton Steinberg, *Anatomy of Faith* (New York: Harcourt, 1960), 130–52.

35. Cf. Vogel, *Quest* 38 n. 22: "Thus, for example, one gets the strong impression from Buber's handling of this issue that when a head-on collision between religion and ethics occurs (as it may well have occurred in the past), the religious pole wins—one is to obey the divine even at the cost of suspending the ethical." Notice, however, that Vogel admits that this aspect of Buber's thought is *not* in keeping with mainstream Judaism.

36. See "Imitatio Dei," in Kellner, *Contemporary Jewish Ethics*, 152–61.

Chapter Six

Does Secular Moral Philosophy
Rest on a Mistake?

1. Reason and Dogmatism

Anyone familiar with the development of moral philosophy in
the twentieth century will recognize at once that my title is adapted
from a famous essay by H. A. Prichard: "Does Moral Philosophy
Rest on a Mistake?"[1] In one respect, the insertion of the word *secular* is superfluous: Prichard never mentions religious ethics, so that
as far as his essay is concerned, moral philosophy and secular moral
philosophy are identical. In another respect, however, it makes all
the difference in the world, since the goals of secular philosophy
are quite different from those of a philosophy which operates within
a religious tradition.

To understand that difference, we have only to look at the distinction between the content of a moral imperative and its source.
The secular philosopher admits that some of the injunctions found
in the Bible are valid but refuses to accept their validity on biblical
authority. If it is true that we should not commit murder or bear
false witness, secular philosophy must show this on the basis of a
rational argument. Part of what is meant by *rational* is that one cannot take a text or interpretive tradition for granted. The reason one
cannot is simple. It is a matter of historical fact whether a particular
imperative is part of a book. But it is impossible to offer a historical
fact as a reason for accepting a moral obligation. This is a variation
on a well-worn theme: that one cannot deduce an "ought" from an
"is." The fact that an imperative is part of a book cannot obligate me
to do anything unless it can be shown by an independent argument
that I ought to do everything the book enjoins. To show this, I
would have to examine the concept of obligation by itself. To cite the
book in defense of its own authority would be to beg the question
in the most egregious fashion.

In this way, secular moral philosophy is Kantian: it claims to
substitute reasoned argument for dogmatic assertion. Instead of

telling us *that* something is commanded it seeks to tell us *why* it is our duty to obey it. It views with suspicion anyone who claims that an imperative is binding merely because it has issued from a privileged source. Even if that source be God, the secular philosopher has no choice but to ask whether there is a reason to act as the imperative commands. But recall Allen Wood's observation that Kant is unable to conceive of the human situation except theistically. The underlying theme of the Critical Philosophy is that God is a necessary postulate of moral reason. Bracket any question of "privileged sources," and reason will discover God on its own. Thus Kant claims (*Lectures*, 110):

> Without God I would have to be either a visionary or a scoundrel. I would have to deny my own nature and its eternal moral laws. I would have to cease to be a rational man.

Secular moral philosophy accepts Kant's desire to substitute reasoned argument for dogmatic assertion. But to the degree it insists on its secular prerogatives, it does not maintain that the idea of God is necessary. The question is: Can it get along without this idea?

2. Ethical Malaise

Prichard begins his essay with the following observation: "Probably to most students of Moral Philosophy there comes a time when they feel a vague sense of dissatisfaction with the whole subject." Although these words were written in 1912, they could just as easily have been written yesterday. Dissatisfaction with moral philosophy is still a popular theme—particularly if one means the moral philosophy we inherit from the Enlightenment.[2] So I hope it will not seem presumptuous if I confess a certain amount of dissatisfaction as well. The question is not whether secular philosophy has found a justification for this or that belief—although it should be said that there are important areas of moral life for which it has hardly attempted one.[3] Nor is it a question of rejecting secular philosophy in toto. If the choice is between a secular philosophy which strives for rigorous argument and a religious philosophy that relies heavily on the notion of "commanding presence," the former is clearly preferable. Rather, the question is whether moral philosophy can succeed without any religious commitments, that is, whether it can offer a defense of morality that is purely secular, or in Prichard's terms, whether it can *prove* that I am justified in fulfilling my obligations rather than following my immediate interests.

Prichard divides previous efforts to answer this question into two groups. One group, which he associates with Plato, Butler, Hutcheson, Paley, and Mill, argues that we ought to behave as morality dictates because doing so will be for our own good or advantage; in short, that it pays to be moral. The other group, with which he probably associates Kant, argues that we ought to behave as morality dictates because doing so would produce something that is intrinsically valuable. He then disposes of both arguments. If I claim that a certain type of action is my duty because performing it will enhance the prospects for a happy life, the action ceases to be a duty in the true sense of the term. According to Prichard, the argument may cause me to *want* the action, but what I want and what I am obliged to do are separate things. Put in a different way, if one offers a prudential argument in favor of a moral judgment, he destroys its character *as* moral. To recover the sense of duty which morality presupposes—what I ought to do even if it is *not* in my interest—one would have to abandon any reference to want or desire. Otherwise I would be guilty of resolving obligation into inclination.

That brings us to the second argument. This group maintains that there is something, for example, a good will, which is valuable in itself and therefore should be realized. In short, it maintains that it is my duty to bring about what is intrinsically good. The problem here is that from the fact that something is intrinsically good, it does not follow that I am under an obligation to bring it about. Again, an "ought" can only be derived from another "ought." There is, then, no argument to take me from a perception of goodness to a sense of duty. According to Prichard, if there is any connection between goodness and duty, it is the other way around: our perception that something is good presupposes the sense that we ought to do it. The goodness of the action is parasitic on its being the right thing to do. If so, our sense of duty is primary and cannot be explained by reference to a good, however impersonal or objective it might be.

How, then, can we prove that we ought to do what morality enjoins? Prichard concludes we cannot. The sense of obligation, of the rightness of an action, is, in Prichard's words, "absolutely underivative or immediate." The mistake of previous moral thinkers was to think that we come to appreciate the rightness of an action on the basis of an argument. In truth, we come to appreciate it on the basis of direct intuition. So previous moral philosophy has, indeed, rested on a mistake.

It is clear that Prichard's intuitionism bears a number of similarities to Moore's—a fact which Prichard felt no obligation to mention even though Moore's work was published first.[4] In any case, Moore argued that previous moral theories were mistaken not because they offered false definitions of goodness but because they offered any definition at all. Goodness, according to Moore, is a simple, nonnatural property. By *simple*, he means that it is not susceptible to further analysis: it cannot be broken into more primitive terms. By *nonnatural*, he means that it cannot be equated with or reduced to an empirically verifiable quality. Even if it were the case that all good things happen to produce pleasure, according to Moore, it would be a mistake to identify the good with the pleasant. The reason it would be a mistake is that the question "Is pleasure good?" still makes sense. If "pleasure" and "good" were identical, the question would amount to a simple tautology—like asking "Is pleasure pleasant?" According to Moore, this sort of identification is faulty even if the property we identify with goodness is a supersensible one like the will of God. The question "Is the supersensible property good?" would also make sense, so that, by parity of reasoning, the two properties could be coextensive but never one and the same.

If one asked how it can be shown that something is good, the answer is that one cannot produce the sort of arguments that moral philosophers used for centuries. One cannot secure agreement on a set of claims about human nature, desire, or the will of God and expect to derive moral consequences as a result. As we have seen, it makes no difference whether these properties are empirically verifiable or not. The only way one can tell whether something is valuable is to hold it before one's mind, isolate it from other things, and try to intuit the presence of the unique property: goodness itself. It is on the basis of such mental inspection that Moore concluded the only things good in an unrestricted sense are the contemplation of beautiful objects and the pleasures of social intercourse.

Before going further, it is important to make some qualifications. Moore's intuitionism was not just a moral theory; it was connected with a particular view of logical analysis, a particular view of subjects and properties, and an epistemology of direct acquaintance. Goodness is a simple, objective property grasped by the mind in an act of mental inspection. The intuition of this property is immediate in the sense that one cannot infer its presence from other things. Later generations of intuitionists would not necessarily agree with Moore on all these points. In any case, what binds intuitionists together is their relative lack of dependence on principles. Whether it is Moore's intuition of goodness or Prichard's sense of duty, intuitionists do not obtain this knowledge by starting with a principle and tracing its implications. They consider actions or subjects one at a time and try to detect the presence of a morally significant feature. From a Kantian perspective, this amounts to sheer dogmatism, because it removes from ethics any reference to volition. According to Kant, one cannot make moral judgments by examining properties external to the agent. No moral significance arises from the fact that property P inheres in object X unless an agent *wills* that it be there. That P is a nonnatural property in Moore's sense counts for nothing. As long as the element of rational choice is missing, the presence of the property in the object is not a moral good.

Why all of this talk about intuitionism? Let us return to the goals of secular philosophy. There was a time when philosophers did not insist on the secular nature of their discipline. First philosophy or metaphysics was exactly what Aristotle said it was: the study of immovable substance, by which he means the divine. Ethics, too, took its lead from Aristotle. It begins with a set of precepts that the student already accepts. It proceeds by way of dialectic from the fact (*hoti*) to the reasoned fact (*dihoti*), from the precept to the principle from which it follows.[5] Notice, however, that on this view, moral philosophy takes a great deal for granted. Although the philosopher is not obliged to accept every precept handed down by a culture, it must be assumed that the majority of them are true— that behind the judgments expressed in such precepts is a body of wisdom worth investigating. It is the philosopher's job to identify the principles behind the beliefs that reasonable people hold. In this way, moral philosophy is not addressed to skeptics or to people not sufficiently acquainted with existing practices and institutions. Rather than construct moral knowledge from the ground up, the philosopher simply provides a rationale.

To be sure, Aristotle did not mean by a moral fact what subsequent philosophers meant by it. For him it meant nothing more than a received doctrine or opinion. For subsequent philosophers it came to mean the body of religious law handed down by tradition. As Alan Donagan points out in a recent study, "in the great ages of religious philosophy, even those who did not question the philosophical demonstrability of the moral system contained in the Mosaic Torah, nevertheless considered that system to have been far more solidly established by divine revelation than it could ever be by philosophical reasoning."[6] That is why no one felt the need to justify the system *de novo*. If we look at a work like Maimonides' *Mishneh Torah*, we can discern two goals: (1) to set forth the ordinances, customs, and decrees mandated by Jewish law; and (2) to identify the philosophical assumptions that lie behind them or the general principles of which they are specific applications. Recall that for Maimonides, the commandments are not arbitrary; every commandment has human perfection as its end. The point is that rather than start with a single principle or hypothetical contract, he, too, starts with a body of wisdom already in place. It would be fair to say, then, that in the great ages of religious philosophy, ethics was more interpretive than demonstrative.

This picture began to change when philosophy no longer accepted anything on religious authority. Appeals to authority were regarded as intellectually dishonest. Rather than beginning with precepts whose truth is accepted on other than philosophic grounds, it would attempt to construct a system from the bottom up. In this way, philosophy would take as little as possible for granted. If the conclusions of moral philosophy overlap with the precepts of biblical faith, fine; but these conclusions would not owe anything to that faith. They would be supported as far as possible by the inexorable logic of clearly formulated ideas. Again, the purpose of secular philosophy is to replace dogmatic assertion with reasoned argument.

It is out of this tradition that Prichard and Moore emerged. But to say this is to recognize that by the turn of the twentieth century, secular philosophy reached a crisis. The discipline that once extolled the virtues of reasoned argument now maintained that when it came to moral questions, argument was impossible. Prichard states:

> The negative side of all of this is, of course, that we do not come to appreciate an obligation by an *argument*, i.e., by a process of nonmoral thinking, and that, in particular, we do not do so by an argument of which a premise is the ethical but nonmoral activity of appreciating the goodness either of the act or of a consequence of the act: i.e., that our sense of the rightness of an act is not a conclusion from our appreciation of the goodness either of it or of anything else.

What, then, is it? We have seen that for Prichard our sense of obligation is "absolutely underivative or immediate." It is an intuition not unlike Moore's intuition of a simple, nonnatural and therefore utterly unique property. What happened to the notion of argument? Had moral philosophy abandoned it altogether?

The intuitionists would answer that they had not. They would, of course, deny that one could argue for a moral proposition in the way one argues for a factual one—like who is going to be the next President of the United States. They would reply, however, that if the normal sort of arguments are not applicable, there is still intellectual work to be done. The intuition of goodness or of a sense of duty may require intense levels of concentration. The point is that rather than a matter of argument, it is a matter of mental inspection. We can therefore appreciate John Maynard Keynes's description of how Moore and the rest of the Bloomsbury circle sat for hours trying to decide whether they could detect the presence of goodness in particular situations.

Yet as Alasdair MacIntyre points out in *After Virtue*, what was supposed to be a process of mental inspection soon became something quite different.[7] According to Keynes, victory went to those who could speak with the greatest conviction and keep up an air of infallibility. More than any argument, it was cold stares, gasps, and guffaws that carried the day; in short, simple theatrics. How ironic that the discipline that promised to liberate us from dogmatic assertion now enshrined it in its holiest of places! Under the aegis of intuitionism, the Bloomsbury group put forward a set of values as arbitrary and exclusive as any the world had seen.

Following MacIntyre, it was a short step from intuitionism to emotivism. What seemed to one generation like the detection of a unique property seemed to another like a report of one's personal preference. Hindsight suggests that the emotivists were right: when they desired to be intuiting a peculiar property, Moore and his colleagues were expressing their own likes and dislikes—a fact which in later life, Moore found difficult to deny.[8] Yet the real victor in this plot was Kant. When we read Keynes's description of how intuitionism was actually practiced at Bloomsbury, we can hear the ghost of Kant saying: "I told you so." For Kant, any moral philosophy that does not begin with the autonomous subject will soon be reduced to emotivism, which is, Kant would say—and I would agree with him—equivalent to reducing it to absurdity.

3. Rawls to the Rescue

It is no accident that the greatest moral thinker in the English-speaking world since Moore thought of himself as reviving Kant. I refer here to John Rawls. Although Rawls does not pretend to offer a textually precise reformulation of the Critical Philosophy, he does claim to capture its spirit. In the words of Steven Schwarzschild, he is "proto-Kantian."[9] Whatever one may think of his conclusions, Rawls has succeeded in at least this much: he has made reasoned argument fashionable again, at least in England and America.

How does such argument proceed? As indicated above, it takes as its starting point the concept of an autonomous subject. It attempts to show that from such a conception, we can derive the basic principles of a just society. We begin, therefore, with the notion of a *moral person*, by which Rawls means a free agent whose voice or share in the determination of a well-ordered society is equal to that of every other agent so designated. Notice how the element of choice is critical. The people who participate in Rawls's exercise are not trying to intuit the presence of a unique property but asking themselves what kind of social order they want to legislate. The usual criticism of Kant is that in putting forward the categorical imperative, he identified the *form* of moral reasoning but not the *content*. In other words, Kant gives us a logical criterion with which every moral judgment must be consistent but not a fleshed-out moral theory or sufficiently detailed conception of the ideal human life. I think the answer to this is that Kant *thought* he was doing both: only from a correct understanding of the form of moral reasoning can one derive the specific duties to which every rational agent is bound. It is not my purpose to review almost two centuries of literature on this point. What interests me is Rawls. Rawls wants to keep the Kantian insight that morality concerns the laws that free and equal persons would impose on themselves at the same time that he avoids the charge of formalism. In other words, he wants to show that we can begin with the notion of an autonomous agent and end up with moral flesh. The question is how he can be sure that the conclusions he derives are the ones real autonomous agents would agree to. Let us recall that for Kant, autonomy excludes any reference to selfish interests or personal preference. We conceive of ourselves as autonomous agents only when we conceive of ourselves as rational beings, *rational* meaning that our actions are not the effects of external causes but of a deep understanding of our own humanity. If Rawls can remain true to the Kantian conception of autonomy and come up with genuine moral content, he will have answered the formalist objection.

He does this by introducing a hypothetical notion called the *original position*. In the original position, rational agents go behind a veil of ignorance: they presume no knowledge of their individual histories, likes, dislikes, talents, or privileges. All they know about themselves and each other is that they are free and equal. In short, the only knowledge they have is the knowledge Kant would attribute to an autonomous agent. They know nothing of their empirical selves, nothing that would interfere with their "self-imposed" legislation of the ideal social order. In one respect, this exercise seems ridiculous. A social order does not come into existence the way a game of Monopoly does.[10] It does not begin with a set of self-interested agents taking equal shares of money and guaranteeing that everyone has the same chance to make a fortune. To this criticism Rawls would reply that there are certain rules which people behind the veil of ignorance would invariably adopt, and that these rules are the content of Kantian morality, again Kantian in spirit. According to Rawls (*A Theory of Justice,* 256):

> The original position may be viewed, then, as a procedural interpretation of Kant's conception of autonomy and the categorical imperative. The principles regulative of the kingdom of ends are those that would be chosen in this position, and the description of this situation enables us to explain the sense in which acting from these principles expresses our nature as free and equal rational persons.[11]

Many people have objected to the hypothetical nature of the original position. For Kant, the moral standpoint is not a hypothesis in Rawls's sense of the term. We cannot help but think of ourselves as rational agents even if we do not always respect this conception. Although we cannot prove that reason is practical, once we admit the possibility that it can be, the moral law follows as an a priori necessity. To deny the moral law would be tantamount to denying the possibility of moral truth.[12] The advantage Rawls has over Kant is that by starting with hypothetical conditions, Rawls avoids many of the epistemological problems in which the Critical Philosophy became ensnared. He readily admits that the principles upon which his ideal order is based are not necessary truths or consequences of self-evident propositions. Along the same lines, he maintains there are no "moral facts" he has to account for:

> I should emphasize that what I have called the "real task" of justifying a conception of justice is not primarily an epistemological problem. The search for reasonable grounds for reach-

ing agreement rooted in our conception of ourselves and in our relation to society replaces the search for moral truths interpreted as fixed by a prior and independent order of objects and relations, whether natural or divine, an order apart and distinct from how we conceive of ourselves. The task is to articulate a public conception of justice that all can live with who regard their person and their relation to society in a certain way. . . . Apart from the procedure of constructing the principles of justice, there are no moral facts.[13]

Rawls's defense of the ideal social order is simply that it is the one that rational people would agree to *if* they took seriously their status as autonomous agents. By a constructed order, he means that it does not owe its persuasiveness to a particular interpretation of history, nor to the intuition of special facts, nor to an exercise of faith. It stands or falls on one's conception of a moral person.

It follows that Rawls is the consummate secular philosopher. He neither affirms nor denies the existence of religious knowledge. By denying it, the atheist implies that if the claims of religion turned out to be true, moral philosophy would have to take notice. In so doing, the atheist concedes that the question of religious knowledge is significant. Rawls does not. What goes on behind the veil of ignorance concerns only those factors that moral persons would agree to without knowing anything about the political, religious, or philosophical doctrines they will hold in real life—even their conception of what the good life is. On this matter, Rawls is honest to a fault. He realizes that a consequence of his view is that the veil of ignorance may exclude relevant beliefs that all of the individuals behind it consider true.[14] A person might argue that any relevant belief for which there is good evidence ought to be taken into account. But Rawls does not concur. He is willing to put such beliefs out of play—that is, to render them *ir*relevant—in order to insure impartiality. So if it should happen that all people in the original position are members of a religious sect, and could secure agreement on a body of doctrine, they could not use this information in their deliberations. In this way, Rawls can insist he is looking at people from the standpoint of autonomy. There must be no reenactment of Bloomsbury behind the veil of ignorance.

Did he succeed? The question is difficult not only because Rawls has offered a lengthy and intricate account of the ideal social order, but because to criticize it, one would have to have an independent conception of what autonomous subjects would agree to.

Still, it is noteworthy that the social order that Rawls constructs is essentially that of modern liberal democracies. There are controversial points here and there; but on the whole, the society which emerges is one in which most of us would feel at home. Schwarzschild went so far as to call it a philosophical idealization of the United States.[15] In so doing, he put his finger on a real problem: is the similarity between Rawls's ideal order and the actual one in which we live a strength or a weakness? Remember that Rawls went to great lengths to avoid particular judgments or prejudices. He wanted to look at people from the standpoint of autonomy.

It is hard not to feel a tinge of doubt when told that autonomous agents put behind the veil of ignorance would choose a version of liberal democracy—or else face the charge that they were not acting rationally. Liberal democracy may have much to recommend it; but can we really claim that our preference for it has nothing to do with the biases or prejudgments we have inherited? The reason for excluding such prejudgments is, once again, Kantian. Rawls's veil of ignorance is nothing but a colorful way of expressing Kant's conviction that moral philosophy must be kept pure, that is, free of empirical content. The veil of ignorance is supposed to guard us from the passions and inclinations that Kant thought would rob moral theory of its universality. Here it is worth remarking that Schwarzschild's criticism of Rawls is also directed at Kant, though in somewhat muted terms.[16] Kant, too, could not keep prejudgments out of his philosophy, even though his philosophy was intended to be a model of vigor. As Donagan put it, Kant arrived at the position that the morality he learned from his pietist parents was not a matter of revelation or feeling but of ordinary human reason (*gemeine Menschenvernunft*).[17]

The question, then, is whether "ordinary human reason" can free itself of cultural or historical biases. The typical answer is that however difficult this may be in practice, there is no reason to think it is impossible in principle. According to Rawls (*A Theory of Justice*, 50), "we may suppose that everyone has in himself the whole form of a moral conception." If this were not the case, there would have to be limits on who could go behind the veil of ignorance and the impartiality of the process would be compromised. But where does this conception originate? Recall the words of Deuteronomy 30.14: that the law is written on the heart of every person. Although Rawls cannot cite the Bible as an authority, it is clear he must assume that something like this is true. He must assume, for example, that every rational agent possesses the wherewithal to see that social inequality is objectionable. But, again, it may be asked: where does this conception originate? A lot of societies have not only tolerated inequality but canonized it. On what basis can Rawls maintain that rational agents would never agree to it and therefore these societies are unjust? Surely the judgments we regard as rational are products of the literary and historical traditions we have inherited. How can we decide how to distribute goods in a hypothetical context unless we have a glimpse of how people have fared in distributing them in actual ones? Consider Rawls's discussion of the difference principle: that the social order is not to improve the lot of the more fortunate unless doing so works to the advantage of the less fortunate. Can this be demonstrated by reason alone or must that reason work within the egalitarian framework established by the Western moral tradition, in particular the Hebrew prophets? The objector will point out, with MacIntyre, that we are born with a past. Much of that past is a reflection on biblical characters and themes. If so, it is not irrelevant that the God of the Bible loves the stranger, the orphan, the widow, in short, the less fortunate elements of society. God, the morally perfect individual, opposes the social inequality Rawls's contractors oppose. The question is: Should the philosopher admit that our moral values are informed by a religious heritage, or should the philosopher regard that heritage as one more prejudgment from which philosophy must free itself?

4. Kant to the Rescue of Rawls

On the question of religion, Rawls's position is much more extreme than Kant's. For Kant, morality does not need religion to determine the duties that rational agents impose on themselves, nor does it need religion to provide an incentive for obeying them. In this sense, Kant regards morality as self-sufficient, a description that, in the present context, is the same as saying that he regards it as secular. But Kant goes on to say that morality needs religion if it is to have a suitable concept of the highest good. Morality puts before me an end that I am obliged to pursue. Yet what if it should happen that there is no hope of this end being realized? In that case, morality would oblige us to pursue something which in Kant's words, is vain and imaginary.[18] To avoid this outcome, morality needs the idea that the universe is hospitable to agents attempting to realize the moral law, which is to say it needs the idea of God. We have seen that when it comes to moral theology, Kant's position is not all that different from the scholastics'. God is a free agent who creates the world in a spontaneous act in which intellect and will are identical. There is, of course, the stock qualification: this picture of the world cannot be *known* to be true. Still, Kant thinks it *is* true if morality has any claim to being legitimate. Without God to insure the possibility of realizing the moral law, we get either extreme optimism or a complete rejection of the concept of duty—the visionary or the scoundrel.

In an earlier passage, I remarked that this argument is not valid. Still, Kant's account of the relation between morality and religion may be supplemented by additional considerations. The purpose of Kantian morality is to identify the principle that all moral judgments presuppose. It may be said, therefore, that he is not putting forward a new morality as much as identifying the logical foundation of the one we already have.[19] In his words (*Critique of Practical Reason*, 8): "Who would want to introduce a new principle of morality and, as it were, be its inventor, as if the world had hitherto been ignorant of what duty is or had been thoroughly wrong about it?" So Kant is not overthrowing the duties imposed by the Ten Commandments or the moral sentiments expressed by the prophets. All he is doing is showing what lies behind them. He accepts "ordinary human reason" and would no doubt accept the contribution that religious figures have made to it. His quarrel is not with the content of religion but with dogmatic uses of it. To see this, we need only return to his notion of twofold revelation. To know that a written commandment is from God, I must compare it to my idea of perfection. Where do I get this idea? Kant answers with a passage reminiscent of Deuteronomy 30.14 (*Religion*, 169):

> There exists . . . a practical knowledge which, while resting solely upon reason and requiring no historical doctrine, lies as close to every man, even the most simple, as though it were engraved upon his heart—a law, which we need but name to find ourselves at once in agreement with everyone else regarding its authority, and which carries with it in everyone's consciousness *unconditioned* binding force, to wit, the law of morality.

In the *Lectures* (160–61) he claims that our idea of perfection comes from God. In *Conflict of the Faculties,* he goes so far as to say that if we use inner revelation to interpret the words of Scripture, then "God in us is Himself the interpreter."[20]

It should be clear, then, that the purpose of the Critical Philosophy is not to find a moral standard over and against God. Rather, it is to assure that *our* conception of divinity is worthy of *His* perfection. The moral law does not replace God; it acts as a check on what we can say about Him. Once the check is applied, however, moral philosophy is free to make use of religious material. In particular, it must turn to religion to obtain the concept of a supremely perfect being. Minimally, this concept is of a creator who wills an end which we ought to will but often do not. In *Religion Within the Limits of Reason Alone*, Kant is more explicit: God is an agent who judges people not on the basis of outward behavior or material circumstances but on the purity of their hearts, an agent who bids us to overcome the natural propensity of the human heart for evil. Where did this conception originate? According to Kant (*Religion*, 47), the first truly moral religion in history is Christianity. He regards Judaism as a purely statutory religion and therefore not a real religion at all. As Kant would have it, Christianity provides a concept of moral perfection that can serve as the basis of a pure or universal faith. The essentials of such a faith would be derived by a rational, that is, moral interpretation of Scripture. Insofar as this faith is cleansed of all elements of particularity, it would be a religion that appeals to autonomous agents regardless of their historical circumstances. Kant never tires of pointing out that the validity of the moral law is context independent. As we saw above, it is engraved on the heart of even the simplest people. The purpose of *Religion* is to argue that a pure faith provides the best chance for the human race to secure the ultimate victory of good over evil and establish the kingdom of God on earth. Progress toward such a goal can be seen in the gradual transition from ecclesiastical religion to moral religion. It follows that the study of religion holds out an element of hope that morality alone can never provide. Religion cannot validate my obligations, but it can help me to develop the disposition to fulfill them. A moral action results from an agent's free choice to act for the sake of duty. By promoting the establishment of a moral commonwealth, religion either encourages people to make this choice or removes the obstacles that stand in their way. It is in this sense that religion contributes to the moral progress of the human race: it prepares people to make the choices that morality demands of them.[21] In so doing, it fosters the conviction that our moral strivings are not in vain.

Kant does not have a veil of ignorance. Yet it is clear that he would have no objection to the discussion of religious issues behind it, and in some cases, would insist on such discussion. Autonomous agents would have to look to the Christian conception of God to understand what perfect autonomy is like. On a more mundane level, if a universal religion provides the best hope of bringing about the kingdom of God, then, as Kant says near the beginning of *Religion* (5), morality cannot be unconcerned with it. There is, of course, one condition: that the religion be "freed from all empirical determining grounds." If this condition is met, and there is nothing in principle that prevents it from being met, the study of morality would not have to insist on its secular prerogatives. It could consider the progress that the human race has made toward the establishment of a moral commonwealth. In this respect, Kant departs from Rawls. There is, however, another respect in which he does not. Kant allows for progress in human attempts to realize the moral law; but he does not allow for progress in our basic conception of it. If he did the latter, the moral law would be subject to empirical conditions and no longer unconditional. In *Religion* (21), Kant maintains that it is consciousness of the moral law that informs us of the freedom of our will (*Willkür*) and the accountability of our actions. As we saw in a previous chapter, the only "proof" we have that we are free is our sense that we are obliged to act in specifiable ways. It follows that if consciousness of the moral law were subject to historical evolution, freedom and responsibility would be subject to it as well.[22] A person in a primitive culture who lacked an adequate understanding of the law would lack the status of a rational agent. In effect, such a person would not be a person at all. This conclusion flies in the face of the entire Kantian moral philosophy. That is why he argues that *everyone*— even the simplest of people—has such a conception, that it is engraved on the heart. So while there may be progress in the degree to which people are prepared to answer the call of duty, there is no progress in the mere fact that they have such a call. It is well known that Kant goes even further: not only does every *person* have it but so does every rational agent in the universe. Here Kant's ahistoricism is just as severe as Rawls's. On the question of duty, the empirical conditions of one's life are absolutely irrelevant.

But if this is so, Kant has painted himself into a corner with respect to religions other than Christianity. How can it be the case that, like all peoples, the ancient Israelites had the requisite understanding of duty and freedom but failed to incorporate that understanding into their religious literature? How can it be that their religion does not show any significant recognition of the universal morality that Kant has to attribute to them? To repeat: Kant can argue that we are better prepared to realize the moral law, but he cannot claim that *we* are aware of it and our ancestors not. No matter how foreign some of their practices may seem, Kant has to hold that the moral law was, if not explicit, then at least implicit in their understanding of themselves. In *Religion* (102), he argues that the predisposition to a moral faith "lay hidden in human reason," but this response is clearly inadequate.

5. From Kant to Cohen

It is at this point that we can understand Cohen and the notion of a rational religion derived from the sources of Judaism. Cohen's project was to show that Kant was wrong about Judaism: properly understood, the ancient sources and their received interpretations are much closer to a morally pure faith than Kant thought. From a methodological standpoint, Cohen's project is the same as Kant's: to submit the products of external revelation to the critique of internal. To the degree that he is successful, he would be supporting the Kantian assertion that recognition of the moral law is not historically specific. Early in *Religion of Reason* (4), he writes:

> Even if I am referred to the literary sources of the prophets for the concept of religion, those sources remain mute and blind if I do not approach them with a concept, which I myself lay out as a foundation in order to be instructed by them and not simply guided by their authority.

To understand the meaning of the prophetic utterances, we must approach them with a concept of moral perfection. That is why the study of religion is not just the study of its historical development. According to Cohen (*Religion of Reason*, 2): "The history of religion has no means whatever of securing the legitimacy of religion." To secure legitimacy, we must regard history as the unfolding of a principle that reason can extract from the records at its disposal. For Cohen that principle is monotheism. The history of the people is therefore the history of a logical progression. If there is one God, there must be one law. If there is one law, there is no *moral* difference between the stranger and the rest of the community, between rich and poor, or between powerful and weak. Here it is well to remember that the stranger is not necessarily a member of one's community, one's nation, or even one's religion. So the injunction "One law for you and the stranger in your midst" (Leviticus 24.22) is a recognition that no one is outside the scope of universal moral principles. And the constant injunction that one must *love* the stranger (Deuteronomy 10.18) indicates that the Israelites must see a connection between themselves and the other peoples of the earth, a connection that can only be founded on a common humanity (cf. Exodus 22.20).

According to Cohen, the ethical significance of monotheism is that it offered a perspective from which people could see beyond the empirical differences that separate them and focus on their humanity. The ancient Israelites were not the first people to formulate a legal code. But they were perhaps the first people to formulate a code which applies *both* to them *and* to people in foreign lands. In this way, Cohen tries to show that a universal law has "wrestled" its way into the literary development of a particular people. Recall that according to Deuteronomy 4.6–8, the special gift of this people was to have a law whose wisdom would be apparent to everyone.

It should be clear that Cohen's account of biblical religion is not history as much as it is historical reconstruction. If it is true that the history of religion is the history of human moral evolution, then the purpose of a reconstruction is to start with the end product of that evolution and see how it is expressed in the actual documents. Cohen finds in the writings of the prophets ideas that were not given philosophic expression for centuries. In the biblical emphasis on repentance and atonement, he sees the origin of the concept of the autonomous moral subject.[23] The fate of such a subject is not in the hands of some cosmic force but in one's own willingness to become master of oneself. In the Book of Job, Cohen sees a principled distinction between the empirical circumstances of a person's life and his or her moral worth—a point which Kant himself recognized.[24] In the concept of Sabbath observance, he sees a distinction between the individual and his or her status as a wage earner. On this day, social standing is put on the other side of a divinely decreed veil of ignorance. More generally, Cohen sees in the prophets a rejection of mysticism and a preoccupation with the economic realities of life: in particular, poverty (*Religion of Reason*, 23):

The poor became for them the symbol of human suffering. If their messianic God is to annul suffering by establishing morality on earth, he has therefore to become lord over poverty, the root of human suffering. Thus, their God becomes the God of the poor. The social insight of the prophets recognizes in the poor the symptomatic sign of the sickness of the state. *Thus, their practical view is diverted from any eschatology of the mysteries.* They do not view death as suffering; death can offer no magic mysticism to them. Their view is concerned with men in the economic stream of the state and with its seemingly deep-rooted poverty, which manifests for the prophets the root of social suffering, the only one that can be redressed and therefore the only one worthy of notice.

It is as if Cohen is attempting to reconstruct Rawls's difference principle. To this we should add that Kant's central claim about religion—one cannot find favor with God in ways that imply no improvement in character—is expressed time and again in the writings of the prophets. The crux of their argument is that the people have retained the outward shell of religion but fallen away from its true meaning. Observing the Sabbath does not help one if he or she goes on to oppress the poor during the rest of the week. The same is true of sacrifices and festivals. Thus the words of Amos (5.21–24, cf. Hosea 6.6, Isaiah 1.11–17):

> I hate and I despise your feasts,
> And I will take no delight in your
> > solemn assemblies.
> Though you offer me burnt-offerings and
> > meal offerings,
> I will not accept them. . . .
> Take away from me the noise of your
> > songs;
> And let me not hear the melody of your
> > psalteries.
> But let justice well up as waters,
> And righteousness as a mighty stream.

This and the dozens of passages like them give the lie to Kant's contention that Judaism is a purely statutory religion. On the other hand, it has to be said that, like other religions, Judaism needed people to remind it of the fact that it is not from time to time.

To the objection that ancient Judaism was not morally pure and contained traces of mythology, tribalism, even paganism, Cohen would agree. He would simply point out that no people can grasp the principles of a universal religion all at once. So if the ancient sources contain the idea of universal humanity, they do so in a fragmented of philosophically imprecise way. It took a number of literary genres including narrative, poetry, social commentary, legal code, and prophetic utterance for the idea to receive its original formulation. And it has taken centuries of commentary for it to be refined. There have been setbacks and corrections, but through it all, the idea has so firm a hold on people's minds that it is impossible to imagine Judaism without it.

In keeping with his Kantian heritage, Cohen does not say that Judaism is *the* religion of reason; no historical faith could ever make such a claim. His point is that the ideas of a purely rational faith can be found in Jewish sources. He admits without hesitation that they can be found in the sources of other religions as well (*Religion of Reason*, 123–25, 364). In fact, the more universal such ideas are, the more we can believe that consciousness of the moral law is context-independent. We saw in a previous chapter that Cohen tried to demythologize the concept of revelation. It is not a historically significant event in which God addresses a particular person but, in general, the awakening of moral consciousness. To the question "Where does this consciousness originate?" Cohen answers that its origins are logical rather than causal. I take this to mean that it is pointless to look for the first moment in history when people heard the call of duty. Still, if Cohen is right, it is not pointless to look at the development of this idea in the religious writings of different cultures. It follows that consciousness of the moral law (or what Rawls terms "the form of a moral conception") has a history. It is not the sort of history one ascribes to an event: there is no temporal beginning. Its history is that of the gradual unfolding of an idea and the conceptual scheme within which to make sense of it. To the objection that people in primitive cultures do not have an adequate conception of this idea, Cohen would answer that in one respect, neither did Kant and neither do we. We have enough understanding of moral reason to be accorded the status of free and responsible agents. But a fully adequate understanding is an infinite task that no historically specific person has yet completed.

6. Rawls Revisited

Between Kant, Cohen, and Rawls there is agreement that morality is a system of laws that autonomous agents legislate for themselves. The question at issue is whether religion is needed for these agents to understand the implications of their autonomy and have a legitimate hope of realizing them. To put this a different way, Is the course of human moral development relevant to the act of legislating for ourselves in an imaginary situation? There is an obvious objection to allowing people to have knowledge of their *own* histories behind the veil of ignorance, but surely this objection does not apply to the history of an idea. The question then becomes: What would this history look like? Here I want to agree with Alan Donagan that "as a matter of historical fact, the biblical tradition has determined the substance of the received morality of the Western world. . . ."[25] That tradition insists on the freedom and moral equality of every human being, the immorality of lying, murder, and envy, and the possibility of realizing a social order superior to the present one. To repeat the basic question: Why should the people behind the veil of ignorance not admit the entire project upon which they are embarked is the outgrowth of a moral tradition that derives from the prophets? Why should they not admit that their exercise is the continuation of something that has been going on for millennia?

To this question Rawls would reply that one of the advantages of the veil of ignorance is that morality is not dependent on historical facts. According to Rawls, there are no bodies of information that the rational contractors must account for prior to entering into their deliberations. In this way, they can generate a plan for the ideal social order by making as few assumptions as possible. By admitting that the ideal order owes something to a historical tradition, we weaken its claim to universality. To paraphrase Schwarzschild, it would be an idealized version of Western democracy—in much the way that Cohen's religion is an idealized form of Judaism. Is this necessarily bad? I submit that my modified way of looking at Rawls's theory does not diminish its importance and offers a realistic account of what it is. More important, it allows Rawls to answer the charge of being ahistorical. The people who go behind the veil of ignorance are not performing a superhuman feat. They are doing the best job they can of constructing or *re*constructing the principles that lie behind our sense of justice. If they are to be completely self-conscious about what they are doing, they will have to acknowledge their debt to people like Amos. One way to see this is to go back to Rawls's contention that the principles upon which the ideal social order is built are not necessary truths. According to Rawls (*Justice*, 21), the justification of these principles is "a matter of the mutual support of many considerations, of everything fitting together into one coherent view." As Rawls makes clear in the rest of the book, principles have to be tested against considered judgments, and vice versa. But considered judgments about right and wrong are the products of centuries of moral conflict and exegesis.

It is always possible for someone to object that if the people behind the veil of ignorance see themselves as operating within the Western moral tradition, they relinquish a measure of certainty. Maybe the Western moral tradition is in error. Here Rawls could reply, again with Donagan, that if it is in error, the error must lie very deep. It must include prophets, poets, and philosophers from very different cultures and very different intellectual climates. It must permeate many of the legal institutions upon which Western democracies are based and much of the social criticism which attempts to reform them.[26] All of this is possible, but it is far from clear that it is true.

The upshot is that secular philosophy can remain secular and still admit that it owes a debt to religion. Following Kant, it cannot accept ethical judgments on rabbinic or clerical authority alone: it must put content ahead of source. But it can do this and still admit that its purpose is to find a philosophic justification of ideas that, as a matter of fact, have a source in the sacred literature of Judaism. Seen in this light, the purpose of secular philosophy is as much interpretive as demonstrative. It clarifies ideas we inherit from people with less analytic precision than we have but with similar convictions on social equality. This is as much as we need to say to effect what has traditionally been called a "synthesis" of faith and reason.

Notes

1. H. A. Prichard, "Does Moral Philosophy Rest on a Mistake?" *Mind* 21 (1912), 487–99.

2. See, for example, MacIntyre, *After Virtue*, 2:

What is the point of constructing this imaginary world inhabited by fictitious pseudo-scientists and real, genuine philosophy? The hypothesis which I wish to advance is that in the actual world which we inhabit the language of morality is in the same state of grave disorder as the language of natural science in the imaginary world which I described. What we possess, if this view is true, are the fragments of a conceptual scheme, parts which now lack those contexts from which their significance derived. We possess indeed simulacra of morality, we continue to use many of the key expressions. But we have—very largely, if not entirely—lost our comprehension, both theoretical and practical, of morality.

3. Among the areas I have in mind are: (1) obligations to spouses, family members, or friends; (2) forgiveness and compassion as moral virtues; (3) the issue of how to cope with guilt. I recognize that there are exceptions to my claim that these areas have been neglected, but exceptions do not necessarily invalidate a general observation.

4. G. E. Moore, *Principia Ethica* (Cambridge: Cambridge University Press, 1903). Note that Prichard's essay was published some nine years later.

5. Aristotle, *Nicomachean Ethics* 1095b1–13, cf. *Posterior Analytics* 78a22–79a16.

6. Alan Donagan, *The Theory of Morality* (Chicago: University of Chicago Press, 1977), 8.

7. MacIntyre, *After Virtue*, 14–17.

8. G. E. Moore, "Reply to My Critics," in P. Schilpp (ed.), *The Philosophy of G. E. Moore* (La Salle, Ill.: Open Court Press, 1942; rpt. 1968), 536–54.

9. Steven Schwarzschild, "An Agenda for Jewish Philosophy in the 1980s," in Samuelson, *Studies*.

10. For this comparison, see Bryan Magee's interview with Ronald Dworkin in *Men of Ideas* (New York: Viking Press, 1978), 248.

11. Rawls, *A Theory of Justice* (Cambridge: Harvard University Press, 1971).

12. *Groundwork*, 408.

13. John Rawls, "Kantian Constructivism in Moral Theory," *The Journal of Philosophy*, 77 (1980), 518–19.

14. Rawls, *Theory of Justice*, 541–42.

15. Schwarzschild, *Agenda*, 65.

16. *Ibid*. His primary objection is to Kant's acceptance of capital punishment in *Metaphysical Principles of Justice*.

17. Donagan, *Theory of Morality*, 9.

18. Kant, *Critique of Practical Reason*, 114.

19. For further discussion, see Paul Stern, "The Problem of History and Temporality in Kantian Ethics," *Review of Metaphysics* 505–45.

20. Kant, *Conflict of the Faculties*, 48. For further discussion, see Allen W. Wood, *Kant's Moral Religion* (Ithaca: Cornell University Press, 1970), 205–77.

21. See Stern, P., 535 ff.

22. Cf. Stern, P., 522 ff.

23. *Religion of Reason*, 194, 203, 207. The biblical text is Ezekiel 18.31: "Cast away from you all your transgressions, wherein ye have transgressed; and make you a new heart and a new spirit." For more on autonomy in the Bible, see Goodman, *Monotheism*, 89–109.

24. For discussion of this point, see the following chapter.

25. Donagan, *Theory of Morality*, 28.

26. On the issue of the prophetic contribution to contemporary social criticism, see Michael Walzer, *Interpretation and Social Criticism* (Cambridge: Harvard University Press, 1987), especially chapter 3.

Chapter Seven

Job and the Problem of Evil

1. Innocent Suffering

In its classical form, the problem of evil is easy to state. God is omniscient, omnipotent, and omnibenevolent. Therefore if innocent suffering occurs, God must know about it, be able to prevent it, and desire to prevent it. Since whatever God desires comes to pass, the existence of innocent suffering is incompatible with the existence of God. It follows that to uphold belief in God, one must either deny that innocent suffering occurs or show that it is not evil in an absolute sense because it is needed to accomplish a greater good.

The medievals treat the problem of evil as a problem about the scope of divine providence: Does God's knowledge extend to individuals or is it restricted to natural kinds?[1] The Book of Job is seen as a philosophical dialogue between competing answers to this question. Job originally puts forward a view associated with Aristotle: providence is completely general. His friends put forward various forms of the theory that God knows individuals *as* individuals. The "thesis" and "antithesis" are overcome in the person of Elihu, who argues that divine providence extends to some individuals but not all. In brief: God's providence extends to prophets because of their superior knowledge of general truths.

I am going to part company with the medieval philosophers in some respects. Instead of concentrating on divine knowledge, I am going to direct my attention to human. And rather than looking backward to previous ages, I intend this chapter to prepare the way for a discussion of Fackenheim and the Holocaust. It will be clear, however, that my response to the problem of innocent suffering is a traditional one. After looking at the plight of Job and the plights of concentration camp victims, I shall argue that traditional conceptions of God, virtue, and human dignity are the most reasonable alternative. It could be said, therefore, that my treatment of these issues is in keeping with the arguments advanced in chapters 2 and 3. In that respect, my treatment of them is an outgrowth of the view

I ascribed to Maimonides: that broadly speaking, religious knowledge is either critical or practical. On my reading, Job's heroism consists in the fact that he admits ignorance of the forces which rule the cosmos without abandoning his own moral integrity.

The book takes up the issue of innocent suffering right from the start. No one who has read it can fail to be moved by the depth of its wisdom or the majesty of its rhetoric. Its poetry rivals that of the Psalms. Yet this impression is matched by an equally vivid sense of disquiet. It is not just that God refuses to offer a justification of Job's calamities. It is that for all its probing, the book never does provide an explicit answer to the problem of evil in its classical form. There are elaborate speeches and equally elaborate replies, but in no case does the book put forward an argument, much less an argument formulated in so abstract a way. Most of the speeches, including those of the comforters, are a mixture of wisdom, poetry, and folly, with the reader never quite sure which is which. If a philosophic lesson is to be derived from the text, it must be constructed.

Another troubling feature is the matter of plot. If instead of doing philosophy, the book offered a narrative, our sense of disquiet would be less pronounced. But with the exception of the epilogue and prologue, there is nothing approaching a story line. A problem, the suffering of a righteous man, is talked to death. God appears; but for all their beauty, His words are as enigmatic as any in the book. Job repents, is rewarded, and the book ends. Unlike the story of Adam and Eve, there is no allegory whose meaning would allow us to reach a general conclusion about the causes of innocent suffering.

Not surprisingly, the text has generated extensive debate. Some people think the prologue is a later addition because it exonerates God. In contrast to the rest of the book, the prologue allows us to see *why* God has permitted Job to suffer: He wants to show that Satan's skeptical view of human piety (1.9–10) is mistaken. Supporting this hypothesis is the fact that the wager between God and Satan is never mentioned again. Others think that the epilogue is a later addition because it provides the book with a happy ending. Still others think that editorial changes have been made in the body of the text to mollify Job's anger. Zophar's third speech is missing. A popular explanation is that lines from this speech were transferred to the mouth of Job to make the hero's position more acceptable to religious audiences (for example, 24.18–25, 27.13–23). Similar considerations apply to the hymn to the inscrutability of

God in chapter 28. The sentiments expressed in this passage seem out of character with the ones expressed by Job in previous speeches. Why the sudden change of heart? The speeches of Elihu have long puzzled scholars, in part because they repeat the views of the other comforters, in part because they prepare the way for the speeches of God. Medieval thinkers like Maimonides and Gersonides put great stress on the latter. Still, there is no reference to Elihu in the epilogue. There are even problems with translation. It has not escaped the notice of biblical scholars that the Septuagint's Job is not nearly the rebel who emerges from the lines of the Hebrew text.[2] Allowing themselves linguistic and editorial liberties, the Greek translators created a character who is much less willing to challenge God. There is even evidence that the Hebrew text was altered.[3]

I prefer to leave questions about textual authenticity to others. Note, however, that even if the theories of multiple authorship are true, it does not follow that the text we have is a hodgepodge. Gothic cathedrals took as much as two hundred years to construct. In that time, there were thousands of artists at work and a series of design changes. But this information is compatible with the claim that the resulting structure is a unified work of art. So, too, with the Book of Job. Aesthetic questions about the organization of the parts cannot be decided by historical arguments. We can therefore agree with Marvin H. Pope when he says:

> There is a considerable degree of organic unity despite the incongruities. Even the Elihu speeches, though probably interpolated, are blended into the whole with such skill that some scholars have seen Elihu as a reflex of the author of the Dialogue.[4]

To the degree that the work is unified, the question of multiple or single authorship can be put aside.

Yet even if we assume the book is coherent, its enigmatic character still haunts us. Without a well developed story line or a clear-cut resolution of the problem of innocent suffering, the early Christian and Jewish interpreters tended to ignore the rebellious Job in favor of the saintly character who serves as a model of patience and humility, for example, James 5.11. Perhaps the Septuagint's rendering was a factor here. Clement of Alexandria portrays Job as a true worshiper of God who, along with Abraham and Moses, heralds the coming of Christ.[5] In Talmudic literature, Job is the subject of conflicting opinions. On one view, he feared the Lord, as the text says three times (1.1, 1.8, 2.3), but his fear, unlike that of Abraham, was not coupled with love.[6] It is argued that Job did not bear his suffering without reproaches against the Almighty. According to another view, however, Job did serve the Lord out of love; we learn this at 13.15: "Though he slay me, yet will I trust in Him."[7] It should be said, however, that this famous line is itself the subject of debate because it is not clear whether the Hebrew *lo aya-hel* contains a negative. On one reading, Job is expressing defiance. But the ambiguity did not prevent this school from arguing that Job loved God as much as Abraham did. As to his anger at God and near blasphemy, it was pointed out that one is not responsible for things said under duress.[8]

On the issue of blasphemy, it is important to remember that the Hebrew prophet enjoyed much greater latitude in his relation with God than is usually recognized. As we saw in the discussion of Abraham, the basic idea is that God does not rule the world like an arbitrary despot. Although superior to man in knowledge and power, He, too, has something to answer for. That is why Abraham can challenge Him over Sodom and Gomorrah without fear of being swept away. And Abraham is not the only one to approach God in this manner. Moses implores Him to change His mind at Exodus 32.12–22 and again at Numbers 14.13–20. According to the interpretation of a Talmudic master, Moses grabbed on to God's cloak and would not let go until He had forgiven Israel.[9] The idea that God can be held to account by one of His creatures is a recurrent theme in the Bible and is found in the book of Psalms (13.2, 44.24–27), Jeremiah (12.1–2), Isaiah (62–63) and Habakkuk (1.2–3). Jeremiah's words are worth quoting because they have a direct bearing on Job:

> Right would Thou be, O Lord,
> If I were to contend with Thee,
> Yet I will reason with Thee:
> Why does the way of the wicked prosper?
> Why are all they secure that deal
>   treacherously?
> Thou has planted them, and they have
>   taken root;
> They grow, they bring forth fruit;
> Thou art near in their mouth,
> But far from their reins.

The interesting thing is not that such protest literature exists but that it is not considered blasphemous. These are people of enduring piety, God's chosen servants, but they do not exhibit blind faith and are ready to speak out when they think they see injustice. It is in this context that Job's protest must be considered.

In fact, Job's speeches contain some moments of genuine devotion. Notice how closely the following lines (9.2–10) resemble the voice from the whirlwind (38–39):

> How can a man be just before God?
> If one wanted to contend with Him,
> One could not answer Him once in a
>   thousand times.
> He is wise in heart and mighty in
>   strength. . . .
> It is God alone who stretched out the
>   heavens,
> And treaded on the waves of the sea;
> Who made the Bear, Orion, and the
>   Pleiades,
> And the chambers of the south.
> Who does great things beyond
>   comprehension,
> And marvelous things without number.

But they also contain moments of doubt (23.5: "Oh, that I knew where I might find Him"); of despair (9.20–21: "Though I am righteous, He condemns me out of my own mouth. . . . I despise my life"); of self-pity (19.21: "Pity me, pity me, you who are my friends"); of self-confidence (13.18: "I know that I shall be justified"); and of outright defiance (9.22–23: "He destroys the innocent and the wicked alike; when a sudden flood brings death, He mocks the plight of the innocent"). These things are all said under duress, but that does not mean they are anything but sincere. Rather than discuss the problem of innocent suffering in the abstract, the author has chosen to exhibit the range of emotions felt by an innocent, God-fearing person in pain.

The result is that while the book does not engage in philosophic speculation, it opens the door to such speculation by presenting its ideas in a cryptic fashion. By the time God speaks to Job, there is still nothing resembling an explicit solution to the problem of evil in its abstract form. It is as if the author is begging us to supply one on our own. My general line of argument will be that the book deals with evil on a human rather than a theoretical level. Put otherwise, the key to reading the book is not to ask a metaphysical question—What are the origins of evil?—but an ethical one: How should the hero cope with it? In regard to the latter, I think it is a mistake to focus on humility or rebellion without seeing that both are parts of Job's personality. A completely humble Job who embodies infinite resignation is a character who closes his eyes to the injustice around him. On the other hand, a purely rebellious Job is a character who feels no need to repent. Neither is true to the character in the book and it is important to see why.

2. The Scandal of Theodicy

Kant once argued that traditional theodicy is a case where the defense is worse than the charge.[10] He concluded that it is certain to be detested by anyone with the slightest spark of morality. Nowhere is this clearer than in the book of Job. Called upon to comfort a sick and bereaved friend, Eliphaz, Bildad, and Zophar do exactly the opposite. Suffering is the consequence of sin. Therefore if Job is in pain, he must have transgressed—if not openly, then secretly. In the mouths of the comforters, this explanation is nothing but a cliché which Job disposes of in short order. But it is a cliché whose consequences are decidedly inhumane. Their "comfort" is little more than an indictment: "Know that God exacts from you less than your sin deserves" (11.6). As the book develops, the indictment becomes more and more severe. Job's cries for pity are ignored and by chapter 22, Eliphaz accuses him of everything from stripping clothes from the needy to assaulting widows and orphans: "Your depravity knows no bounds" (22.5).

The fact that neither Eliphaz nor anyone else has ever witnessed this depravity is irrelevant: it is required by the view that suffering is the consequence of sin. So Kant is right; traditional theology has gotten in the way of Eliphaz's natural feelings of compassion. Earlier Job had told him that if their situations were reversed, "the solace of my lips would assuage your pain" (16.5). It is not that Eliphaz or the others are stupid. They simply think that acknowledging innocent suffering is detrimental to belief in God. The atheist assumes the same thing. The atheist holds, however, that because innocent suffering is undeniable, belief in God is groundless. For the traditional theologian, it is just the opposite: because God is undeniable, innocent suffering cannot occur.

Faced with living proof that innocent suffering does occur, the comforters try out a number of diversions: suffering brings one closer to God (5.17), no one is truly innocent (25.4–6), God is such a mystery to us that we cannot do or know anything (11.6–8). The effect of these claims is to belittle Job's pain. Either there is a simple explanation for it or else the world is too vast for us to explain anything. What is missing in all of this is a sense of indignation. None of them seem troubled by Job's plight or anxious to plead on his behalf. Job's insistence that "the upright are appalled at this" (17.8) falls on deaf ears. We have seen that Abraham, Moses, and Jeremiah spoke out when they thought they saw injustice. The comforters resort to theodicy.

Not only do the comforters not sympathize with their friend, they never really come to grips with the question he has posed. Job never denies that God exists. And while he questions God's justice several times (9.22–24, 12.5–6, 221.7–8), he never makes what could be considered an outright denial. On the contrary, it is *because* God exists and is just that Job cannot make sense of his situation. The poignancy of his question owes everything to the fact that he has not given up his belief in cosmic justice. Without a just God, there would be no court in which to argue his case (9.15–16, 13.20–23, 23.1–6), no avenger (*goel*, 19.25) to right his wrong.[11] As Paul Ricoeur put it in a recent essay: "Suffering is only a scandal for the person who understands God to be the source of everything that is good in creation, including our indignation against evil, our courage to bear it, and our feeling of sympathy toward victims."[12]

That is why Job insists repeatedly that all he needs is a fair hearing. It is true that God has laid His hands on Job and treated him like an enemy (13.21–42). But in addition to a slayer, God is described as Job's avenger, his witness (16.19, 19.26), his judge. The notion that God is adversary, advocate, and judge is more than a confused picture given by a tormented man. Job is, in effect, citing God against Himself. In so doing, he repeats Abraham's question: Shall not the judge of all earth do what is just? It is as if God's unfailing sense of justice will correct the wrong He Himself has done or is about to do.[13] For the metaphysician convinced of God's radical unity, this literary division is a nightmare. What it shows is that Job does not think acknowledging innocent suffering is detrimental to belief in God. For Job the problem is never that God might not exist but that He has temporarily hidden Himself: "Oh, that I knew where I might find Him" (23.3).

When Job does find God in the whirlwind, he does not receive a direct answer to his question. In fact, his question is met by still more questions. The lack of any explicit theodicy in God's speech has caused some scholars to proclaim it irrelevant and others to doubt its authenticity.[14] We must ask, however, what would be gained if God had answered with a treatise on natural theology. Suppose, for example, that He had answered Job with the principle of plenitude, arguing that "localized privations" such as Job's pain are needed to achieve the greatest amount of perfection overall. Or suppose He had claimed that Job's misfortune is a necessary evil that must be endured in order to achieve a greater good. Would Job's or anyone else's plight be more bearable?

I suggest it would not. All it would do is allow another generation of "comforters" to look human misery in the face and take refuge in platitudes. My contention is that the book of Job implicitly rejects any theory that views suffering as a good, even a qualified good needed to achieve a higher purpose. That is, it rejects such theories insofar as God does not avail Himself of them and expresses anger at those who do (42.7). There is no reference in God's speech to "chastisement of love," no attempt to show that suffering is necessary or to generalize from Job's suffering to others'. God simply refuses to say anything from which a theodicy could be derived. According to Robert Gordis, God does not deny there is innocent suffering, and in some passages, such as 40.9–14, comes close to admitting it.[15] If a solution to the problem of evil means we must convince ourselves that Job's pain serves a religious purpose and is good when viewed from the long run, then, I submit, *a solution cannot and should not be found.* Anyone who justifies suffering, or attempts to view it with equanimity by adopting a "long-run" perspective, is, as Kant claimed, making a defense worse than the charge.

It is sometimes argued that the Book of Job is powerless to solve the problem of evil because it lacks a sufficiently developed notion of the afterlife. Some scholars have seen in Job's remarks at 19.26 a veiled reference to the doctrine of resurrection, but the line is obscure and quite possibly corrupt. According to the normal interpretation, *sheol* is a place where people go whether they have led a just life or not (3.17–19). Like Hades, it does not offer any prospect of reward or atonement. Job describes it as a land of gloom and chaos (10.21–22), and while he prefers it to his current condition, he does not contemplate anything like salvation (cf. Psalms 6.6, 88.11–31).

It is important to see, however, that even if a fully developed notion of the afterlife were known to him, Job would be no closer to a resolution of his problem. The prospect of finding happiness in the world to come might make Job feel less despondent, but it would do nothing to assuage the indignation he feels right now. He is suffering unjustifiably. Though he does not claim to be perfect, he protests that his pain is far out of proportion to his guilt (13.23–26; cf. Isaiah 40.2). What he wants is recognition of this fact, not compensation at a future date. Whatever happens to innocent souls in the world to come, the upright will be appalled at the misery they must experience now. This point is made in a forceful way in *The Brothers Karamazov*.[16] After going into intricate detail about the torture of a young child by her parents, Ivan protests that nothing, not the rewards of heaven or the punishments of hell, nor the greater, more comprehensive good for which the child's suffering is supposedly necessary, can overcome the injustice done to her. There are no grounds for saying that the world is "better off" because a human being was subjected to torture. Even if the victim is compensated in a future life, the outrage persists.

Note, however, that if the author wants us to sympathize with Job and feel indignant at his plight, the book seems to lead us into a dilemma. On the one hand, we are shown the inhumane consequences of theodicy. God Himself does not attempt to justify innocent suffering when given a perfect opportunity to do so. Nor does He offer an explanation of Job's plight. On the other hand, we are encouraged to regard Job's plight as outrageous. We, too, want to know why a righteous man has been reduced to an ash heap. We want someone to be held to account. But when we put the two together, we find ourselves in a situation where we are indignant at something that can neither be justified nor explained. How does the book resolve this tension? Does it point to a reconciliation between Job and God or does it leave us with nothing but a futile protest over something we cannot possibly understand?

There is no question that Job is comforted by God's speech. The man who raised the finger of protest to heaven and demanded to confront his accuser claims in chapter 42 that he has spoken of things too great for him to know and repents in dust and ashes. Is he, at this late stage, denying his innocence? Has he been frightened by the thunder and bluster of God's voice? A standard interpretation of the book is that God has the right to shroud Himself in mystery. But if this is true, what becomes of the moral indignation we feel on Job's behalf? Does it get submerged in a theological skepticism according to which we have no choice but to resign ourselves to the will of God? It is to these questions that we must now turn.

3. Morality and the Limits of Human Knowledge

In addition to theodicy, the book raises a number of questions about the scope of human knowledge.[17] To his friends who have come with "maxims and proverbs of ashes," Job replies with scorn: "What you know, I also know; in no way am I inferior to you" (13.2). To God he protests: "Make me know my transgression and my sin" (13.23). To everyone he proclaims that he knows his avenger lives (19.25). When their theodicies begin to crumble, the comforters resort to an extreme form of skepticism. Bildad maintains that we are but of yesterday and "know nothing" (8.9). He even foreshadows the final speech of God (11.7–8):

> Can you find out the deep things of God?
> Can you find out the ultimate purpose of
> 　　the Almighty?
> It is as high as heaven; what can you do?
> Deeper than sheol, what can you know?

So, too, Elihu (37.14–16):

> Do you know how God commands them?
> And causes the lightning of His cloud to
> 　　shine?
> Do you know the balancings of the clouds?
> The marvelous works of Him who is perfect
> 　　in knowledge?

Maimonides (*Guide* 3.23) interprets the speeches of Elihu as further evidence of the truth of negative theology. We have seen that the inability of humans to penetrate the unfathomable wisdom of God is also put in the mouth of Job in the disputed speech of chapter 28. This speech ends with the famous claim that fear of the Lord is wisdom.

Strictly speaking, this sort of skepticism is incompatible with theodicy. For theodicy to work, it must be the case that this world is the best possible, that suffering serves a higher purpose, and that God's intentions can be discerned from a consideration of earthly events. But if human wisdom is as limited as the comforters say, if, when it comes to God's ultimate purpose, we know nothing at all, how can we make the judgments theodicy requires? This inconsistency is most apparent in the speech of Eliphaz in chapter 15. He repeats Job's scorn: "What do you know that we do not know?" (15.9) But in the next dozen lines, he takes it upon himself to speak for God. If man has nothing but "windy knowledge," by what authority can Eliphaz discover a divine purpose in the misery of his friend?

When God speaks for Himself, the limits of human knowledge are very much at issue: "Who is this that darkens counsel by words without knowledge?" (32.2) In fact, God is not above sarcasm in responding to Job's protest. At several places (38.5, 18, 21, 33), He asks Job a question and follows it with a taunt: "for surely you know." The picture which emerges from God's speech is that of a universe where forces of good and evil far beyond the scope of human understanding are controlled by a ruler who insists on His kingly prerogatives: "Will you condemn Me that you may be justified?" (40.8) It is true, as Charles Hartshorne points out, that despite the thunderous tone of God's oration, Job is never in physical danger.[18] At no time does God threaten him with violence. But the point of these taunts is not lost. In his final speech of the book, Job humbles himself before divine perfection: "I have uttered what I did not understand, things too marvelous for me, which I did not know" (42.3). So while God does not violate human reason in the manner suggested by Kierkegaard, He certainly points out its limits.

The lesson to be drawn from Job's humility seems obvious. We have no comprehension of what it is like to create entire galaxies or to control natural forces on a cosmic scale. We therefore have no basis on which to protest divine rule. The moral concepts we live by are limited to the actions we are capable of understanding. Hence there is no reason that God should justify Himself in our eyes. As Isaiah (55.8) says about God: "My thoughts are not Your thoughts."

This is an easy lesson to draw but not one which preserves the integrity of the book. The humble Job who repents in dust and ashes may replace the angry, impatient Job who demands an explanation of his plight, but simple humility is not the end of the story. Both are replaced in the epilogue by a new Job who prays for his friends—Job the prophet. The tradition for regarding Job as a prophet is established as early as Ezekiel (14.12–14), where a righteous man named Job is mentioned alongside Noah and David.[19] In any case, the editors of *The New Oxford Annotated Bible* are right to point out that Job's restoration follows not his repentance but his willingness to intercede on behalf of others.[20] In view of the precedent established by Abraham, Moses, and Jeremiah, intercession involves trust in God's saving power but falls short of what is normally meant by submission. The prophet is someone who pleads with God, even argues with Him, not someone who accepts divine decrees without question. As Abraham J. Heschel put it, the soul of the prophet exhibits an extreme sensitivity to human suffering: when he is with the people, he takes the side of God; but when he is with God, he takes the side of the people.[21] So the prophet does not necessarily think that once one has heard God, everything is right with the world. Nor is he a lonely knight of faith. The stormy relationship between God and Moses is enough to refute both suggestions. The prophet never relinquishes his status as a free-thinking, moral agent.

Job may not know the dimensions of the heavens or the ordinances which govern the Pleiades; yet by the end of the book, he does have the proper standing to argue a case before the heavenly court. What, then, of his own case? Here is the one place where skepticism is never an issue. In the midst of his torment, he is told by his three closest friends to stop proclaiming his innocence and repent of the heinous crimes he has committed. Confused, betrayed, and racked by pain, a lesser character would have followed his friends' advice, thinking that he must be mistaken about his innocence and that even if he is not, a little servility never hurts. In short, he would throw himself in the dirt and grovel for forgiveness. Job, however, will have none of it. He will not allow his friends to proclaim moral superiority and will not confess a crime he did not commit. In defiance of everything he has heard, he stands up like a hero and affirms his innocence (27.3–6):

> All the while my breath is in me,
> And the spirit of God is in my nostrils,
> Surely my lips shall not speak
> > unrighteousness,
> Neither shall my tongue utter deceit;
> Far be it from me that I should justify
> > you;
> Till I die I will not put away my
> > integrity from me.
> My righteousness I hold fast, and will
> > not let it go;
> My heart shall not reproach me so long as
> > I live.

If this character were to become totally submissive—even in the face of God—the book would lose whatever claim it has to being a unified whole. The hero's most important speech would amount to a lie and his elevation to the status of prophet, a gratuitous addition to an unbelievable story. Note, for example, that while God rebukes Job for speaking about things he does not understand, He never rebukes him for proclaiming his innocence. The challenge, then, is to see how Job can retain his moral integrity at the same time he admits his intellectual limits.

Kant has a ready-made answer. When Job repents before God, he is confessing not that he has spoken sacrilegiously but that he has spoken unwisely about things beyond his comprehension.[22] We have seen that for Kant, there is no inference by which we can move from experience of the world to knowledge of its Creator. In particular, we cannot infer the intentions of the Creator by looking at the objects of His creation. That is why theodicy is impossible. The ultimate purpose served by things in the physical world is hidden from us. Even more hidden is the connection between the physical order and the moral. God's ways are known only to Him. In this scheme, the comforters represent the attempt of speculative reason to understand God on the basis of principles extrapolated from experience. Hence the charge that Job is a sinner. Kant takes this as a dogmatic assertion that presupposes that experience must be in harmony with our conception of divinity. Job represents the attempt to make morality rather than speculative reason the basis of faith. Citing the speech quoted above (27.3–6), Kant claims that Job's faith was founded on the uprightness of his heart rather than a metaphysical understanding of God.

Although it presupposes philosophical sophistication beyond anything available to the author of the text, Kant's interpretation is right to this extent: the world is not a book from which we can infer the intentions of the author. Every time God says to Job "for surely you know," he underscores this point. Kant is also right in saying that Job's confession is not a retraction of his earlier claim of innocence. The inability of our minds to fathom the will of God does not imply inability to insist on our own moral worth. It is still true, after the confession, that Job is a righteous man who was falsely accused by his friends.

In the last analysis, though, Kant's Job is yet another version of the patient hero who endures pain with stoic resolution. Put otherwise, Kant maintains that Job's primary virtue is honesty. Unlike the comforters, Job does not try to flatter God by concocting a dogmatic theodicy: he is sincere about what he knows and what he does not. Since he cannot know the reason for his suffering, he has little choice but to bear it. On the reading I have suggested, it is honesty coupled with indignation. It is true that this indignation is tempered by awe in the face of God's infinite wisdom and strength, but it is never extinguished; if it were, Job could not assume the role of prophet. It may be said, therefore, that the prophet is both a servant and an adversary. Like Jeremiah, the prophet admits God's superiority but argues his case all the same.

We can understand this duality by returning to the question of analogy. I have argued that in one respect, there is an analogy between human beings and God, in other respects not. When it comes to knowledge of the origins of the universe, or power in controlling it, the analogy is impossible. Maimonides writes (*Guide* 3.13):

> Be not misled in your soul to think that the spheres and the angels have been brought into existence for our sake. For it has explained to us what we are worth: *Behold, the nations are as a drop of a bucket.* Consider accordingly your substance and that of the spheres, the stars, and the separate intellects; then the truth will become manifest to you, and you will know that man and nothing else is the most perfect and the most noble thing that has been generated from this [inferior] matter; but that if his being is compared to that of the spheres and all the more to that of the separate beings, it is very, very contemptible.

All we can say about God is that He is not limited in the way we are. This does not mean that He has greater knowledge and power if "knowledge" and "power" are understood in a conventional way; it means that His knowledge and power bear no relation to ours. But knowledge and power are not the whole story. We can agree with David Hartman when he says that for all Maimonides' insistence on the insignificance of human beings before God, the great philosopher *also* insists on God's adherence to the Sinai covenant and the rationality of its terms.[23] The fact that we are insignificant from a physical standpoint does not mean that God can treat us in an arbitrary fashion when it comes to morality. Both God and humans are rational agents capable of willing the moral law. And the law is the same for both no matter how different the details of their respective situations. So the moral judgment that recoils at the sight of innocent suffering has application beyond the small part of the universe we occupy. It is this duality on which the movement of the book rests. Job confesses ignorance of creation but still has the right to plead a case before the Almighty. From a philosophic perspective, the duality resolves itself in the following claims: (1) We cannot conceive God except as a moral agent who guarantees the possibility that the world can be perfected; (2) in regard to empirical facts, we cannot tell when perfection has been realized; we have no way of telling whether God wills a specific event as an end, a means, or a third possibility.

In the last analysis, then, Jeremiah is right. As moral agents, we have no choice but to protest when we see innocent people afflicted. Since every human being is an end in him- or herself, innocent suffering is *always* outrageous. But as beings of limited knowledge and power, we have no hope of understanding the fine points of God's creation. The result is that we cannot allow the physical circumstances of a person's life to determine our estimate of his or her worth and are wont to cry out in anguish when the two seem out of joint. According to Cohen (*Religion of Reason*, 22), the fact that they can be out of joint implies one thing: "that all measuring and comparing of the inner *dignity* of man with the outward appearance of his earthly lot is futile and meaningless, shortsighted and deluded." If this is right, we do not please God by failing to recognize human dignity either in others or in ourselves. In its own way, failing to recognize human dignity is as serious an error as asserting a resemblance between God and humans with respect to knowledge or power. The depth and sensitivity of Job's character derive from the fact that he refuses to do either.

4. Coping with Evil

To return to the point with which this chapter began, the Book of Job does not discuss the problem of evil in the form in which Augustine, Leibniz, and Hume do. It is unlikely that the author of the book ever encountered the philosophical formulation of the problem, but even if the author had, there are good reasons for thinking that he would have rejected it. God's speech implies that human understanding has no purchase on divine wisdom or strength. There is a question, then, whether the terms we use to state the problem have any clear sense. Hartshorne argues they do not. He says that Job

is not scared or bribed with humility, he is simply shown his actual cognitive situation. And what is that situation? That he has been brought up on a theory of all-mightiness whose meaning no one understands. What is the use of trying to derive consequences from a concept that one does not possess? There was no clearly understood notion of God's power to give rise to a problem of evil, of why God 'does' this or 'does' that. What does it mean to say, 'God does something'? To accept such language as clear, but find a puzzle in the divine motive, *why* God does things, is, as Berdayev said, once and for all, to treat as a mystery a problem which one has 'already over-rationalized.' The puzzle begins one step earlier. Human 'power' we know something about, but what sort of analogy enables us to speak of 'divine power'? Until we have this analogy straight, there is no clearly defined problem of evil.[24]

This takes us back to Maimonides. Without an analogy between God's power and ours, we cannot apply the vocabulary of human causality to God. And even if the event defies explanation in human terms, we cannot know for sure *if* God has acted or *why*. It follows that the question of why God "does this" or "permits that" is incoherent. The creation of the universe bears no relation to the instigation of a specific act within it. Spontaneous action arising from perfect self-knowledge bears no relation to restricted action which is affected by external conditions. If the abstract version of the problem of evil requires us to apply the vocabulary of human action to God, then it is incoherent as well. The analogy exists only at the level of purpose. How God accomplishes His purpose we cannot say. Again from Cohen, our understanding of God is normative; it concerns what ought to be done and how such an "ought" is possible. But it has no bearing on the explanation of individual events.

I submit that the Book of Job rejects both of the alternatives to which the traditional version of the problem of evil leads: atheism and theodicy. Atheism allows for innocent suffering but has no grounds for regarding it as scandalous. Theodicy assumes we know how God works, when we really do not. If we put aside unanswerable questions about God's purpose in permitting evil to occur and ask how an upright person ought to cope with it, the problem of evil will have more to do with us than it does with God. It arises from the fact that we can conceive of ourselves in either of two ways: as ends in ourselves or as creatures fashioned from the dust. The key to understanding the problem is to see that both are legitimate.

Consider the first. A common response to personal tragedy is to blame oneself. The survivor of an accident in which several people are killed feels guilty even though the evidence shows he was not at fault. A person who is stricken by a serious illness rationalizes it by saying fate has only dealt him what he deserves. In fact, the tendency to find oneself guilty is so prevalent that Freud claimed it has a share in every neurotic illness.[25] So when Job affirms his innocence in chapter 27, it is not just the advice of his friends he must overcome but a powerful force in human psychology. Again, the easy thing would be to fall on the ground and beg forgiveness—even if he is not totally sure what the forgiveness is for. The author seems to be aware of this tendency at 15.15–16 when he has Eliphaz say that "if God puts no trust in His holy ones, and the heavens are not clean in His eyes, how much less so is man, who is loathsome and rotten and drinks iniquity like water." Job, however, does not play what Ricoeur terms "the cruel game of the expiatory victim."[26] Whatever the risks of blasphemy, his emotion of indignation is far preferable to the self-contempt Eliphaz tries to instill in him.

On the other hand, Job is able to see that however deserved, his own happiness is not the focal point of the universe. What comfort he receives comes from his ability to marvel at the vastness of creation and the terrible forces within it. As committed an atheist as Bertrand Russell saw in the spectacle of death and the endurance of intolerable pain "a sacredness, an overpowering awe, a feeling of the vastness, the depth, the inexhaustible mystery of existence."[27] It is just such a perspective that is afforded by the voice from the whirlwind. From this perspective, innocent suffering is still an outrage. But Job comes to see that the question such suffering poses is neither the beginning nor the end of human curiosity. If he is right to insist on his innocence, he is also right not to become consumed by it. In the end, he repents with dignity: he admits to narrowness of vision without succumbing to neurotic guilt.

The emotions of indignation and awe are as close as we will ever get to a "solution" to the problem of evil because they are the only legitimate ways of coping with it. The book suggests they are capable of existing together in the person of the prophet. This does not mean that we mix hot water with cold and get something in the middle: the prophet continues to agonize over human suffering and run up against the limits of human knowledge. Like Isaiah (Isaiah 62.1: "For Zion's sake, I will not be silent"), the prophet never reaches a state of complacency. The point is that even if there is no explanation of how everything fits together, the prophet is able to live with himself and attain a measure of dignity. It is significant, therefore, that Job never achieves superhuman modes of awareness. In the end, he is content with the recognition of his limits and the certainty of his own inner worth. In principle, his achievement is available to anyone. In this respect, there is nothing exclusive about his development as a character. So when the psalmist asks, "What is man that Thou art mindful of him?" (Psalms 8.5), the Book of Job answers: a being who even in agony can rise to heroic proportions. Such heroism does not constitute a "justification" of innocent suffering as that term is normally used. But it does provide a model for the only honest way to respond to it. The question we must now ask is whether this model holds up in the face of an evil that even Job may not have been able to imagine.

Notes

1. See *Guide* 3.22–23, as well as Gersonides, *Wars of the Lord* 3.11–77. The reader is further advised to consult the notes and critical discussion of Seymour Feldman's edition of *Wars of the Lord*.

2. The earlier versions of the Greek text are shorter than the Hebrew and even when the missing lines are supplied, the translation is not always exact. Compare the two at 3.20, 9.13, 9.22, 12.6, 14.16, 16.13–14, 19.6, and 23.7. For the literature on this problem, see H. S. Gehman, "The Theological Approach of the Greek Translator of Job 1–15," *Journal of Biblical Literature* 68 (1949), 231–40; D. H. Gard, "The Concept of Job's Character according to the Greek Translation of the Hebrew Text," *Journal of Biblical Literature* 72 (1953), 182–86; and H. Orlinsky, "Studies in the Septuagint of the Book of Job," *Hebrew Union College Annual* 28 (1957), 53–74, 29 (1958), 229–71, 30 (1959), 153–67.

3. The most telling example is that of 13.15, mentioned below. The wording and the context suggest that Job is expressing defiance, but an editorial note changed "defiance" to "faith." For further discussion, see Marvin H. Pope, *The Anchor Bible Job* (Garden City, N.Y.: Doubleday & Company, 1965), 95–96. Notice, however, that Pope accepts the editor's change in order to propose a decidedly Christian reading of Job in his introduction, lxxvii–lxxviii.

4. Pope, *Anchor Job,* xxviii.

5. *The Apostolic Fathers,* trans. K. Lake (New York: Loeb Classical Library, 1930), vol. 1, 39.

6. *Babylonian Talmud, Sotah* 31a, *Baba Batra* 16a. For further discussion, see E. E. Urbach, *The Sages,* trans I. Abrahams (Jerusalem: Magnes Press, 1979), 406–13.

7. *Sotah* 31a.

8. *Baba Batra* 16b.

9. *Babylonian Talmud, Berahot* 32a. For further discussion of the theme of protest in the Bible, see Sheldon H. Blank, "Men Against God: The Promethean Element in Biblical Prayer," *Journal of Biblical Literature* 72 (1953): 1–13.

10. Immanuel Kant, "On the Failure of All Attempted Philosophical Theodicies," trans. M. Despland, in Michel Despland, *Kant on History and Religion* (Montreal: McGill-Queen's University Press, 1973), 283–97.

11. A *goel* is a redeemer or kinsman who typically seeks revenge for a murder. See Leviticus 25.25, Numbers 5.8, 35.9ff., Ruth 3.13. The fact that Job says his *goel* will stand on earth has no tendency to show that Job must be referring to someone other than God. There are simply too many passages in Biblical literature where God is referred to as a *goel*, e.g., Exodus 6.6, 15.13, Isaiah 41.14, 43.14, 44.6, 47.4, 48.17, 59.20, 60.16, 63.16. The idea is that God will make His presence known and correct the wrong Job is suffering. Compare Pope, *Anchor Job*, 134–35, who sees a reference to a personal god of Sumerian theology.

12. Paul Ricoeur, "Evil, A Challenge to Philosophy and Theology," *Journal of The American Academy of Religion* 53 (1985), 647.

13. For further discussion of this theme, see Robert Gordis, *The Book of God and Man* (Chicago: University of Chicago Press, 1965), 87–89.

14. This literature is reviewed and disposed of by Robert Gordis, ibid., chapter 10.

15. Ibid., 119.

16. Fyodor Dostoevsky, *The Brothers Karamazov*, trans. C. Garnett (New York: Random House, 1950), 286–87. Cf. Augustine, *On Free Choice of the Will*, translated by A. S. Benjamin (Indianapolis: Bobbs-Merrill, 1964), 140–41: "Some raise a greater and, as it were, more merciful objection, concerning the bodily suffering with which young children are afflicted. Because of their age, they say children have committed no sins (assuming that their souls have not committed sin before animating their bodies). Hence they ask: 'What evil have they done that they should suffer so?' But what reason is there to believe that anyone should be rewarded for innocence before he could do harm? Since God works some good by correcting adults tortured by the sickness and death of children who are dear to them, why should this suffering not occur? When the sufferings of children are over, it will be as if they had never occurred for those who suffered. Either the adults on whose account the sufferings occurred will become better, if they are reformed by temporal troubles and choose to live rightly, or else, if be-

cause of the hardships of this life they are unwilling to turn their desire toward eternal life, they will have no excuse when they are punished in the judgment to come. Moreover, who knows what faith is practiced or what pity is tested when these children's sufferings break down the hardness of parents? Who knows what reward God reserves in the secret place of his judgment for the children who, though they have not acted rightly, are not, on the other hand, weighed down by sin?"

17. This theme is discussed in Nahum N. Glatzer's introduction to *The Dimensions of Job: A Study and Selected Readings* (New York: Schocken Books, 1969), 6–11. This is a valuable anthology, not only for Glatzer's essay and the other selections, but for the bibliography at the end.

18, Charles Hartshorne, *A Natural Theology for Our Time* (LaSalle, Ill.: Open Court Press, 1967), 116–20.

19. Here it should be noted that the crux of Maimonides' position in *Guide* 3.22–23 is that Job is described as a righteous man at the beginning of the story but not as a wise one. Wisdom does not come until he hears the voice from the whirlwind. But this is still compatible with saying that the knowledge he gets is critical in nature. This is exactly how Maimonides interprets the speeches of Elihu.

20. *The New Oxford Annotated Bible*, ed. H. G. May and B. M. Metzger (New York: Oxford University Press, 1962), 655.

21. Abraham J. Heschel, *The Prophets*, vol. 1 (New York: Harper & Row, 1955), 121.

22. Kant, "On the Failure," 283–97.

23. Hartman, *The Living Covenant*, 126. Overall, Hartman's book is a study in how this duality manifests itself in rabbinic literature. I find his conclusions quite compatible with my own.

24. Hartshorne, *A Natural Theology,* 118–19.

25. Freud, *The Complete Introductory Lectures on Psychoanalysis*, J. Strachey, trans. and ed. (New York: W. W. Norton, 1966), 572.

26. Ricoeur, *Evil, A Challenge,* 646.

27. Bertrand Russell, "A Free Man's Worship," in *Why I Am Not a Christian* (1957; rpt. New York: Harper & Row, 1963), 113.

Chapter Eight

Fackenheim's Dilemma

1. Transformation of the Existentialist Challenge

In his essay on the suspension of the ethical, Buber confronts the following paradox. God is personal and therefore beyond the reach of philosophic systems. But in our time, God is in eclipse. We cannot be sure whether it is God's voice which addresses us or someone else's. To avoid catastrophe, we must assume that God does not demand anything more than what is contained in Micah's formula. It is clear, however, that between *I and Thou* and *Eclipse of God*, Buber's thought underwent a change. The God of the former is always present, the God of the latter hides His face. Still, "our time" is a cryptic way to refer to one of the most devastating experiences in history.

I do not wish to suggest that Buber ignored the Holocaust. In "The Dialogue between Heaven and Earth," he begins where the essay on suspending the ethical leaves off:

> In this our time, one asks again and again: how is a Jewish life still possible after Auschwitz? I would like to frame this question more correctly: how is a life with God still possible in a time in which there is an Auschwitz? The estrangement has become too cruel, the hiddenness too deep. One can still "believe" in a God who allowed those things to happen, but *how can one still speak to Him? Can one still hear His word?* Can one still, as an individual and a people, enter at all into a dialogical relationship with Him? Can one still call on Him? Dare we recommend to the survivors of Auschwitz, the Jobs of the gas chambers: "Call on Him, for He is kind, for His mercy endureth forever?"[1]

Like Job, Buber poses a question he cannot answer. His earlier notion of dialogue led him to believe that it is impossible to do evil

189

with one's whole soul.[2] If so, the medieval philosophers were right: evil has no reality of its own; it is a lack or deficiency. But however one defines it, evil has gotten in the way of the divine/human encounter. In the passage just quoted, Buber suggests that dialogue may no longer be possible. The God who has hidden His face may be out of reach. Worse, we in our anger may not *wish* to call upon Him. As it happens, Buber did not pursue these thoughts very far. That job was taken up by Emil Fackenheim. In Fackenheim's hands, the cryptic phrase "in our time" becomes a catalogue of human atrocity.

To understand why Fackenheim feels the need to supply such a catalogue, we must understand the degree to which he has gone beyond Buber. If the primary metaphor in Buber's attack on traditional philosophy is the concrete, the primary metaphor in Fackenheim's is immanence. Time and again, he argues for a God who is "engaged," "involved," a God who enters into what Fackenheim terms "flesh and blood" history. Hence the titles of two of his major works: *God's Presence in History* and *The Jewish Return Into History*. In his criticism of Cohen, Fackenheim maintained that a modern Jew can put less trust in the God-Idea than in the ancient God of Israel. If the latter acts *in* history, the former is "divorced from history and therefore impotent." The argument behind this criticism is that great ideas are not validated by abstract arguments. To remain in the realm of the abstract is to escape from reality rather than confront it, to be inauthentic. Ideas are confirmed only when people witness to them in specific situations. That is how we break through the circle of idealism. Thus Fackenheim writes:

> Authentication is possible only by a witness who *exists in* his particular situation, not by scientific observers, philosophers, or theologians who fancy themselves as transcending every all-too-particular situation.[3]

This does not mean that Fackenheim denies the possibility of transcendence or the legitimacy of universal truths. If he did, he would cease to be a Jewish thinker. His point is essentially a Kierkegaardian one: that even if we seek universality, we must do so from the standpoint of our own existential uniqueness, in short, from the standpoint of the particular.[4] For Fackenheim, all universal claims must be tested in the light of Jewish particularity. Add to this the writings of Heidegger and Rosenzweig and we get the qualification: Jewish *historical* particularity. The passage quoted above continues:

One can be witness to a Transcendence which transcends the historical situation only *within* one's historical situation; nor can others who could appraise or respond to this testimony do so except from within *their* historical situation.

With Rosenzweig, Fackenheim thinks that history imposes existential limitations that are untranscendable.[5] If this is true, the purpose of philosophy is not to escape from history but to bring ideas down *into* it.[6]

We must keep these points in mind if we are to understand why Fackenheim thinks the Holocaust constitutes a rupture in the fabric of rationality. One does not normally claim that an event *refutes* a philosophic theory. No one would argue that Socrates' trial is a refutation of his thought. The point is that by "refute" Fackenheim does not mean what a traditional philosopher means by it. For Fackenheim, an idea is refuted when it ceases to affect the flow of events, when people no longer commit themselves to it or care whether anyone else does. This is what Fackenheim means by "impotence." Unless people witness to ideas, then, in his words, they become "weak," "abandoned," or "betrayed." Much of his writing is an attempt to show that while traditional philosophy has suffered such a fate, Judaism has not. But it is significant that Fackenheim allows for the possibility that Judaism *might be* abandoned or refuted. In a thought-provoking essay, he claims that God is "empirically manifest in the world," so that Judaism may be subject to empirical *dis*confirmation.[7] In a more recent publication, he goes further. He asks us to imagine a world in which the Holocaust occurred exactly as it did but the State of Israel did not come into existence. Would there be any reason to continue to practice Judaism? Fackenheim suggests there would not:

In a world with a Holocaust but without a Jewish state, all Jews truly sensitive to what has occurred would surely be in a flight from their Jewish condition that would dwarf anything known as "assimilation" now. And who could blame them: Not long ago the world was divided into one part bent on the murder of every available Jew, and another that did less than was possible to prevent it, to stop it, or at least to slow the process down. If after that there had been no *radical* change, who would want to be a Jew? Who could be expected to remain one?[8]

It may be said, therefore, that like Russell and Buber, or for that matter, Rosenzweig and Heidegger, Fackenheim has a robust sense of reality. The real test of an idea is whether it is realized in "flesh and blood."

How can an idea like monotheism be disconfirmed? Better yet, how can an ethical idea like human dignity be disconfirmed? Did Kant not maintain that the categorical imperative is valid even if no one lives up to it? Fackenheim's response is to ask about the place of the categorical imperative in history (*To Mend the World*, 273):

> Taken as a serious philosophical doctrine, his philosophical *Idea* of Humanity *must* have, and according to Kant *does* have, a matrix or *Boden* in *actual* humanity. Kant, in short, *believes* in humanity: *but is that belief warranted?* Perhaps it was so in Kant's time. Arguably it was once warranted at *any* time if only because, while undemonstrable, this belief was at least also irrefutable. (Who can refute a "good will" in the "common man" which is not admittedly "overlaid with selfishness" and hence, "not manifest in action"?) But is this belief warranted in the age of Auschwitz? Then and there, one kind of common man—the *Muselmann*—was made into a uniquely uncommon victim, while the other, the manufacturer of the victim, was made—*let himself* be made—into a uniquely uncommon criminal. And "uniquely uncommon" in both cases was this, that personality was destroyed. It is true that Kant's belief in humanity could at no time be verified. However, not until the advent of the Holocaust world was this belief *refuted*, for here the *reality* that is object of the belief was *itself systematically annihilated*. That this was possible is the awful legacy of Auschwitz to all humanity.

This is a dangerous road for a Jewish thinker to travel—a fact which cannot possibly have escaped Fackenheim's notice. The classic anti-Semitic argument is that history constitutes living proof of God's displeasure with the Jewish people. As Fackenheim himself remarks, some theologians invoked the Holocaust in just this way.[9] Yet we do not have to cite so preposterous a case to see that historical relevance is a problematic criterion. Did the Holocaust refute Kant's belief in humanity or did it refute the people who thought his belief could be dispensed with? To be sure, Fackenheim is not suggesting that we do historical analysis by counting noses. But to the degree that we rely on historically situated individuals to give vitality to ideas, we run the risk of trivializing those ideas. Kant was invoked both by people who supported Hitler and people who opposed him. What was refuted and what confirmed? Surely we cannot decide this question on the basis of historical evidence alone. And surely Fackenheim does not want to say that without formation of the State of Israel, monotheism would be dead.

On the issue of confirmation, the rationalist has a simple reply: ideas do not have to be realized in "flesh and blood" to be legitimate. The connection between flesh and blood and moral worth was destroyed once and for all in the Book of Job. Again from Cohen: the history of religion has no means of securing the legitimacy of religion. The fact that Jews have suffered for two millennia has no tendency to show that Judaism is true—or false. And if, by chance, the United Nations had voted against formation of the State of Israel, it would still be legitimate to say the *Shema*. But Fackenheim is adamant that Judaism not be rendered impotent, that it somehow find its way back into history.

How is the latter to be accomplished? According to Fackenheim, such a return was facilitated by the Holocaust. Here was an unprecedented event, a form of evil never before contemplated. In previous ages, people were killed for what they *did;* here they were killed for what they *were*. The "offense" that merited death was having one Jewish grandparent. In previous ages enemies of the state were killed; here they were not just killed but systematically degraded—a process that required the commitment and resources of an entire nation. In Fackenheim's eyes, reason is overwhelmed by evil on this scale. We have no words to describe it and no categories under which it can be subsumed. If so, the philosophic categories at our disposal are inadequate to the historical facts. We can ignore the facts but only at the cost of inauthenticity. An unprecedented event demands, if not an unprecedented response, then at least a substantial one. To the degree that no response is forthcoming, and to this date few philosophers other than Fackenheim have offered one, philosophy has failed.

By calling this chapter "Fackenheim's Dilemma," it is clear that I intend to be critical. But before any criticism is advanced, it is important to note that the dilemma I attribute to Fackenheim is one he readily accepts. The interpretation of the Holocaust leads to a paradox that in Fackenheim's view is unavoidable. So there is no question of surprise. Still, *To Mend the World* is a great book—not for any philosophic puzzle it solves but because it represents the denouement of Jewish existentialism.

2. Breaking with the Past

For the idealistic tradition in philosophy, there is an unbreakable connection between goodness and intelligibility. Plato expressed this by saying that Goodness is beyond being in dignity and power. It is, therefore, the pinnacle of the world of ideas; like the sun, it enables everything else to be *and* be known. In the *Republic* (505e), Plato describes it as "that which every soul pursues as the end of all its activities, dimly perceiving its existence, perplexed and unable to grasp its nature with the same clearness and assurance as in dealing with other things, thereby missing whatever value those other things may have. . . ." Since Philo, religious thinkers have tried to assimilate Platonism and monotheism. God is the source of all existence. Since God's will is good, everything in existence must satisfy a purpose. If so, evil can have no reality of its own. It is a privation that arises from the fact that the universe is material and all material things are subject to limitations.[10] Put otherwise, evil is an accident. God produces it only because it is a consequence of having created a universe in the first place. On the human level, evil is the result of ignorance. It is only because people are not aware of goodness that they pursue its opposite. On this scheme, nothing which exists is essentially or irredeemably evil. If something were, it would be completely outside God's providence and therefore completely unintelligible.

In one respect, Fackenheim accepts this view: goodness and intelligibility are related. But he goes on to say that the irredeemable *does* exist, from which it follows that something unintelligible exists—or, to be more accurate, has come to pass. There is no possibility of making the Holocaust intelligible. According to Fackenheim (*To Mend the World*, 233):

> To explain an action or event is to show how they were possible. In the case of the Holocaust, however, the mind can accept the possibility of both how and why it was done, in the final analysis, solely because it was done, so that the more the psychologist, historian, or "psychohistorian" succeeds in explaining the event or action, the more nakedly he comes to confront its ultimate inexplicability.

In the face of the Nazi death machine, reason is paralyzed. There is no hope of explaining why it happened or what purpose it served.

The first part of Fackenheim's argument is that the theological explanations that accompanied previous tragedies are no longer applicable. To make the Holocaust a punishment for sin, or a test of faith, or an opportunity to manifest virtue, is to blaspheme God and mock the death of the six million. What sort of God would devise a test of this kind? Here it is noteworthy that even for a traditional theologian like John Hick, the Holocaust remains an irredeemably evil event, a surd.[11] In Fackenheim's words, its evil cannot be overcome. There is nothing edifying in the systematic degradation of human life.

Plato was not exactly innocent of evil. His description of the tyrant in Book Eight of the *Republic* is a penetrating account of the criminal mind. But however revolting the tyrant may be, his motivation is perfectly intelligible: he is pursuing his own self-interest. The problem is that he has such a distorted image of his self-interest that his behavior is out of control. He has sunk to the ultimate level of human ignorance. In one place, Plato compares him to a wild animal.[12] If nothing else, Fackenheim has shown that this account of evil is inadequate. There is a difference in kind between a wild animal and a demon. The tyrant is not systematic; he has no need of ideology. Although he is ruthless, we cannot imagine him allocating valuable resources to the destruction of people who pose no threat. For the tyrant, killing is a means to his own gratification. According to Fackenheim, however, the demon introduces an entirely new dimension. Here killing is not a means to an end but the end itself. It is something which calls for a national sacrifice, something which expresses the national will. In short, killing is "idealized." It becomes a form of worship.

There is, of course, a danger in introducing a concept like "the Holocaust" into the philosophic lexicon. Immediately people will want to ask a host of questions. When did it begin?—when Hitler came to power? on *Kristallnacht* ? or when the death camps were built? Does it include groups other than Jews, such as gypsies, homosexuals, Marxists, the physically handicapped, and the mentally ill? What is meant by saying that the Holocaust is unique? Does this mean that every other instance of mass killing in history *is* intelligible and has a place in God's plan for the world? Are numbers crucial? Would it be a Holocaust if 60,000 people had been killed, or 600, or 60? Could there be a Holocaust without modern technology? What if Hitler's victims had been killed with bows and arrows? There is a danger in thinking that by invoking a term like "the Holocaust," we know exactly what we are talking about. No doubt, the term produces an intense reaction. But we must be careful not to confuse intensity with clarity.

Let us assume, however, that Fackenheim is right: we have a clear idea of what we mean by the Holocaust, and there is no historical precedent for such a catastrophe. If goodness and intelligibility are connected, then at least one event on a world scale is unintelligible. This does not mean that historians are incapable of keeping accurate accounts of the facts, only that there is no meaning in the facts, no possibility of seeing how outwardly rational people could have wanted them to *be* facts in the first place. According to Fackenheim (*To Mend the World*, 237–8), "those manipulated *let themselves* be manipulated; those obeying ever-escalating orders *chose* to obey without limits; those surrendering in a blind idealism *made a commitment* to blindness." There is no way to understand a conscious commitment to blindness within the scope of traditional philosophy. To be sure, reason balks at the suggestion that there is something it cannot penetrate. As Fackenheim indicates (239), there is a tendency to think that if only we could get inside the mind of an Eichmann or a Himmler, we could make sense of their world. Here, too, Fackenheim is right: we cannot. A world which idealizes human degradation is a world forever inaccessible to rational analysis. Again from Fackenheim (200), "where the Holocaust is, *no* thought can be, and . . . where there is thought it is in flight from the event." In a way, Fackenheim's writing on this subject is like the discovery of irrational numbers: a worldview incommensurate with our own exists. And just as the discovery of irrational numbers was a shattering blow to previous theories, so, Fackenheim contends, this discovery is equally shattering to previous systems of philosophy. The old paradigms are destroyed. Confidence in the power of reason is overturned. There is nothing in the thought of previous thinkers to prepare us for such an outcome or to allow us to make sense of it.

According to Fackenheim, this is the risk we run when thought is exposed to "the rigors of history." Indeed, the mention of history brings out yet another respect in which a rupture has occurred. Fackenheim's objection is not just that the old theories fail to provide an adequate understanding of the event. According to him, no such understanding is possible. Worse than the failure of explanation is the failure of individual philosophers to oppose the evil around them. Recall that for Fackenheim, ideas are confirmed when people witness to them. That is why he cannot forget that the inheritor of the German philosophic tradition, Martin Heidegger, supported Hitler (*To Mend the World*, 169):

> The scandal would be minor if at issue were merely Heidegger's personal behavior. The indisputable and undisputed fact is, however, that when he endorsed in advance the Führer's actions as German "reality" and "law," he did so not, like countless others, impelled by personal fear, opportunism, or the hysteria of the time, but rather deliberately and *with the weight of his philosophy behind it*.

The mistake was compounded after the war when Heidegger not only did not apologize but, in Fackenheim's opinion, continued to talk as if no rupture had occurred.[13] The philosopher who insisted on historical situation could not confront the history he helped create. This is particularly troubling for Fackenheim since there is a great deal in Heidegger's thought he knowingly accepts. It is impossible not to notice that Fackenheim's concern with historicity is of a piece with Heidegger's emphasis on land, blood, and peoplehood. So while Fackenheim is outraged by the direction of Heidegger's life, his outrage is tempered by the fact that there is much in Heidegger he wants to appropriate. From a philosophical perspective, Fackenheim's criticism of Heidegger is that he did not take historicity seriously enough: by ignoring the Holocaust, Heidegger himself lapsed into inauthenticity.[14]

In Fackenheim's study, the only German philosopher to oppose Hitler was Kurt Huber, an obscure neo-Fichtean. If the idea of human dignity was weak, abandoned, and betrayed, then, in Fackenheim's eyes, Huber gave it strength. But to the degree that he was the only philosopher to do so, the philosophic tradition stands condemned.

3. Responding to the Break

Assuming that a rupture has occurred, what is one to make of it? Consider two possible answers. (1) The Holocaust shows beyond a doubt that the God who acts in history is an illusion. There is simply no way to explain this kind of evil in a world ruled by a loving God who acts on behalf of His people. To see this, we have only to consider the following argument: If God could have acted to prevent the Holocaust, He would have acted. He did not act. Therefore the idea of a God who acts in history is illegitimate. If it is, the entire scheme founded on covenant, revelation, and redemption is illegitimate as well. (2) The Holocaust proves what should have been evident all along: that there is no inference by which we can go from the physical circumstances of a person's life to his or her moral worth. Of course the standard theodicies are inadequate to explain this event; but they were shown to be inadequate long before Hitler came on the scene. According to the Book of Job, they could not explain the suffering of one person. With respect to history, all we can affirm is the *possibility* that God can act, which is enough to allow us to *hope* that He will. But it is impossible for reason to go from possibility to actuality. We therefore have no grounds for saying that God has acted or for criticizing Him for not acting. What the Holocaust shows is not that human dignity has been refuted but that the consequences of ignoring it are too evil to contemplate. The first response is essentially that of Richard Rubenstein, the second, Immanuel Kant. It is noteworthy that both responses reject theodicy: the first because God is dead, the second because history does not allow us to draw conclusions about the will of God. Fackenheim denies both.

He rejects the "God is dead" alternative because he regards it as incompatible with the future of Judaism. He rejects the Kantian alternative, which, as we have seen, is not much different from the scholastic one, because it does not have a God who acts *in* history. According to Fackenheim, it gives us a distant God, a *deus absconditus*.[15] Whoever is right in this debate, one thing is clear: all three possibilities are consistent with the facts. There is no historical evidence which favors one theory over another. So it is misleading to talk about disconfirmation.

The main reason Fackenheim cannot assert the "God is dead" alternative is that Jewish martyrs in the concentration camps did not assert it. If historically situated people remained faithful to God despite death and humiliation, *he* cannot abandon God after the fact. If he did, then according to his own principles, he would give the lie to their heroism. And if the event is as important as he claims, he cannot hold that God hid His face. Somehow there must be a theological interpretation of the event. Steven Katz interprets Fackenheim's predicament as follows:

> The two radically opposite things he wants to maintain are that: (1) the Holocaust is unique; but (2) it does not lead to a denial of the existence of God à la Rubenstein. The dialectic he wishes to affirm is that: (1) the Holocaust is without "mean-

ing"; and yet (2) out of Auschwitz the commanding voice of the Living God of Israel is heard. This complex structure is necessitated by the concern not to do injustice to the martyrs of the death camps nor to speak against God. It recognizes, indeed insists upon, the awesome nature of the Holocaust and its "unique" significance for theology, yet it also demands that this event be located within the structures of theistic beliefs rather than be allowed to break these structures apart in an irreparable manner that would mark the end of religion in any traditional sense.[16]

In the writings which lead up to *To Mend the World*, Fackenheim drew two lessons from the Holocaust. The first is the famous 614th commandment: that Jews may not give Hitler a posthumous victory and therefore Jewish survival after the Holocaust is a sacred obligation. If we interpret the 614th commandment as a law on a par with the previous 613, insuperable difficulties arise. A more charitable reading is that this commandment is not a formal addition to the Mosaic code but a way for modern Jews to respond to, and oppose, the evil unleashed by Hitler.[17] Without such a "commandment," there is nothing *specific* one can do to resist it. The second lesson is that God's presence in history has been reconfirmed by the formation of the State of Israel. Both lessons assume that God is not dead and that religiously significant acts are still possible.

His response to Kant is more complicated. As Fackenheim himself points out, Kant recognized the category of the demonic.[18] In fact we have seen that Kant *warned* about the demonic when discussing the idea that God might be approached outside the confines of morality. The crux of Kant's position is this. Human beings exhibit a propensity toward evil. Contrary to the usual explanation, this propensity cannot arise from our sensuous nature or the inclinations that follow from it.[19] Evil implies responsibility. But we are not responsible for the sensuous qualities with which God has created us. One can no more blame a person for having a sensuous nature than one can blame a person for having two arms and two legs. If the source of evil cannot be found in our sensuous nature, neither can it be found in moral reason. Kant considers it inconceivable that reason could destroy the authority of a law it gives to itself. Thus the only source of evil is the will. Evil arises when an agent freely adopts an incentive to deviate from the moral law. Yet here an objection presents itself: Why should an agent choose to pervert the law that follows from one's awareness of oneself as a rational being? Why act in such a way that one undermines the possibility of affirming one's own infinite worth? To this question Kant admits there is no answer (*Religion Within the Limits of Reason Alone*, 38): "The rational origin of this perversion of our will whereby it makes lower incentives supreme among its maxims, that is, of the propensity to evil, remains inscrutable to us. . . ."

There is no explanation for why one should act systematically to degrade human existence, one's own or someone else's. Since this propensity must be sought in the will, it *is* evil. If it were sought elsewhere, the command *not* to do evil could not be an obligation. And since it corrupts all maxims, it is *radical* in nature. Kant terms such radical evil a perversity of the heart. To the degree that such perversity remains inscrutable, there is no chance of getting inside the minds of Eichmann, Himmler, or anyone else who engages in the worship of death. Notice, however, that if Kant is right, Nazi evil is not unique. *No* agent who wills evil for its own sake can be understood. There may have been a thousand acts of incomprehensible evil before the Holocaust and a thousand after it. The Holocaust may be an instance where such perversity of the heart is "writ large," but on this view, it is not a new phenomenon. So while the Holocaust may have no historical precedent, from Kant's perspective, it is indicative of a moral tendency that has always been with us. The Kantian directive for how to respond to this perversity is clear: if understanding is impossible, the only thing we can do is turn from it and accept goodness in its full purity.

From Fackenheim's perspective, anything which compromises the uniqueness of the Holocaust is inauthentic. It is therefore inauthentic to maintain that there is no moral difference between the degradation of one human being and that of six million. But this is exactly what a Kantian has to maintain. If every human life is of infinite worth, then once a single life is destroyed by a conscious effort to subvert the moral law, we reach the limit of moral reason. There is no criterion by which to say that this act is better or worse than six million others. To put this in a different way, if we reach the limit of reason, we have no moral basis on which to compare the Holocaust with atrocities committed by other agents. No moral insights would be gained by juxtaposing Hitler with Stalin, Pol Pot, or Charles Manson. There may have been many Holocausts, each one as incomprehensible as the next. What worries Fackenheim about this view is that Jewish particularity is surrendered: the victims of Auschwitz are just one among many of history's nameless dead.[20]

On the other hand, he cannot reject Kant entirely. In *To Mend the World* (239), his response to radical evil is pretty much the one contained in the 614th commandment—if you cannot understand the Holocaust, at least you can oppose it:

> The truth disclosed in this shudder is that to grasp the Holocaust whole-of-horror is not to comprehend or transcend it, but rather to say no to it, or resist it. The Holocaust whole-of-horror is (for it has been); but it *ought not* to be (and *not* to have been). Thought would lapse into escapism if it held fast to the "ought not" alone; and it would lapse into paralyzing impotence if it confronted, nakedly, the devastating "is" alone. Only by holding fast at once to the "is" and "ought not" can thought achieve an authentic survival. Thought, that is, must take the form of resistance.

Notice the distinction between "is" and "ought." In the very next paragraph, Fackenheim distinguishes his position from Kant's by claiming that this distinction cannot be confined to the realm of thought alone. Resistance to evil must become an ontological category, a way of being. Once again, Fackenheim wants vitality. The problem is that vitality is no substitute for content. If the final lesson of the Holocaust is that we must resist evil with everything at our disposal, what is unique about this response? Why would a person not draw the same conclusion after having studied other atrocities as well?

The outlines of Fackenheim's dilemma are now in place. Faced with incomprehensible evil, we have no choice but to resist. If we cannot overcome it in thought, we can attempt to overcome it in action. But resistance cannot be haphazard. The forms of resistance which Fackenheim admires are ones in which people stick to traditional conceptions of God and human dignity. Kurt Huber went to his death committed to philosophic idealism; millions of believing Jews went to theirs proclaiming monotheism in the form of the *Shema*. Having rejected the "God is dead" alternative, and the possibility of atheistic resistance, Fackenheim has no choice but to reappropriate tradition. This is what he calls mending (*tikkun*). But if there can be a reappropriation, in what sense was there a rupture? This dilemma would be particularly acute if there were a martyr who came right out and said that Kant is right: that the lesson of the Holocaust is not that human dignity was refuted but that it must be affirmed now more than ever before. If there were such a person, the distinction between "is" and "ought" would return in exactly the form in which Kant stated it. And if someone *witnessed* to this distinction, Fackenheim could no longer proclaim it "impotent."

4. Statement of the Dilemma

Such a person presents herself in the testimony of a Polish woman (not a Jew) named Pelagia Lewinska. Fackenheim refers to her often in *To Mend the World:*

> At the outset the living places, the ditches, the mud, the piles of excrement behind the blocks, had appalled me with their horrible filth. . . . And then I saw the light! I saw that it was not a question of disorder or lack of organization but that, on the contrary, a very thoroughly considered conscious idea was in the back of the camp's existence. They had condemned us to die in our own filth, to drown in mud, in our own excrement. They wished to abase us, to destroy our human dignity, to efface every vestige of humanity. . . . to fill us with horror and contempt toward ourselves and our fellows.
> . . . From the instant when I grasped the motivating principle . . . it was as if I had been awakened from a dream. . . . *I felt under orders to live.* . . . And if I did die in Auschwitz, it would be as a human being, I would hold on to my dignity. I was not going to become the contemptible, disgusting brute my enemy wished me to be. . . . And a terrible struggle began which went on day and night.

These words affirm as radical a distinction as can be imagined between physical circumstances and moral worth. In this respect, they follow the Book of Job. Recall that the title character rejects appeal to theodicy and continues to insist on his own moral worth. In this respect, the quality we admire in Job is the same quality we admire in Pelagia Lewinska; she would not allow herself to become a disgusting brute. But if this is so, Fackenheim's admiration for her is fraught with peril. Here admidst the filth and slime, with death and degradation all around, she learned to love herself—*as an idea.*

And what was the lesson she drew? Did she suspend the ethical in favor of a leap of faith? Did she proclaim that traditional conceptions of morality are no longer applicable? Did she protest that previous conceptions of human dignity are inauthentic? According to her own words, she responded to evil by recognizing an obligation. To repeat: *I felt under orders to live.* In one respect, she confirms the basic conviction of Fackenheim's 614th commandment: the preservation of life is a sacred obligation. But in another respect, she departs from it. Pelagia Lewinska's obligation does not mention a particular people. It can be appropriated by anyone. Fackenheim's 614th commandment imposes an obligation on Jews. To be sure, Fackenheim insists that Jewish survival after Auschwitz is really survival *in behalf of* all humanity.[21] But it is noteworthy that even Jewish survival has to be particularized. According to Fackenheim, the spearhead of Jewish survival is the State of Israel, so that one state comes to stand for the entire human race and its opposition to evil. It could be doubted whether any state—Jewish or otherwise— could possibly accept such a burden. More to the point, we must ask whether Fackenheim has enhanced the sacredness of the commandment to preserve life by particularizing it in this way or whether it is much more compelling in the terms in which Pelagia Lewinska stated it.

A lesser thinker would avoid the problems this testimony creates or would not have seen them in the first place. Not so with Fackenheim. Near the end of the book, he asserts his dilemma with perfect honesty. If we hold fast to the innocent and nameless victims of the Holocaust, we must despair of any mending or reappropriation. The tragedy is too great. The only response is to recoil in horror. But if we despair, we neglect the few who, like Pelagia Lewinska, resisted on principle. It is this resistance which, in Fackenheim's opinion, makes mandatory our own. Since resistance to evil is the primary lesson we learn from the Holocaust, we cannot neglect the few. Since the horror is unforgettable, we cannot neglect the nameless victims either. The conclusion is that Holocaust theology has to move between two extremes: the "God is dead" alternative and the view that either nothing unique happened or, if it did, all is mended. Fackenheim's solution is typical of existential philosophers: instead of solving the dilemma, he affirms it with renewed vigor. According to Fackenheim (309–10), Holocaust theology "must dwell, however painfully and precariously, between the extremes, and seek a *Tikkun* as it endures the tension." Put otherwise, Holocaust theology is fraught with risk and must proceed with fear and trembling. Unable to appropriate neat, logical solutions, it has no choice but to invoke a collective leap of faith—an image which recurs in much of Fackenheim's writing.

Buber's dilemma arose over the suspension of the ethical. On the one hand, he did not want it to be suspended; on the other, he wanted the immediacy of a personal God who stands above universal laws. Fackenheim's dilemma is similar. He wants a rupture at the same time he talks about the possibility of a cure. Both want to disengage from the idealistic tradition. Both want a tradition that speaks to people in the particular situations in which they find themselves. But in the end, neither can make a clean break. Somehow the need to resort to traditional ethical categories and insist on human dignity keeps asserting itself. Having looked at the horrors of the Nazi death machine, both fall back on the moral law—Buber by citing Micah, Fackenheim by quoting Pelagia Lewinska and calling for resistance to evil. The question we must put to Fackenheim is this: Is there really a dilemma? Why not assert that the only "lesson" we can learn from the systematic destruction of human life is the sacredness of human life? How do we remain true to the memory of the nameless dead by asserting anything else? In short, why not claim that Pelagia Lewinska is right and that the "tension" of hanging between extremes is an illusion?

The answer is clear: by asserting the dignity of human life and forgetting the rest, we would be drawn back to idealism. According to Fackenheim, we do not do justice to the people who were denied such dignity, the nameless dead, if we fall back on the certainty of ethical postulates and pretend there was no rupture. Faced with incomprehensible evil, we cannot return to business as usual. Fackenheim wants a response that is "Jewish" in some sense of the term. But, like Buber, he hastens to add that any response will be fragmentary and laden with risk. A return to idealism would rob us of the "unredeemed anguish" that the Holocaust inspires—a solution which, in Fackenheim's eyes, is too easy, too secure. Worse, a return to idealism would ignore "the curse of historicity." If the conditions for realizing the dignity of human life are destroyed, the idea of human dignity cannot be confirmed. Thus Fackenheim agrees with Elie Wiesel that at Auschwitz, not only humanity died but the *idea* of humanity as well.[22] Yet far from solving the dilemma, this comment reinforces it. If the idea died, why do we admire Pelagia Lewinska for affirming it?

5. Its Resolution

Can an idea die? A moral idea is not a description of human behavior but an imperative. Suppose the conditions for realizing the imperative are taken away. Do we fault the imperative or the people who have prevented it from being acted on? To put this in a different way, when is an imperative confirmed and when disconfirmed? What lesson do we draw when people want to fulfill it but cannot? The reason Fackenheim cannot give a simple answer to this question is his commitment to an ontology of immanence. The idea of human dignity was realized in "the few and select" who, like Pelagia Lewinska, resisted the evil around them, but not realized in the nameless dead. So it was realized and not realized: hence the dilemma. Yet this ontology is problematic. Does an idea become more valid when it is present "in flesh and blood"? Does it become less valid when it is not?

In one respect, the moral law is indifferent to its realization. It is binding whether the agent who acts for its sake secures the desired end or not. Cohen took this as reason for moving from morality in the strict sense to religion. From the standpoint of compassion for one's fellow human beings, it makes all the difference whether the action succeeds or fails. It follows that in discussing the moral law, we must take notice of two points: the respect in which it is isolated from historical considerations and the respect in which it is not. We can admit this difference by distinguishing between realization and confirmation. Any ideology can be realized in the flesh; but only one that upholds human dignity can be confirmed. Nazism can never be confirmed—no matter how numerous or how successful its adherents. It is impossible to confirm something that denies the freedom and infinite worth of even a single person. This is true even though individual Nazis underwent enormous personal sacrifice to deny it. They may have given strength and vitality to their cause but did not validate it. By the same token, the moral law cannot be *in*validated. There is no circumstance in which I can be obliged to degrade another human being. Even if no one realizes the moral law, its validity remains intact. Against Fackenheim, we can say the same thing about monotheism. Monotheism is *not* a timeless idea if that means that our understanding of it has undergone little change from one century to the next. It *is* timeless in the sense that its validity is unaffected by historical circumstances. It would be true even if, in the words of Fackenheim, nothing "radical" happened after the Holocaust.

To repeat: it makes a big difference whether the moral law is realized. In this respect, the existentialists are right. It is logically possible for everyone to act for the sake of the moral law but for no one's life to be improved as a result. To prevent such a possibility, I must treat the other person not just as an exemplar of humanity but as a Thou, a person in a specific situation whose welfare matters to me. It is here that we encounter the need for moral emotions like pity, compassion, and forgiveness. The issue of success and failure is important not only for my relation to others but for my own sense of self-worth. The moral law obliges me to act but does not provide any consolation when I fail. Nor does it provide me with a reason to think that failure is only temporary. It is only by turning to religion that we move from obligation per se to the hope of realizing it. To ignore the issue of realization is, as Cohen put it, to perpetuate the illusion that ethics deals only with law and rule, never with actual people.[23] But the move from possibility to actuality does not mean that ethics is invalid, only that it is incomplete. It is still true that the moral law imposes an obligation on me no matter what circumstances I am in. That I must work for its realization, and need to be consoled when I fail, is clear. All the same, failure to realize the moral law has no tendency to show that it is not *worthy* of realization.

Once we distinguish the validity of the law from the conditions for realizing it, the dilemma vanishes. Our outrage at the specter of the nameless dead arises from the fact that human dignity was denied them; but it does not follow that the idea of human dignity was somehow refuted. Nor does it follow that the way to preserve the memory of the nameless dead is to "despair of any possibility of *Tikkun*." In this context, the notion of refutation makes no sense. Take away the conditions for treating people as ends in themselves and the necessity of the idea will be evident all the more. By running together confirmation and realization, not only do we block any chance of resolving the dilemma, we rob morality of its normative force. If, in fact, the idea of humanity died at Auschwitz, on what authority will we resist what happened there? Resistance is justified only if historical circumstances leave the idea untarnished.

The see this, consider Fackenheim's claim that resistance to evil has become an ontological category. For an inmate in a concentration camp, this makes perfect sense. But how are people no longer living in those conditions to interpret a concept like *evil*? It will not do to leave the question unanswered. That runs the risk of making resistance blind. Nor will it do to so particularize evil that the primary way of understanding it is in terms of threats to the survival of Israel. That runs the risk of political extremism. Fackenheim is in much the same predicament as Buber. The latter argued for an unmediated relation with God but saw that his position led to the problem of worshiping false absolutes. Frightened by the consequences of such worship, he had little choice but to turn back to philosophy and ask for the wherewithal to critique the "absolutes" that demand human sacrifice. Fackenheim calls for resistance to evil. But without the classical notions of human dignity and respect for human freedom, his call is hollow. The problem is that to appropriate classical notions of good and evil, he has little choice but to return to "old" thinking.

All of this is a way of saying that the moral law is the measure of human history rather than something measured by it. According to the rationalist tradition, monotheism demands nothing less. If God is unique, He stands apart from the world as judge and creator. The world may turn its back on God, but it cannot alter the standards by which He evaluates it. The Psalmist (113.4–6) maintains that He is above the nations, above heaven and earth. The rationalist tradition takes this to mean that authority has nothing to do with empirical manifestation. Those who insist on having God present in history are like those who once insisted on having Him present in nature. What both overlook is that uniqueness implies transcendence. Although they did not have a philosophic vocabulary at their disposal, the prophets saw at least this much: (1) even the most terrifying forces are subject to moral rule, and (2) the Ruler who pronounces judgment on them cannot be likened to anything given in sense. That is why, despite all appearances to the contrary, despite the weight of historical testimony, the poor have equal standing with the rich. Indeed, they have greater standing. The prophets tell us on almost every page that God loves the sick, the poor, the dispossessed, the nameless dead of ages past. What is this love other than a way of saying that their dignity *cannot* be taken away from them, cannot be disconfirmed? It cannot be disconfirmed even if no one witnesses to it. To disconfirm it is to disconfirm God.

To remain within this tradition, we must reject the rhetoric of strength, vitality, and impotence—a rhetoric to which Fackenheim really should have objected. Nietzsche was right in saying that Judaism was a slave revolt, an attempt to invert these values and replace them with peace, tranquility, the Sabbath. Behind this inversion is the idea that moral authority does not *need* vitalization. It derives its legitimacy from the fact that we cannot understand our status as human beings without it. From Nietzsche's perspective, ideas that do not require vitalization are nothing but ways of apol-

ogizing for impotence. Thus the concept of a moral authority above
the flow of history is linked with the paradox that God loves the
poor. And again, Nietzsche is right: the prophets gave us both. The
point is that we do not do justice to the nameless dead by breaking
with the prophets and taking up the rhetoric of their most important existential critic. Without the paradox and the concept of authority that goes with it, the nameless dead might just as well be
forgotten.

6. Denouement

In defense of Fackenheim, it must be stressed that his dilemma
is not an inconsistency. A dilemma is a decisive objection to a philosophy that patterns itself along the lines of science. *To Mend the
World* does not. Rather than a treatise which sets forth a body of
truths, it is a process for helping us to arrive at them, an intellectual odyssey. In this respect, its model is the Book of Job. We have
seen that the latter is not a simple statement of the problem of evil.
It is the story of a man who feels a variety of emotions including
anger, devotion, confusion, and self-pity. Indeed, it is the story of a
man who *grows* as a result of his anguish. With this model in mind,
we can understand why the conciliatory tone at the end of Fackenheim's book stands together with the "restrained outrage" prevalent
at the beginning. Faced with the awful legacy of Nazi Germany, he
turns to traditional philosophy and finds no answers. He rejects the
notion that the Holocaust can be understood and proposes resistance as an alternative. He sees that resistance must be made on
behalf of something if it is to be meaningful. The desire to have
meaningful resistance leads him back to human dignity and Jewish
survival. Such a "return"—at one point Fackenheim likens it to re-
covering from an illness—is in essence a reappropriation. He re-
turns to the old categories but not with the feeling he once had. It is
like making up with a friend after a bitter disappointment. There is
love, but it is mixed with trepidation. The return thus makes possible a mending or *tikkun.*

This scenario would enable a person in the rationalist tradition
to say that for all his striving, Fackenheim does not break through
the circle of idealism any more than Buber did. Ultimately the "dilemma" in which Fackenheim finds himself—despair or principled
resistance—is tipped in favor of the latter. This is a reasonable account of Fackenheim's odyssey except for one thing: he still insists
on particularity. The Holocaust is unlike the evil of previous ages.

The Holocaust victim is a novum. Since Jews were the paradigm victims, it is essentially a Jewish event. Therefore it merits a specifically Jewish response. Any attempt to assimilate Auschwitz to the Gulag, Cambodia, or the Spanish Inquisition is inauthentic. In short, the lesson of the Holocaust cannot be universal. It cannot be a moral rule, or a condemnation of modern technology, or an indictment of fascism.[24] It must be a response *about* Jews directed primarily *to* Jews. Everything else is secondary. This is the existentialist insistence on particularity all over again. An authentic response must be tied to historically specific situations. That is how we move from an impotent God-Idea back to the ancient God of Israel.

Or do we? The prohibition against murder and the recognition that every human being is made in the image of God was given to Noah (Genesis 9.6), a non-Jew whom Jewish tradition regards as the representative of all humanity. In short, respect for the dignity of human life has nothing to do with national boundaries. No less a person than Moses was criticized for killing an Egyptian. To be sure, there are passages in the canonical sources of Judaism that disparage gentiles and contain strong ethnic or nationalistic affirmations. But why should these sentiments take precedence over universal ones in the present context? On what basis can we claim that exclusionary interpretations of Jewish law are mandated by the Holocaust? Is not the death of Pelagia Lewinska, a woman Fackenheim deems "an honorary Jewess," as tragic as that of anyone else?

If the prohibition against murder is universal, there is no relevant principle by which to distinguish the murder of a Jew from the murder of anyone else. The historical circumstances in which the murder is committed may differ; but if it *is* a murder, the religious heritage of the victim is of no consequence. We can blame the categories at our disposal for not drawing a distinction where one should be drawn. But we will not get back to the ancient God of Israel by doing so. I suggest, therefore, that attempts to compare the victims of one atrocity with those of others or to distinguish victims of the same atrocity on the basis of national origin are misconceived. So far from providing a basis for Jewish particularity, they rob Judaism of the one idea which separated it from other ancient religions: universal humanity. In this day and age, no one denies that this idea is too abstract to stand alone. But it cannot be made specific by arguing that the death of a Jew is fundamentally different from the death of someone else. If existentialism requires that we forgo the idea of universal humanity, either because it mediates between the individual worshiper and God or because it was rendered invalid by historical events, then, I submit, the existentialist challenge has to be seriously reformulated.

Notes

1. Buber, "Dialogue Between Heaven and Earth," in W. Herberg (ed.),*Four Existentialist Theologians* (Garden City, N.Y.: Doubleday & Company, 1958), 203.

2. On this issue, see "Reply to My Critics," in Schilpp (ed.), *op. cit.*, 720–21.

3. Fackenheim, *The Jewish Return Into History* (New York: Schocken Books, 1978), 105.

4. Fackenheim, *Encounters*, 202.

5. Fackenheim, *To Mend the World* (New York, Schocken Books, 1982), 63.

6. Fackenheim, *To Mend*, 78. Cf. *Encounters*, 201–2.

7. Fackenheim, "Elijah and the Empiricists," in *Encounters*, 11.

8. Fackenheim, *What Is Judaism?* (New York: Summit Books, 1987), 38.

9. Fackenheim, *To Mend*, 133.

10. For a typical account of this position, see Maimonides, *Guide* 3.10–11. Notice how readily he accepts the "Socratic Paradox" that virtue is knowledge.

11. John Hick, *Evil and the God of Love* (London: Macmillan & Company, 1966), 397. But this admission occurs late in the book and does not seem to have much effect on Hick's overall thesis.

12. *Republic* 565e–566a.

13. Fackenheim, *To Mend*, 265–66.

14. Fackenheim, *To Mend*, 190–200. For more on Fackenheim's relation to Heidegger, see *Encounters*, 213–23.

15. Fackenheim, *What Is Judaism?*, 283.

16. Steven T. Katz, *Post-Holocaust Dialogues*, 205–6.

17. For a discussion of this point and criticism of Katz, see Michael Morgan's review of Katz's book in *The Journal of Religion* 65 (1985), 433–34.

18. *To Mend*, 9–10, esp. n. 6.

19. Kant, *Religion Within the Limits*, 16–17.

20. On this point, see Fackenheim, *The Jewish Return Into History*, 27–28.

21. See *The Jewish Return Into History*, 139. "The whole Israeli nation is collectively what each survivor is individually: a testimony *in behalf of all mankind* to life against the demons of death; a hope and determination that there must be, shall be, will be no second Auschwitz; and on this hope and this determination every man, woman, and child in Israel stakes his life." This is only one of many passages that make this point.

22. *To Mend*, 273. He is here referring to Elie Wiesel in *Legends of Our Time* (1968, rpt. New York: Schocken Books, 1982), 230.

23. *Religion of Reason*, 20–21.

24. Fackenheim, *The Jewish Return Into History*, 92:

"Can either Nazism or its murder camps be understood as but one particular case, however extreme, of the general technological dehumanization? Or (to use language which theologians are equipped to understand) does not a scandal of particularity attach to Nazism and its murder camps which is shied away from, suppressed or simply forgotten when the scandal is technologically universalized? To be sure, there have been "world wars"—but none like that which Hitler unleashed on the world. There have been (and are) "total" political systems—but none like Nazism, a truth suppressed when "fascism" is used as a generic term in which Nazism is included. And while there have been (and are) "cults of personality" there have been no *Führers* but only one *Führer*."

25. *Sanhedrin* 56a.

Chapter Nine

Universality and Particularity

1. The Age-Old Struggle

Throughout this study, one theme has been dominant: the conflict between those who stress the universal qualities of Jewish thought and those who stress cultural or religious particularity. The terms *universal* and *particular* may be a bit dated but the conflict is as alive as ever. In any case, it is clear that I am on the side of those who stress universality. I have characterized "Jewish" philosophy in a way which deemphasizes the ethnic dimension and gives prominence to the philosophic. I have argued that we can make sense of prophecy without supposing that certain individuals have special modes of access to God. According to this view, much of the prophets' contribution is to indicate how little we understand about the divine nature. I have also argued that it is impossible to have an immediate relation with God in any meaningful sense. We cannot conceive of God except under the description of moral perfection. We can think of morality in terms of Micah's formula or in terms of the sense of duty engraved on our hearts. In either case, God is part of a complex system of judgments and beliefs. One cannot break through this system and expect to encounter God as He is in Himself. All we can encounter, all we *need* to encounter, is God's goodness. To talk about a *system* of judgments and beliefs is to talk about the enterprise of interpretation and critique. Our understanding of moral perfection derives from Jewish sources. But the construction of this system is a rational process that must proceed according to universal principles. When it comes to the weighing of evidence or the evaluation of arguments, there is no advantage to being Jewish.

It is clear that I am not sympathetic with the claim that arguments that apply to other people do not apply to Jews—that when it comes to philosophic truth, Jews have privileged status. Jews may have been the first people to express universal ethical principles in their literature. But once having been expressed, these principles can be accepted by everyone. It is equally clear, however, that my

213

understanding of Jewish philosophy is partisan. To many people, the concept of universal validity is suspect and the ethnic dimension of Jewish philosophy paramount. According to Michael Wyschogrod, Judaism cannot survive unless there is a personal relation between Jews and their God. For Wyschogrod, the central fact of Judaism is the election of Israel, an election that he insists must be understood in corporeal terms. It follows that "a Jew remains in the service of God no matter what he believes or does. The Jewish body as well as the Jewish soul is therefore holy. . . ."[1] In Wyschogrod's view, there can be Jewish ethics but it will always be subordinate to the heteronomy of God's commands and the "historical and existential soil of Jewish peoplehood." Although Wyschogrod and Fackenheim strongly disagree about the Holocaust, they do not disagree about the philosophic significance of the Jewish people. According to Fackenheim, the single most important event of this century is a Jewish event and calls for a distinctively Jewish response. The only authentic response is that Jewish survival is now a sacred obligation. Fackenheim admits he was once critical of Jewish philosophers who argued that survival is an end in itself.[2] From a philosophic standpoint, any people who recognize no value beyond their own survival are morally bankrupt. But he thinks that after the Holocaust, *Jewish* survival is different. It must be understood not as a tribal response but as a profound act of faith in an age of crisis.

It is important to recognize that the conflict between universality and particularity is not unique to this century. In many ways, the terms of the debate were established by Maimonides and Judah Halevi.[3] The former defends a philosophic conception of God and reinterprets the Bible in light of it. More important, Maimonides suggests that the moral and intellectual challenges confronted by the Jewish people are similar to those which confront others, the most significant being idolatry. The biblical narrative indicates that the Jewish people have fought an ongoing battle with idolatry and have suffered numerous reversals. To the degree that Jewish law opposes idolatry and everything it implies, Jewish law, on this view, overcomes a powerful human tendency: a bias toward the empirical. The natural inclination is to put more trust in what we can see than in what we cannot. Like a disease, this bias affects Jews and gentiles alike. David Hartman writes:

> Maimonides, unlike Judah Halevi, does not attribute any special ontological dimension to the Jewish people. He believes that the same basic psychology . . . is operative both in Jews

and other human beings. When, therefore, he speaks of the susceptibility of the Israelites to idolatry, he is describing how he sees the primitive religious impulses of humankind in general.[4]

Another way to see this point is to consider Maimonides' account of the ancient history of the Jews in Book One of the *Mishneh Torah*. At the age of forty, Abraham rejected the idolatry of his culture and came to recognize the true God. He had arguments to support his position and prevailed over his opponents. His arguments won over large numbers of people and were passed on to Isaac and Jacob. But when the Israelites entered Egypt, most of the people forgot these arguments and reverted to idolatry. The situation was not corrected until the time of Moses and Sinai. The clear implication is that one of the purposes of the Mosaic code was to succeed where arguments alone had failed. The people were given a body of ritual to lure them away from idolatry in stages. This account would make no sense unless the Israelites were attracted to idolatrous worship and required divine guidance to have any hope of avoiding it. If so, the ultimate goal of the Mosaic code is the inculcation of a truth which is universal in scope: God's uniqueness.

Judah Halevi agrees with Maimonides to this extent: the Torah contains nothing abhorrent to reason (*Kuzari* 1.89). But there is a substantial disagreement on what reason will allow. Judah Halevi rejects the philosophic conception of God in favor of the living God of Scripture, a God whose legitimacy is established by miracles and who can shroud Himself in mystery if it suits Him. It is this conception of God that makes possible a unique mystical relation with the Jewish people. Both Maimonides and Judah Halevi have textual citations to support their positions. Both have attracted devoted followers through the centuries. There are obvious echoes of Maimonides in Cohen, almost as obvious echoes of Judah Halevi in Buber and Rosenzweig.

I call attention to the historical dimension of the problem because it would be foolish to expect this book, or any book, to resolve it. It is not that one side stresses universality to the exclusion of particularity while the other side does the opposite. It is rather a question of priority. The universalist accounts for the historical mission of the Jewish people not in terms of a unique property but in terms of a commitment to fundamental truths. Following Deuteronomy 4.6–8, the universalist describes the Jewish people as the custodians of wise doctrines and sound laws. There is no way to establish wisdom and soundness without argumentation. To the universalist, then, the people are unique because they have dedicated themselves to ideas which transcend the peculiarities of their own situation. In regard to ancient Israel, Cohen writes (*Religion of Reason*, 127–8) "that national history is understood as a support for the love of the stranger, which, psychologically as well as objectively, is the foundation for the love of the fellowman." Jewish particularity is made legitimate by the legitimacy of the idea of universal humanity. The idea of universal humanity is a direct consequence of the commitment to monotheism. Take away this idea and the literary sources of the Jewish people would be of limited philosophic interest.

The particularist reverses the order. Abstract ideas are legitimate not because they possess a spiritual reality of their own but because they are realized in flesh and blood. Unless there were people who profess monotheism, and are willing to die for it, monotheism would cease to matter. That is why Fackenheim puts so much emphasis on Jewish survival. It is the people who give legitimacy to the idea, not the other way around.

The terms of the debate are such that each side claims the other has God in eclipse. To the universalist, monotheism is ultimate and cannot derive its legitimacy from something else. Historical circumstances cannot refute it, flesh and blood cannot enhance it. The danger of making monotheism subordinate to, or even on a par with, Jewish survival is that the Jewish people will forget God and come to think of themselves as the supreme reality. Or, what amounts to the same thing, they will conceive of God as an arbitrary ruler who grants special privileges and puts the welfare of one people above that of another. No people can be an object of worship or veneration. To be regarded as holy, a people must recognize something *more* valuable than their persistence through time— something whose legitimacy could, in principle, outlive their own.

The particularist replies that it is the universalists who make God subordinate to a higher authority. Judaism is not Platonism. To argue that God cannot do otherwise than as the moral law directs is to limit God and deny Israel's status as a chosen people. Worse, it is to limit God by conceiving of Him under the description of an abstract principle. This is not how the God of Israel wishes to be understood. Unlike a principle, He loves His worshipers and demands that they love Him in return. He needs witnesses. Following Fackenheim, God is both infinite and intimate. Without a people to return His love, the element of intimacy would be lost, and in a sense, God would no longer *be* God.[5]

My reason for discussing this debate is not to make the usual scholarly move of opting for a middle position but to argue that no one contribution can put an end to it. There is no question that my sympathies are with universalism. But there is also no question that since Buber and Rosenzweig, particularism has held sway. If it is mentioned at all, universalism is usually brought in to allow the author to repeat the stock criticisms: It is too abstract. It puts undue emphasis on the power of reason. It ignores the historical experience of the Jewish people, in particular the Holocaust. It offers a distant God to whom it is impossible to pray. Most important, by stressing autonomy, it undermines the sanctity of Jewish law. If it is unrealistic to seek resolution of an age-old problem, it is not unrealistic to try to raise the level of the debate. In this connection, I submit that the stock criticisms are wide of the mark and have been voiced so many times that they have lost their effectiveness.

2. Universalism as Straw Man

To appreciate the hollowness of these criticisms, we must consider them more closely.

Undue emphasis on the power of reason. It is often suggested that God has the right to shroud Himself in mystery and that it is pointless to approach Him by way of proofs and demonstrations. What this criticism fails to see is that the philosophers in whose footsteps I have followed are concerned primarily with the *critique* of human knowledge and warn repeatedly of the dangers of metaphysical speculation. Recall that Maimonides denies that we can demonstrate doctrines like creation, miracles, or divine providence. And while he offers a demonstration of God's existence, there are serious questions about how to interpret it. In any sense in which we can understand it, "existence" is not applicable to God. Kant and Cohen are very much in this tradition. If God is conceived as a morally perfect agent, it is important to remember that there is no proof that the premises of morality are true. All the Critical Philosophy can do is set before us the principles which morality presupposes. In the last analysis, morality remains a hypothesis—something we can hope for or believe in. According to Hilary Putnam, understanding the legitimacy of that hope is itself a use of reason.[6] But this use of reason is a long way from scientific demonstrations.

From the standpoint of the Critical Philosophy, the attempt to approach God with scientific demonstrations amounts to fanaticism.

Ahistorical treatment of religious ideas. This criticism is valid if it means that history cannot *refute* a transcendental idea. It is groundless if it means that our understanding of such ideas is fixed once and for all. Here it is important to consider how Cohen reworked Kant. The basic categories with which we make sense of experience do not constitute a static system but an infinite series of tasks. The historical and literary sources of Judaism indicate how understanding of transcendental ideas has evolved and is continuing to evolve. This does not mean that social and political institutions will always keep pace with philosophic developments. Progress in realizing the moral law is something that ought to happen, but in any particular age, there is nothing to guarantee that it will. Like other moral and religious ideas, messianism is something it is rational to hope for but not something susceptible to demonstration—either empirical or conceptual.

No response to the Holocaust. As indicated above, the Critical Philosophy does not make empirically verifiable predictions about the future. So there is no respect in which the Holocaust can be regarded as "countertestimony." There is, of course, a great danger in taking a catastrophic event like the Holocaust and attempting to draw "lessons." Why is the lesson of this event not the conviction that the sacredness of human life is indispensable? Or, to carry the battle to the other camp, why is the lesson not that appeals to blood, land, and ethnicity are dangerous unless put forward under some kind of moral corrective? The people who argue that traditional ideas of human dignity are bankrupt, or inaccessible, or impotent put us at tremendous risk. For without these ideas, the chance of worshiping not the Absolute but one of its apes increases tenfold. Is this not a perfectly good reading of the life of Heidegger or de Man?

A parallel argument can be made with respect to our idea of God. Why not say that the lesson of the Holocaust is essentially the same as the lesson of Job: the notion of God's "doing" this or "not doing" that makes no sense because it implies an analogy between human activity and divine. If the Holocaust refutes anything, it is that God can be engaged or involved in human history in the way Fackenheim often demands. We cannot expect divine incursions to happen all the time, but it is part and parcel of Fackenheim's argument that Auschwitz constitutes a special case. A perfectly rational response to this question is to say that the usual understanding of divine presence has to be revised, hence the need for a transcendent God.[7] To be sure, it is not the *only* response. But the suggestion that particularism is the only position able to deal with catastrophe on this scale is false.

No possibility of praying to a distant God. This criticism totally misses the mark because the significance of prayer has nothing to do with whether God is "near" or "far." If one conceives of prayer as a way of circumventing one's duties to oneself or others, then prayer is not only impossible but objectionable. Moral duties are binding whether one is praying or not. If anything, they are *more* binding when one is praying because it is in prayer that we examine ourselves and attempt to rededicate our lives. By allowing the worshiper to seek repentance and redemption, prayer is itself a morally significant act. It is not enough to point out what our duties are. There must be a way of dealing with the inevitable cases in which we fail to fulfill them. Prayer asks us to purify our hearts and start over. It evokes important emotions such as humility, forgiveness, sympathy, awe, and love—emotions without which it would be impossible to live a human life. It educates us about God and His radical uniqueness. It bids us to turn away from the transitory and focus on the eternal. When done in private, it forces us to be honest with ourselves. Like most religions, Judaism not only allows but requires petitionary prayer. We do not have to think of it as trying to make the impossible possible. We do not have to think that God will physically feed the hungry and clothe the naked to see value in asking Him to do so. The question of efficacy is beside the point. What matters is that we are asking for the realization of a noble end.

As a final point, let us not forget that prayer always takes place *before God*, which is to say that prayer is directed to the ideal personality. It occurs during those moments when we are conscious of facing the ideal and trying to bring ourselves in conformity with it. In this respect, it is set off from the activities of the workaday world. Provided that we understand "Thou" as a perfect moral exemplar, it is the time when we confront the eternal Thou.

Autonomy undermines religious law. The subject of autonomy requires a book unto itself. For present purposes, it is important that we recognize that in its classical formulation, the doctrine of autonomy is not a justification of individual choice. In many discussions, the prefix *auto* (self) dominates the root *nomos* (law). It is true that autonomy means self-legislation, but we should not think of such legislation along the lines of a parliamentary body which can choose whatever it wants, even if what it wants today is different from what it wanted yesterday. Strictly speaking, autonomy is the imposition of a morally necessary law on oneself or the recognition that one is obliged to follow law. The normal way of characterizing autonomy is to contrast it with heteronomy: self-legislation versus legislation by another. But autonomy is also opposed to arbitrariness or caprice. An autonomous agent is one whose actions are governed by principle: not a scientific principle but a moral one. We saw in our discussion of miracles that autonomy is needed to explain how it is that God is free but cannot do otherwise than will the moral law. Deny either of these and God could no longer be thought under the description of moral perfection. With respect to humans, part of what is involved in the concept of autonomy is conditions even a pre-Critical philosopher like Maimonides would accept. To be morally significant, an action must result from a free choice and be such that the agent understands the reason behind it. Recall that Maimonides opposes the idea that the statutory part of Jewish law is nothing but a test of human obedience to divine authority. He believes in divine authority but insists that the commandments are ways of perfecting human nature. If so, the performance of a commandment does not involve a leap of faith. For the person able to "decode" the commandments, observance goes hand in hand with understanding. As Twersky put it: "The purity and naturalness of the motivation is a moral desideratum for Maimonides."[8] This does not mean that if one fails to see the reason for a commandment, one is free to disregard it. Maimonides' rationalism does not allow an individual worshiper to pick and choose. What it maintains is that everything God commands is in accordance with principles we are capable of understanding: that reason and revelation are "congruent."[9]

Kant's new insight is that to be free an action must be reflexive: it must fall under a law the agent imposes on him- or herself. As he put it (*Groundwork* 431): "The will can only be subject to a law of which it can regard itself as the author." The usual criticism of this position is that morality becomes a human product and God drops out of the picture.[10] Why do we need reflexivity? According to Kant, it is reflexivity that distinguishes us from animals and inanimate objects. The latter obey laws but not ones which are self-imposed. It is, therefore, reflexivity that accounts for our status as sacred and irreplaceable beings. Again, we must not confuse reflexivity with personal choice. Kant's position is that *reason* must regard itself as the author of the law, where reason is the faculty by which we apprehend universal truths. He does not say, and *cannot* say, that the self which imposes the moral law in a reflexive way is the empirical self. So it is not true that any law can be obeyed in an autonomous fashion. Like Maimonides, Kant does not allow the individual agent to pick and choose. The only law that can be obeyed in an autonomous fashion is one according to which the agent respects the dignity of all other autonomous agents. This law is as necessary in the realm of morality as the law of gravity is in nature.

Has God dropped out of the picture? The answer is yes *if* we assume that God wants us to obey laws that are not congruent with reason, laws that do not uphold the dignity of every moral agent. If that is the case, the law we impose on ourselves cannot be divine and we will have to rely on something like "commanding presence" to understand what God wants of us. But why assume this? Why not assume that the Creator has left a mark of His perfection on the soul of every being made in His image: respect for the law that God imposes on Himself and that we can impose on ourselves if we make the effort? In short, why not assume, with Cohen, that revelation does not present us with a "commanding presence" but with a sacred obligation written on our hearts? Although Maimonides does not think of moral agency in terms of reflexivity, there is still a strong parallel between his position and Cohen's: ideally God does not want simple obedience as much as purity and understanding of purpose. No doubt, Kant's description of autonomy makes it seem as if reason creates the moral law anew. Cohen corrects this by arguing that Judaism denies any possibility of a conflict between God and moral reason. God's will is not alien. It is the paradigm by which we understand our own. He is in that sense the infinite possibility of my realization of myself as a person.

The opposite view is that God wants obedience above all else. A lot of people think that the more subservient we are in obeying God, the more we display respect for Him. But let us be very clear about what such subservience or heteronomy involves. It requires us to say that God, having created a rational or self-conscious agent, commands that agent in such a way that he or she must disregard his or her rationality. Put otherwise, God commands in such a way that He seeks to destroy the agent's own sense of dignity. Put in even more graphic terms, God seeks to degrade another rational agent. This is tantamount to saying that God seeks to commit an immoral act. If it is true that we cannot conceive of God except under the idea of moral perfection, then heteronomy is incoherent, even blasphemous. We can therefore accept the idea of "commanding presence" if it means one comes to see the obligation to treat every rational agent as an end in him- or herself. But if commanding presence takes us outside the moral law, it is an invitation to ascribe less than perfect motives to an admittedly perfect agent. As to how one would apply the principle of *imitatio Dei* to a heteronomous God, we can only shudder. A heteronomous God would be an invitation to tyranny.

This account is subject to an important qualification: the doctrine of autonomy may arise from philosophic reflection on Scripture, but in no sense is it a simple interpretation. The classic texts do not present a completely consistent picture of revelation. Some suggest that God imposed the Torah on a frightened audience, some that the Torah was accepted without understanding, some that it was accepted with understanding.[11] Like everything else in his treatment of Judaism, Cohen's account of revelation is an idealization. If God is the source of moral reason, He is not an empirical cause. The lightning and thunder have disappeared. There are, of course, other ways of reading the Bible. But let us not forget that the process of idealization did not originate in Marburg. It has been going on ever since people realized that literal interpretation is not always required. From a philosophic perspective, there are two considerations which support the claim of no conflict between God and moral reason. The first is that autonomy makes sense only within the context of the prophetic tradition in morality. Without the concept of universal humanity, it would be impossible to say how we can legislate for ourselves in a rational fashion. The concept of autonomy was put forward to inspire exactly the kind of moral judgments we find in the prophetic writings. The second consideration is that the meaning of Scripture is not always obvious. Philosophic critique is needed if Scripture is to be regarded as an eternal vehicle of truth. In this way, reason and revelation complement each other. Neither is simplistic; neither dogmatic.

These considerations do not show that a universalist reading is necessary. To use Maimonides' image, the most they could do is tip the scales. My purpose in stating them is to show that universalism is a more reasonable position than many people think. It is not a historical relic or a way of legitimating lawlessness. The problem with the present age is that the universalist message has been drowned out.

3. "Jewish" Philosophy Revisited

Let us return to the point with which we began: philosophy is not indigenous to Judaism. For two thousand years, kings, priests, prophets, poets, scribes, rabbis, and ordinary worshipers got along without it. Even in the Middle Ages, when the philosopher and the talmudic commentator could be found in the same person, the fit between philosophy and Judaism was not perfect. The Bible is not a treatise. To become a subject of philosophic reflection, it has to be interpreted. Interpretations always leave doubts. Do the first lines of Genesis really imply creation *ex nihilo*? Did Abraham think of himself as suspending the ethical? Does the Book of Job support the claims of negative theology? Perhaps and perhaps not. The fact is, however, that we turn to the Bible for answers to questions that its original audience never thought of. In some cases, the questions we put to it did not arise in a Jewish context. In others, the answers we get, or think we get, require a secular philosophic tradition to make sense. It follows that "Jewish" philosophy will always be problematic. Who counts as a "Jewish" philosopher? How liberal can such a philosophy be in its interpretation of classical sources? What is the relation between "Jewish" philosophy and actual Jewish life?

I want to argue that the problematic nature of this situation is all to the good. There is no procedure by which we can read the Bible and derive philosophic theses that have the same authority as the original text. The philosophic commentator cannot help but put something of himself or herself into the interpretation. And unless such a commentator is philosophically naive, the biases and assumptions that go into the interpretation are the products of long hours of reflection on Aristotle, Descartes, Hume, Kant, and Wittgenstein. There is, then, no possibility of protecting ancient sources from secular influence—unless one decides not to ask questions about creation, ethics, and the limits of human knowledge. This implies that Jewish philosophy is not an authoritative statement of Jewish practice and belief. It does not underwrite what goes on in the synagogue or undermine what goes on in a church or mosque. Its goal is to provide what Putnam calls a *moral image of the world* and offer a reasonable hope that the image can be fulfilled.[12] Such an image is not a state description but an account of how our goals and aspirations fit together. By virtue of the fact that it deals with goals and aspirations, it cannot proceed by way of strict demonstration. It would be better to say that it proceeds by way of hypothesis. It is tentative, probing, and testing rather than affirming with certainty. In addition to putting forward arguments, it tries to stimulate appropriate forms of behavior. To return to a word used earlier, it is *messianic*. It offers a picture of how things could and should be.

By characterizing Jewish philosophy as messianic, we make it possible to see continuity between the masters of Jewish philosophy and the prophets. The contribution of the masters consists of an argument and a vision, or better yet, an argument *based* on a vision. If this is so, we do not have to think of prophecy as a completely supernatural phenomenon nor philosophy as a completely academic one. The connection becomes even stronger if we follow Maimonides and Cohen in describing philosophy as a moral task. Although the prophets did not view their task in quite the same way, there is little question that they were embarked on a related one. The original body of law had to be systematized and interpreted. Its moral force had to be sharpened. The status quo had to be attacked. The hope for a new order had to be legitimated. Without claiming that Saadia, Maimonides, and Buber speak with the same authority as Amos, Isaiah, and Ezekiel, we can say that they are all visionaries of a sort. If the works of secular philosophers helped the former group arrive at their vision, so much the better. The danger is that people will perpetuate the argument that since philosophy was once foreign to Judaism, it must remain so. If that argument carries the day, the visions which have sustained Judaism for so long will cease.

Notes

1. M. Wyschogrod, xv.

2. Fackenheim, *The Jewish Return Into History*, 21–22.

3. See, for example, *Kuzari*, Book One, 11, 25, 27, 95. Cf. Fackenheim's use of Halevi in "Reflections on Aliyah," in Michael Morgan (ed.), *The Jewish Thought of Emil Fackenheim* (Detroit: Wayne State University Press, 1987), 373–74.

4. Hartman, *A Living Covenant*, 93. The reader should note that I have deleted a reference to Aristotle in Hartman's quotation because in my opinion, he overemphasizes Aristotle's influence on Maimonides.

5. On this point, see Fackenheim, *What Is Judaism?*, 285–86.

6. Putnam, *The Many Faces of Realism*, 50–51.

7. Compare this to Fackenheim's own response in *What Is Judaism?*, 288–92.

8. Twersky, *Introduction to the Code of Maimonides*, 453–59. His position is based on Maimonides' discussion of inclination in "Eight Chapters." According to Twersky, the philosophic view extols spontaneous, voluntary, natural virtue, while the religious view extols virtue resulting from struggle and conquest over evil impulses. But, if this is true, notice how pure a statement of the "religious" view we get in Kant, *Groundwork*, 398. For further criticism of Twersky, see Spero, *Morality, Halakha and the Jewish Tradition*, 343.

9. The word is Twersky's, *ibid.*

10. On the issue of God's becoming irrelevant, see the alternative to my view in Fackenheim, *Encounters*, 48–49.

11. According to *Shabbat* 88a, God held the mountain over the heads of the people and threatened them if they did not accept the Torah; Exodus 24.7 is sometimes taken to mean that the Torah was accepted before the people knew what it said. The problem with (1) is that an agreement made under threat is not binding. The problem with (2) is that the people were relying on a just and saving God when they accepted His Torah. For further discussion, see Novak, "Natural Law," *ibid.*

12. Putnam, *Many Faces*, 50–51.

Bibliography

The following is a list of sources consulted for the preparation of this book. It does not include standard editions of the Bible, Talmud, and philosophic writings of Plato and Aristotle.

Adams, R. M. *The Virtue of Faith*. New York: Oxford University Press, 1987.

Agus, J. *Guideposts in Modern Judaism*. New York: Block Publishing, 1954.

Albo, Joseph. *Sefer ha-Ikkarim*. Edited and translated by I. Husik. Philadelphia: Jewish Publication Society, 1957.

Altmann, Alexander. "The Divine Attributes: An Historical Survey of the Jewish Discussion." *Judaism* (1966), 40–60.

———, ed. *Jewish Medieval and Renaissance Studies*. Cambridge: Harvard University Press, 1967.

———. "Maimonides' Attitude toward Jewish Mysticism." In A. Jospe, *Studies in Jewish Thought*. Detroit: Wayne State University Press, 1981, 200–219.

———, ed. *Between East and West*. London: East and West Library, n.d.

Baeck, Leo. *The Essence of Judaism*. Translated by V. Grubenwieser and L. Pearl. 1936 rpt. New York: Schocken Books, 1948.

Beck, L. W. *A Commentary on Kant's Critique of Practical Reason*. Chicago: University of Chicago Press, 1960.

Berkovits, Eliezer. *Major Themes in Modern Philosophies of Judaism*. New York: KTAV Publishing House, n.d.

Blank, S. H. "Men Against God: The Promethean Element in Biblical Prayer." *Journal of Biblical Literature* 72 (1953), 1–13.

Bleich, J. D. *"Lo Ba-Shamayim Hi;* A Philosophical Pilpul." In N. Samuelson, *Studies,* 463–88.

———. "Is There an Ethic Beyond Halakhah?" In Samuelson, *Studies in Jewish Philosophy,* 527–46.

———. *Contemporary Halakhic Problems,* Vols. 1–2. New York: KTAV Publishing, 1977–83.

Blumenthal, D. R. "Maimonides' Intellectual Mysticism and the Superiority of the Prophecy of Moses." *Studies in Medieval Culture* 10 (1977), 51–67.

Boman, T. *Hebrew Thought Compared to Greek.* Translated by J. L. Moreau. London: SCM Press, 1960.

Borowitz, Eugene B. *Choices in Modern Jewish Thought.* New York: Behrman House, 1983.

Buber, Martin. *Between Man and Man.* Translated by R. G. Smith. London: Kegan Paul, 1947, 273–96.

———. *Eclipse of God.* Translated by M. S. Friedman. New York: Harper & Bros., 1952.

———. *I and Thou,* 2d edition. Translated by R. G. Smith. New York: Charles Scribner's Sons, 1958.

———. "Dialogue Between Heaven and Earth." In W. Herberg, *Four Existentialist Theologians.* Garden City, N.Y.: Doubleday & Co., 1958, 215–25.

———. "Reply to My Critics." In P. Schilpp, *The Philosophy of Martin Buber.* LaSalle, Ill.: Open Court Press, 1967.

———. *Moses: The Revelation and the Covenant.* New York: Harper & Row, 1958.

Cassirer, E. *Kant's Life and Thought.* Translated by J. Haden. New Haven: Yale University Press, 1981.

Cohen, A. A., ed. *Arguments and Doctrines.* New York: Harper & Row, 1970.

———. *The Tremendum.* New York: Crossroad, 1981.

Cohen, Hermann, *Jüdische Schriften*, Vols. 1–3. 1924, rpt. New York: Arno Press, 1980.

——. *Religion of Reason Out of the Sources of Judaism.* Translated by S. Kaplan. New York: Frederick Ungar Publishing Co., 1972.

——. *Reason and Hope.* Translated by E. Jaspe. New York: W. W. Norton, 1972.

Curley, E. M. "Descartes on the Creation of the Eternal Truths." *The Philosophical Review* 93 (1984).

——. "Spinoza on Miracles." In E. Giancotti, *Proceedings of the First Italian International Congress on Spinoza.* Naples: Bibliopolis, 1985, 421–38.

ibn Daud, Abraham, *Ha-Emunah Ha-ramah (Exalted Faith).* Translated by N. Samuelson. Rutherford, N.J.: Farleigh Dickinson University Press, 1986.

Davidson, H. "Maimonides' Secret Position on Creation." In Twersky, *Studies in Medieval Jewish History and Literature*, 16–40.

Dienstag, J. I., ed. *Studies in Maimonides and St. Thomas Aquinas.* New York: KTAV Publishing, 1975.

Diesendruck, Z. "The Philosophy of Maimonides." *Central Conference of American Rabbis Yearbook* 65 (1935), 355–68.

Dietrich, Wendell S. *Cohen and Troeltsch: Ethical Monotheistic Religion and Theory of Culture.* Atlanta: Scholars Press, 1986.

Dodd, C. H. *The Bible and the Greeks.* London: Hodder & Stoughton, 1935.

Donagan, A. *The Theory of Morality.* Chicago: University of Chicago Press, 1977.

Edelheit, J., ed. *The Life of Covenant.* Chicago: Spertus College of Judaica Press, 1986.

Fackenheim, E. "Martin Buber's Concept of Revelation." In P. Schilpp, *The Philosophy of Martin Buber.* LaSalle, Ill.: Open Court Press, 273–96.

——. *Quest for Past and Future.* Bloomington: Indiana University Press, 1968.

———. "Hermann Cohen—After Fifty Years." *Leo Baeck Memorial Lecture* 12 (1969), 3–17.

———. *God's Presence in History*. New York: New York University Press, 1970.

———. *Encounters Between Judaism and Modern Philosophy*. New York: Basic Books, 1973.

———. *The Jewish Return Into History*. New York: Schocken Books, 1978.

———. *To Mend the World*. New York: Schocken Books, 1982.

———. *What Is Judaism?* New York: Summit Books, 1978.

Fakhry, M. "The 'Antinomy' of the Eternity of the World in Averroes, Maimonides, and Aquinas." In Dienstag, *Studies*, 107–23.

Faur, Jose. *Golden Doves with Silver Dots: Semiotics and Textuality in Rabbinic Tradition*. Bloomington: Indiana University Press, 1986.

Feldman, S. "A Scholastic Misinterpretation of Maimonides' Doctrine of Divine Attributes." In Dienstag, *Studies*, 58–74.

———. Critical notes and commentary in Gersonides, *The Wars of the Lord*.

Fox, M. "Kierkegaard and Rabbinic Judaism." *Judaism* 2 (1953), 160–69.

———. "Maimonides and Aquinas on Natural Law." In Dienstag, *Studies*, 75–106.

———. "Judaism, Secularism, and Textual Interpretation." In Fox, *Modern Jewish Studies*. Columbus: Ohio State University Press, 1975, 3–26.

———. "On the Rational Commandments in Saadia's Philosophy: A Reexamination." In Fox, *Modern Jewish Ethics*. Columbus: Ohio State University Press, 1976, 174–87.

Franck, I. "Maimonides and Aquinas on Man's Knowledge of God: A Twentieth Century Perspective." *Review of Metaphysics* 38 (1985), 591–615.

Frankfurt, H. "Descartes on the Creation of the Eternal Truths," *The Philosophical Review* 86 (1977), 36–57.

Freud, S. *The Complete Introductory Lectures on Psychoanalysis.* Translated by J. Strachey. New York: W. W. Norton, 1966.

Friedman, M. S. *Martin Buber: The Life of Dialogue.* New York: Harper & Row, 1955.

Gard, D. H. "The Concept of Job's Character According to the Greek Translation of the Hebrew Text." *Journal of Biblical Literature,* 72 (1953), 182–86.

Gehman, H. S. "The Theological Approach of the Greek Translator of Job 1–15." *Journal of Biblical Literature* 68 (1949), 231–40.

Gersonides, *Gersonides on God's Knowledge.* Translated by N. Samuelson. Toronto: Pontifical Institute of Medieval Studies, 1977.

——. *The Wars of the Lord,* Vols. 1 & 2. Translated by S. Feldman. Philadelphia: Jewish Publication Society, 1984–1987.

Glatzer, N. N. Introduction to *The Dimensions of Job: A Study and Selected Readings.* New York: Schocken Books, 1969.

Goodman, L. E., *Monotheism.* Totowa, N.J.: Littlefield, Adams & Co., 1981.

Gordis, R. *The Book of God and Man.* Chicago: University of Chicago Press, 1965.

Guttmann, J. *Philosophies of Judaism.* Translated by D. W. Silverman. 1964, rpt. New York: Schocken Books, 1973.

Habermas, J. *Philosophical-Political Profiles.* Translated by F. G. Lawrence. Cambridge: MIT Press, 1983, 21–43.

Halevi, J. L. "Kierkegaard and the Midrash." *Judaism* (1935) 13–28.

——. "Kierkegaard's Teleological Suspension of the Ethical—Is It Jewish?" *Judaism* 8 (1959), 291–302.

Halevi, J. *Kuzari.* Translated by H. Hirschfield. New York: Pardes Publishing Co., 1946.

Handelman, S. *The Slayers of Moses: The Emergence of Rabbinic Interpretation in Modern Literary Theory.* Albany: SUNY Press, 1982.

Hanson, N. R. *Patterns of Discovery.* Cambridge: Cambridge University Press, 1965, 4–30.

Hartman, D. *Maimonides: Torah and Philosophic Quest.* Philadelphia: Jewish Publication Society of America, 1976.

———. *A Living Covenant.* New York: Macmillan, 1985.

Hartshorne, C. *A Natural Theology for Our Time.* LaSalle, Ill.: Open Court Press, 1967.

Harvey, W. Z. "A Third Approach to Maimonides' Cosmogony-Prophetology Puzzle." *Harvard Theological Review* 74 (1981), 287–301.

Heller, J. "Maimonides' Theory of Miracles." In A. Altmann, *Between East and West,* 112–127.

Heschel, A. J. *Between God and Man.* New York: Macmillan, 1959.

———. *The Prophets,* Vols. 1 & 2. New York: Harper & Row, 1962.

Hick, J. *Evil and the God of Love.* London: Macmillan & Company, 1966.

Hume, D. *Enquiries.* Edited by L. A. Selby-Bigge. Oxford: Clarendon Press, 1966.

Husik, I. *A History of Medieval Jewish Philosophy.* 1916, rpt. New York: Harper & Row, 1966.

Hyman, A., ed. with J. J. Walsh. *Philosophy in the Middle Ages.* 2d edition. Indianapolis: Hackett Publishing, 1973.

———. "Maimonides' Thirteen Principles." In A. Altmann, *Jewish Medieval and Renaissance Studies,* 22–40.

———. "Maimonides on Religious Language." In Samuelson, *Studies,* 351–65.

Ivry, A. "Revelation, Reason and Authority in Maimonides' *Guide of the Perplexed.*" In Samuelson, *Studies,* 321–49.

———. "Maimonides on Creation." In D. Novak and N. Samuelson, *Creation and the End of Days.* Lanham, Maryland: University Press of America, 1986, 185–213.

Jacobs, L. *A Jewish Theology.* New York: Behrman House, 1973.

——. "The Relationship between Religion and Ethics in Jewish Thought." In Outka and Reeder, *Religion and Morality,* 155–72.

——. "The Problem of the *Akedah* in Jewish Thought." In R. L. Perkins, *Kierkegaard's Fear and Trembling: Critical Appraisals.* Alabama: University of Alabama Press, 1981, 1–9.

Kant, I. *Critique of Pure Reason.* Translated by N. K. Smith. New York: St. Martin's Press, 1929.

——. *Foundations of the Metaphysics of Morals.* Translated by L. W. Beck. New York: Liberal Arts Press, 1959.

——. *Critique of Practical Reason.* Translated by L. W. Beck. New York: Liberal Arts Press, 1956.

——. *The Critique of Judgement.* Translated by J. C. Meredith. Oxford: Clarendon Press, 1952.

——. *Religion Within the Limits of Reason Alone.* Translated by T. M. Greene and H. H. Hudson. 1934, rpt. New York: Harper & Row, 1960.

——. "On the Failure of All Attempted Philosophical Theodicies." In M. Despland, *Kant on History and Religion.* Montreal: McGill-Queen's University Press, 1973, 283–97.

——. *Lectures on Philosophical Theology.* Translated by A. W. Wood and G. M. Clark. Ithaca: Cornell University Press, 1978.

——. *Conflict of the Faculties.* Translated by M. J. Gregor, New York: Abaris Press, 1979.

Katz, S. T. *Post-Holocaust Dialogues.* New York: New York University Press, 1983.

Kaufmann, Y. *The Religion of Ancient Israel.* Translated by M. Greenberg, New York: Schocken Books, 1972.

Kellner, M. M., ed. *Contemporary Jewish Ethics.* New York: Sanhedrin Press, 1978.

——. "Is Contemporary Jewish Philosophy Possible?—No." In Samuelson, *Studies*, 17–28.

——. *Dogma in Medieval Jewish Thought.* New York: Oxford University Press, 1986.

Kenny, A., ed. *Descartes: Philosophical Letters.* Oxford: Clarendon Press, 1970.

Kierkegaard, S. *Fear and Trembling.* Translated by W. Lowrie. Princeton: Princeton University Press, 1941.

Kogan, Barry. "A Response to Professor Kellner." In Samuelson, *Studies*, 29–41.

——. "Reason, Revelation, and Authority in Judaism: A Reconstruction." In Samuelson, *Studies*, 127–60.

——. *Averroes and the Metaphysics of Causation.* Albany: SUNY Press, 1985.

Kuhn, T. S. *The Structure of Scientific Revolutions.* Chicago: University of Chicago Press, 1962.

Leibowitz, Y. *Yahadut, Am Yehudi Umedinat Yisrael.* Jerusalem: Schocken Books, 1976.

Leiman, S. Z. "Critique of Louis Jacobs." In Kellner, *Contemporary Jewish Ethics*, 58–60.

Lichtenstein, A. "Does Jewish Tradition Recognize an Ethics Independent of Halakha?" In Kellner, *Contemporary Jewish Ethics*, 102–23.

MacIntyre, A. *After Virtue*, 2d edition. Notre Dame: Notre Dame University Press, 1984.

MacRae, G. "Miracle in the Antiquities of Josephus." In C. F. D. Moule, *Miracles*, 142–47.

Maimonides. *Guide of the Perplexed*, Vols. 1 & 2. Translated by S. Pines. Chicago: University of Chicago Press, 1963.

——. *Moreh Nevuchim.* Translated by S. ibn Tibbon. Jerusalem: Mossad Harav Kook, 1958.

——. *Le guide des égarés*. Translated by S. Münk. Paris: A. Franck, 1856–66.

——. *A Maimonides Reader*. Edited by I. Twersky. New York: Behrman House, 1972.

Martin, G. *Kant's Metaphysics and Theory of Science*. Translated by P. G. Lucas. Manchester: Manchester University Press, 1955.

Moore, G. E. *Principia Ethica*. Cambridge: Cambridge University Press, 1903.

Moore, G. F. *Judaism in the First Centuries of the Christian Era*, Vols. 1–3. Cambridge: Harvard University Press, 1954.

Morgan, M. L. "History and Modern Jewish Thought: Spinoza and Mendelssohn on the Ritual Law." *Judaism* 30 (1981), 467–78.

——. "The Curse of Historicity: The Role of History in Leo Strauss' Jewish Thought." *The Journal of Religion* 61 (1981), 345–63.

——, ed. *The Jewish Thought of Emil Fackenheim*. Detroit: Wayne State University Press, 1987.

Moule, C. F. D., ed. *Miracles*. London: A. R. Mowbray, 1965.

Neusner, J. "Judaism in the Secular Age." *Journal of Ecumenical Studies* 3 (1966), 519–41.

——. "The Implications of the Holocaust." *Journal of Religion* 53 (1973), 293–308.

Novak, D. "Buber's Critique of Heidegger." *Modern Judaism* 5 (1985), 125–40.

——. *The Image of the Non-Jew in Judaism*. Toronto: Edwin Mellon Press, 1983.

——. "Natural Law, Halakhah and the Covenant." *Jewish Law Annual* 7 (1988), 43–67.

Olafson, F. *Principles and Persons*. Baltimore: Johns Hopkins University Press, 1970.

Orlinsky, H. "Studies in the Septuagint of the Book of Job." *Hebrew Union College Annual* 28 (1957), 53–74; 29 (1958), 229–71; 30 (1959), 153–67.

Outka, G. "Religious and Moral Duty: Notes on *Fear and Trembling.* In Outka and Reeder, *Religion and Morality,* 204–54.

——, ed. with Reeder. *Religion and Morality.* Garden City, N.Y.: Doubleday & Company, 1973.

Owens, J. *The Doctrine of Being in the Aristotelian Metaphysics,* 2d edition. Toronto: Pontifical Institute, 1963.

——. *An Elementary Christian Metaphysics.* Milwaukee: Bruce Publishing Co., 1963.

Pines, S. "The Philosophic Sources of *The Guide of the Perplexed.*" In *The Guide of the Perplexed,* lvii–cxxxiv.

——. "The Limitations of Human Knowledge According to Al-Farabi, ibn Bajja, and Maimonides." In Twersky, *Studies in Medieval Jewish History and Literature,* 82–109.

Plaut, G. *The Torah: A Modern Commentary.* New York: Hebrew Union College Press, 1981.

Polish, D. "Covenant: Jewish Universalism and Particularism." In Edelheit, *The Life of Covenant,* 137–53.

Pope, M. H. *The Anchor Bible Job.* Garden City, N.Y.: Doubleday & Company, 1965.

Prichard, H. A. "Does Moral Philosophy Rest on a Mistake?" *Mind* 21 (1912), 487–99.

Putnam, H. *The Many Faces of Realism.* LaSalle, Ill.: Open Court Press, 1987.

Quinn, P. *Divine Commands and Moral Requirements.* Oxford: Oxford University Press, 1978.

Rawls, J. *A Theory of Justice.* Cambridge: Harvard University Press, 1971.

——. "Kantian Constructivism in Moral Theory." *Journal of Philosophy* 77 (1980), 515–72.

Ricoeur, P. "Evil, A Challenge to Philosophy and Theology." *Journal of the American Academy of Religion* 53 (1985).

Rorty, R. *Philosophy and the Mirror of Nature.* Princeton: Princeton University Press, 1979.

———. *Consequences of Pragmatism.* Minneapolis: University of Minnesota Press, 1982.

———. *Contingency, Irony, and Solidarity.* Cambridge: Cambridge University Press, 1989.

Rosenzweig, F. "Einleitung." In *Hermann Cohen's Jüdische Schriften,* Vol. 1, xiii–lviv.

———. *The Star of Redemption.* Translated by W. W. Hallo, New York: Holt, Rinehart, & Winston, 1970.

Ross, J. P. "Some Notes on Miracles in the Old Testament." In C. F. D. Moule, *Miracles,* 45–60.

Rotenstreich, N. *Jewish Philosophy in Modern Times.* New York: Holt, Rinehart, & Winston, 1968.

Roth, L. *Spinoza, Descartes, and Maimonides.* London: Oxford University Press, 1928.

Saadia, Gaon. *The Book of Beliefs and Opinions.* Translated by S. Rosenblatt. New Haven: Yale University Press, 1948.

Samuelson, N. "On Knowing God: Maimonides, Gersonides, and the Philosophy of Religion." *Judaism* 18 (1969), 64–77.

———. "Revealed Morality and Modern Thought." In Kellner, *Contemporary Jewish Ethics,* 84–99.

———. *Contemporary Jewish Ethics,* 84–99.

———. "Issues for Jewish Philosophy: Jewish Philosophy in the 1980s." In Samuelson, *Studies,* 43–59.

———. Critical notes and commentary in *Gersonides on God's Knowledge.*

———, ed. *Studies in Jewish Philosophy.* Lanham, Md.: University Press of America, 1987.

Sarna, N. M. *Understanding Genesis.* New York: Schocken Books, 1970.

Scholem, G. G. *Major Trends in Jewish Mysticism.* 1941, rpt. New York: Schocken Books, 1961.

Schulweis, H. *Evil and the Morality of God.* Cincinnati: Hebrew Union College Press, 1984.

Schwarzschild, S. S. "Do Noachites Have to Believe in Revelation?" *Jewish Quarterly Review* 52 (1961), 297–308, 53 (1962), 30–65.

———. "The Lure of Immanence—the Crisis in Contemporary Religious Thought." *Tradition* 9 (1967), 70–99.

———. "Moral Radicalism and 'Middlingness' in the Ethics of Maimonides." *Studies in Medieval Culture* 11 (1977), 65–94.

———. "An Agenda for Jewish Philosophy in the 1980s." In Samuelson, *Studies,* 101–25.

———. "A Critique of Martin Buber's Political Philosophy: An Affectionate Reappraisal." *Publication of the Leo Baeck Institute* 31 (1986), 355–88.

———. "The Title of Hermann Cohen's 'Religion of Reason Out of the Sources of Judaism.' " In Edelheit, *The Life of Covenant,* 207–20.

———. *Heidegger and Rosenzweig: The Jewish Turn to Ethnicity.* Forthcoming, SUNY Press.

———. "On Jewish Language." Unpublished manuscript.

———. "De Idolatria." Unpublished manuscript.

Seeskin, K. "Moral Necessity." *New Scholasticism* 51 (1977), 90–101.

———. *Dialogue and Discovery.* Albany: SUNY Press, 1987.

———. "What Philosophy Can and Cannot Say About Evil." In A. Rosenberg and G. E. Myers, *Echoes from the Holocaust.* Philadelphia: Temple University Press, 91–104.

Shapiro, D. S. "The Doctrine of the Image of God and the *imitatio Dei.*" *Judaism* 12 (1963), 57–77.

——. "The Meaning of Holiness in Judaism." *Tradition* 7 (1964–65), 48.

Soloveitchik, J. B. *Halakhic Man.* Translated by L. Kaplan. Philadelphia: Jewish Publication Society, 1983.

Sommers, F. "What We Can Say About God." *Judaism* 15 (1966), 64–66.

Spero, S. "Is the God of Maimonides Truly Unknowable?" *Judaism* 22 (1973), 66–78.

——. *Morality, Halakha, and the Jewish Tradition.* New York: KTAV Publishing, 1983.

Spinoza, B. "The Ethics." In *Works of Spinoza.* Translated by R. H. M. Elwes. 1883, rpt. New York: Dover, 1951.

——. *A Theological-Political Treatise.* Translated by R. H. M. Elwes. 1883, rpt. New York: Dover, 1951.

Stern, J. "The Idea of a *Hoq* in Maimonides' Explanation of the Law." In S. Pines and Y. Yovel, *Maimonides and Philosophy.* The Hague: Nijhoff, 1986, 92–139.

——. "Skeptical Themes in the *Guide of the Perplexed.*" Unpublished manuscript.

Stern, P. "The Problem of History and Temporality in Kantian Ethics." *Review of Metaphysics* 39 (1986), 505–44.

Strauss, L. *Persecution and the Art of Writing.* Glencoe, Ill.: The Free Press, 1952.

——. "How To Begin To Study *The Guide of the Perplexed.*" In *The Guide of the Perplexed*, xi–lvi.

——. *Philosophy and Law.* Translated by F. Baumann, Philadelphia: The Jewish Publication Society of America, 1987.

Swinburne, R. *The Concept of Miracle.* London: Macmillan & Company, 1970.

Tennant, F. R. *Miracle and its Philosophical Presupposition.* Cambridge: Cambridge University Press, 1925.

Twersky, I., ed. *Studies in Medieval Jewish History and Literature*. Cambridge: Harvard University Press, 1979.

——. *Introduction to the Code of Maimonides (Mishneh Torah)*. New Haven: Yale University Press, 1980.

Unger, E. "Modern Judaism's Need for Philosophy." In A. A. Cohen, *Arguments and Doctrines*, 146–58.

Urbach, E. E. *The Sages*, Vols. 1 & 2. Translated by I. Abrahams, Jerusalem: Magnes Press, 1979.

Vogel, M. *A Quest for a Theology of Judaism*. Lanham, Md.: University Press of America, 1987.

Walzer, M. *Interpretation and Social Criticism*. Cambridge: Harvard University Press, 1987.

Wolfson, H. A. *The Philosophy of Spinoza*, Vols. 1 & 2. 1934, rpt. New York: Schocken Books, 1969.

——. *Philo*, Vols. 1 & 2. Cambridge: Harvard University Press, 1968.

——. *Religious Philosophy: A Group of Essays*. New York: Atheneum, 1965.

——. *Studies in the History of Philosophy and Religion*, Vols. 1 & 2. Edited by I. Twersky and G. H. Williams, Cambridge: Harvard University Press, 1973–77.

——. "St. Thomas on Divine Attributes." In Dienstag, *Studies*, 1–28.

Wood, A. *Kant's Rational Theology*. Ithaca: Cornell University Press, 1978.

Wyschogrod, Michael. "Faith and the Holocaust." *Judaism* 20 (1971), 286–94.

——. *The Body of Faith: Judaism as Corporeal Election*. New York: Seabury Press, 1983.

Index

Index of Subjects

241

Index of Names and Principal Philosophic Sources

Index of Biblical and Rabbinic Sources